The Politics of Public

C000263969

The question of public expenditure has proved to be one of the perennial problems for British governments. The 1990s will be no easier for John Major than earlier years have been for past administrations. In fact, given forecasts of low growth and record levels of unemployment, the Government could now be faced with greater dilemmas than any previously experienced.

This text is principally concerned with explaining the political contexts in which public expenditure decisions have had to be made over the last twenty years. It examines the way in which governments make choices according to public pressure and the fact that bargains and compromises have to be made in order to maintain political credibility. Maurice Mullard explains instances where government policy and individual expenditure programmes have been shaped according to the political climate. His approach seeks to combine theoretical frameworks with detailed policy analysis. This revised edition contains new chapters on Conservative and Labour politics and a section on the Government under John Major.

Maurice Mullard has been involved in the study of public policy and the interface of politics and economics since the early 1980s. He has been published extensively and is the author of *Understanding Economic Policy*.

The Politics of Public Expenditure

Second edition

Maurice Mullard

London and New York

First published 1993
by Routledge
11 New Fetter Lane, London EC4P 4EE

© 1993 Maurice Mullard

Typeset in 10 on 12 point Baskerville by Megaron, Cardiff, Wales

Printed in Great Britain by Clays Ltd, St Ives plc
Printed on acid free paper

British Library Cataloguing in Publication Data

A catalogue record for this book is available from the British Library

Library of Congress Cataloging in Publication Data has been applied for.

ISBN 0–415–10222–7 (pbk)

To Jackie, my children and grandchild

Contents

Figures

Tables

Introduction

The major challenge for the 1990s for Britain, Europe and the United States will be the continuing concern for the financing of the public sector. The UK is faced with the long-term problems of high levels of unemployment combined with forecasts of low growth in the economy. The balance of trade deficit, high interests and the growing public sector deficit will continue to hinder UK governments in their attempts to achieve greater economic prosperity. These internal constraints are further exacerbated by external factors. The long-term problems of German unification and the implications of financing a large public sector deficit means that German interest rates will continue to remain high, which in turn means lower growth for Germany, and also for Europe. Furthermore, the USA, after twelve years of Republican government, is also faced with a large public sector deficit which will be a major constraint on the Clinton administration and the prospects of expanding the US economy. Both these internal and external factors will continue to influence public expenditure decisions in the UK during the 1990s.

The text seeks to argue that public expenditure decisions reflect both the dimensions of political choice and of governments seeking to respond to external events. Whilst governments do make political choices in selecting between a number of policy options they are also constrained by contexts which are not within their immediate influence. Governments are therefore continuously involved in bargains and compromises – they do not have complete autonomy in the policy process but neither are they complete prisoners of events. The study of government is similar to that of the biography of the individual, that is, of continuously seeking to make decisions that reflect personal autonomy and events. Governments, like individuals, are shaped by events, but they also seek to give shape to their lives. In making decisions, individuals are continuously involved in seeking and collating information, mapping their options and strategies whilst attempting to decide what is feasible and what is possible. The added implications are that strategies that work today might not necessarily work tomorrow. Contexts that appear as constraints now dissolve and are replaced by new climates and contexts. Individuals live in a world that is fluid, where events and autonomy are not held constant. Governments also share this world of change, where events are difficult to predict, where principles and policies have to be continuously reviewed and revised to respond to new challenges, and where policy decisions are therefore mainly influenced by factors of expediency, feasibility and what is politically possible.

The study of the 'politics of public expenditure' seeks to put an emphasis on the argument that in making decisions on how to provide resources between competing expenditure programmes governments make political choices. Political choice involves negotiations and compromises between political ideology as outlined and defined in party manifestos, political judgement in terms of the attractiveness of the policy and political arithmetic that relates to what is politically possible given the constraints of the electoral cycle.

The analysis of public expenditure requires a multi-layered approach. It is difficult therefore to isolate the concerns of economics, politics and the social implications of public expenditure decisions. Economists might argue that the concern of economics is to provide the analysis of the costs and benefits of specific expenditure decisions and that their objective is to provide governments with the policy options thus allowing the final decision to be made by the politicians. However, such an approach can be judged to be rather narrow and also misleading, since such an argument seems to imply that outlining a series of costs and benefits does not involve political choice. Furthermore, such an approach seems also to 'de-skill' the economist by leaving political decisions to politicians. In the real world economists cannot divorce themselves from the political process, and the study of public expenditure therefore must inherently involve the understanding of the economics of public expenditure as much as the processes of political choice.

Whilst this study concentrates on the experiences of public expenditure in the UK there are themes that could be utilised in comparative studies. Public expenditure decisions need to be analysed at two levels. At one level public expenditure decisions require a macro approach since public expenditure cannot be separated from the national economy. It is an approach that puts an emphasis on public expenditure as an aggregate, where decisions on public expenditure are made in the context of wider decisions relating to the macro economy. In contrast, the micro, or programme, approach implies that the aggregate for public expenditure represents the decisions that are made at the programme level, and it is therefore the expenditure programmes that shape the aggregate rather than the aggregate that shapes the programme.

The analysis of public expenditure confirms that there is a need to separate the rhetoric of policy statements from the reality of expenditure outcomes. Policy statements on public expenditure, whether they are gleaned from party manifestos, policy review documents or documents produced by think tanks, are useful to the extent that they provide indications of political intentions, but to understand the dynamics of public expenditure there is a need to study actual expenditure out-turns. Furthermore, the changes in expenditure cannot be explained by looking at the outcome for an expenditure programme; rather, there is the need to look at changes within programmes to break down expenditure programmes into components, because it is at this level that changes to expenditure programmes are achieved. It is the capital, current and transfer components which add up to an expenditure programme. Planned increases or reductions are targeted at the components of an expenditure programme.

The lessons to be derived from the study of public expenditure in the UK over the last twenty years show that, despite the rhetoric of the 'Thatcher Revolution' after 1979, there has not been a revolution in the financing of the public sector. Whilst major changes have taken place through the privatisation of public utilities including water, gas, electricity and telecommunications together with the selling off of strategic industries including British Airways, Britoil, British Shipbuilders and Rolls-Royce, the structure of subsidies and grants which governments had to allocate to some of these industries during the early 1970s has now been utilised and reallocated to other expenditure programmes. Omitting the processes of privatisation commitments to public expenditure shows that total expenditure will represent over 42 per cent of GDP during the 1990s. This ratio can be compared to the 1960s, when expenditure was some 34 per cent of GDP and included the nationalised industries.

If there has been a 'Thatcher Revolution' within public and social policies, that revolution is much more associated with the administering of the public sector rather than the financing of public services. The reforms in health, education and social security and the introduction of internal markets have resulted in the establishing of new quangos which are no longer accountable to the political process. These new quangos, including hospital trusts, school governing bodies, grant-maintained schools, the regulators of the utilities, and the TECs, are staffed by personnel who are not elected but who are appointed by the Government directly or approved by the responsible minister. This break with public accountability is likely to de-politicise public expenditure in that the Government would be able to claim that it has allocated sufficient resources, arguing instead that the problems of achieving value for money lay with the new managers. To a certain extent this has already become part of the UK experience with the Government blaming the local authorities when there is any attempt to report crisis of funding in education or social services. The recent forecast that some 30,000 jobs could be lost in local government has, for example, been easily dismissed by ministers as being a problem of inefficient management by some local authorities. The Government can always point to those local authorities that are not experiencing crisis as part of their strategy to show that the problem is not one of resourcing but of efficient management. Likewise, within the Health Service repeated reports of hospitals running out of funds before the end of the financial year, and therefore not being able to undertake surgery or take in new patients, is explained by the Government as either being a problem of transition or of managers coming to terms with taking responsibility for their budgets. Whilst such a strategy might be viable in the short term the question of who provides resources for popular public services is still likely to remain part of the political agenda.

Looking to the challenges of the 1990s it might be argued that there are some enduring lessons to be learned from the experiences of the 1970s and 1980s. During the past two decades governments have tended to use one of two strategies to achieve reductions in public expenditure. The first and most popular was to make the brunt of reductions in capital expenditure projects, including public sector housing, roads, hospitals and other infrastructure programmes, despite frequent warning that this form of aggregation was likely to have an adverse impact on the national economy. Furthermore, the neglect of the infrastructure was also likely to lead to public squalor as public buildings and communications fell into disrepair. However, most of the warnings went unheeded as governments sought to achieve reductions at the least political cost. It now seems very clear that a policy founded on expediency was always likely to be flawed. Britain in the 1990s is again faced with problems of inadequate housing. The neglect of public sector housing stock together with the major reductions in the building of new housing means that people entering the housing market for the first time are not likely to be housed unless there is a drastic shift in housing policy. Whilst Mrs Thatcher was Prime Minister suggestions by her Chancellor, Nigel Lawson, of reforming mortgage tax relief were never taken seriously; now, under the leadership of John Major, the estimated costs of £5 billion to the exchequer can no longer be taken for granted, and the sacred cow of mortgage tax relief does not seem so sacred. The emphasis on owner occupation has left many people homeless, young families with little hope of starting up a new home and public sector housing stock in a state of neglect. Repairs to school buildings and roads have also been ignored, and the railways do not offer a dependable public service, yet the infrastructure is essential for our quality of life. The choice of the Thatcher Government was to reduce personal taxation to allow more individuals to buy video recording equipment and new cars. The problem was that whilst we indulged in private consumption our surroundings became more drab and more squalid. We increased our immediate private comforts whilst outside our front doors the roads appeared less clean, weeds were not removed and older people slipped on the previous year's autumn leaves.

The second strategy available to governments has been to explore means of containing the growth of current expenditure. Since current expenditure can be mostly explained in terms of public sector wage costs the problem for governments has been how to contain the rate of wage increases in the public sector. The study of the Heath and 1974–9 Labour Governments confirms that seeking to achieve reductions through dialogue with the trade unions required a series of policy compromises which in the long term both governments found too politically costly to sustain. Despite Mr Heath's many attempts to achieve a better understanding with the trade unions and his invitation for them to become responsible social partners in the conduct of policy, the Heath Government had to abandon this strategy when it became clear that the demands made by the trade unions would have resulted in major policy shifts for the Government. Equally, despite Labour's claim that it had a special relationship with the trade unions, the Social Contract was undermined when the trade unions found they could no longer carry their members with them. The

1974 Labour Government did achieve three consecutive years of wage restraint together with major reductions in capital expenditure, but in the longer term trade unions wanted to return to the process they felt they understood, which was the world of free collective bargaining – a policy to be endorsed by Mrs Thatcher's Government. Wage restraint in the public sector is again a short-term policy because in the longer term there are always problems of re-entry. In the long term public sector workers do catch up in their earnings with their private sector counterparts. The attempt by John Major's Government to limit wage increases to 1.5 per cent can only be seen as a short-term policy unless there is an attempt to widen that pay policy to include the private sector.

However, there are challenges in the 1990s which will be qualitatively different to those of the past two decades. The first major challenge is the challenge of living with longer term unemployment. Whilst both the Heath and Labour Governments sought to use public expenditure as part of their macro economic strategy to reduce unemployment, at least in the short term, such a macro economic objective was abandoned by the Thatcher Government. Mrs Thatcher's Government preferred to reduce taxation and interest rates hoping that these policies would create an environment of increased consumer confidence and that consumer confidence would be used as the engine of growth. In part the recession of the 1990s can be explained in terms of the decline in that confidence. Higher interest rates together with the threat of unemployment have made the recession of the 1990s that much more difficult. Consumers have been left with a huge debt overhang on their credit cards. The reduction in interest rates is not proving an inducement to spend but, instead, to repay debt, whilst the fall in the price of housing has made consumers feel less well off. Despite the fall in consumer confidence the Government cannot utilise public expenditure as the means to increase demand since this is likely to worsen the balance of payments deficit. The path of consumer confidence only seems to offer a short-term solution to the problem of unemployment, since any attempt to go for consumer-led growth is likely to lead to a balance of payments constraint.

The challenge for government in the 1990s therefore is how to finance long-term unemployment. Reductions in unemployment can no longer be assumed to be desirable if the increase in employment is likely to result in the further deterioration of the environment. Expanding car production and consuming more energy are no longer necessarily desirable objectives in themselves. The question for governments, therefore, is whether they see unemployment as purely an economic problem and a problem of public expenditure. The Justice Commission recently set up by the Labour Party under the leadership of Sir Norman Borrie could, for example, provide a platform for a debate about the funding of social security. The major concern for the unemployed is the problem of poverty for themselves and their families – the question facing British society is whether it can be bold enough to face the issue of providing a minimum income which seeks to bring to an end the cycle of poverty. However, providing a minimum income also means the end of a long-held view about giving funds from the exchequer to those who some people judge as being feckless or workshy – a theme which goes back to the days of the Poor Law.

Government expenditure is always likely to increase because of external pressures. Like all governments, the UK Government will come under pressure to sign agreements to care for the environment by providing funds to deal with pollution, and also maybe to make commitments to placing limits on the use of private cars, funding public sector transport projects, and phasing out pollutants.

I have now been writing about public expenditure for the last ten years. The text is an update of the text I wrote in 1987 under the same title. During the last five years there have been changes in public expenditure that needed to be considered in the revised edition, but, more important, however, have been the changes in me as a person that also needed to be reflected in this version. Whilst in 1987 my major concern was an attempt to advance the debate on public expenditure, the objective here has been to try to share with students my experiences not only as a student of public expenditure but also as a tutor who seeks to work at the interface of politics and economics. The emphasis of the present text has shifted, the aim now being to try and make the subject of public finance – a subject that seems to belong to the world of the specialists – that much more accessible; in that sense I hope that more will be willing to enter a debate which is not likely to go away. The financing of the public sector impinges on all our lives; it provides for our quality of life, and it is the best method we know for providing resources to care for the elderly, and to provide pensions, health care and education for us all, making public expenditure a concern to each of us.

Texts never completely belong to the author. They represent a number of processes of reading and discussion, of people willing to share their views with you, to hear your arguments and therefore make your own arguments that much more coherent. In this I feel that there are many debts to acknowledge, and here I can only mention some. First I must acknowledge my family, Jackie, Anna, Lucy and John, for giving me their support, encouragement and understanding. Next, my colleague and friend Harry Fineberg, who is always willing to share with me his ideas, and who patiently reads and comments on what I write. My friend Ken Partington advised on computing techniques and graphics. I also want to thank Gordon Smith and James Whiting at Routledge for their encouragement, advice and support. As always, the limits and omissions of this text remain my total responsibility.

Maurice Mullard
January 1993

Chapter 1

Definitions of politics and public expenditure

APPROACHES TO POLITICS

As the title suggests, this text seeks to provide a 'political' dimension to the explanation of the dynamics of public expenditure within the UK. The central concern is to enable students to utilise a specific series of tools that are seen as being derived from the study of politics and that could be applied to the issues of public expenditure. These political tools are perceived to be complementary to, and an addition to, those concepts which are derived from the study of economics and sociology. The emphasis on the politics of public expenditure provides a framework which shows that decisions on public policy and expenditure outcomes continuously involve political judgement, political calculation and political choice. Public expenditures on health, education and social services present governments with a series of choices and policy options. It is not inevitable that all governments will respond to a common problem such as changes in population structure in a similar manner. Not all governments will necessarily increase spending on health or social services because of, for example, the growth in the number of elderly people in the population. Furthermore, there is no inevitable relationship between the growth in the economy and public expenditure, and there is no automatic transmission mechanism between what is happening within the economic sphere and public expenditure.

Whilst in the United States health care is provided for the majority of people through private insurance, the United Kingdom has a National Health Service funded through taxation. Equally, in the context of the 1990s, whilst the UK Government seems to be moving towards 'internal markets' to deal with the problems of increased demands for health care, within the United States Congress there are pressures to produce a national health system similar to that which already exists in the United Kingdom and which at present the UK Government is seeking to reform. In the UK expenditure on health represents about 6 per cent of GDP; in contrast, the USA devotes 12 per cent of national income to health; France and Germany each spend about 8 per cent. Furthermore, in the new Germany the costs of unification and the demands for public expenditure on infrastructure and employment have resulted in the Government increasing personal taxation to fund these new expenditures and at the same time reducing expenditure on pensions, despite the growing numbers of elderly people.

In both Europe and the USA, there have been consistent high levels of unemployment during the 1980s and early 1990s, yet governments have tended to respond very differently. In the USA unemployment insurance only covers the first 26 weeks of registered unemployment, whilst in Germany and the UK unemployment insurance covers the first 52 weeks – a contrast to France, where unemployment insurance covers the first two years of unemployment. When unemployment insurance is exhausted the long-term unemployed in the UK resort to income support, whereas the USA has no such safety net. In the USA once extended benefits are exhausted the unemployed become dependent on food stamps and soup kitchens. In Sweden, by contrast, benefits stop altogether after 14 months, but during that time the unemployed receive professional counselling and also receive very high-quality training. Sweden spends roughly seven times as much as the UK on training.

There are, always, competing policies available to governments; they can make it their central concern to reduce personal taxation and reduce revenues to government or they can increase taxation to fund new expenditure. Governments can also utilise fiscal drag to bring in new revenues in order to fund higher levels of public expenditure. The study of politics emphasises that there are always available to governments a series of policy choices and options. This means that policy outcomes cannot be explained in terms of explanations which exclude the political dimension. The political dimension implies that, although things happen in a certain way, nothing is inevitable and outcomes can be very different.

THE CONCEPT OF POLITICS

There is obviously a dilemma in providing a definition of the concept of politics. Any attempt to construct a definition of politics might resolve the issue of what, in a specific context, can be termed political, but it is also likely to create problems since definitions tend to be static and reductionist, and can therefore set artificial barriers between what is included within that definition and therefore what is excluded. The attempt to provide a definition would create a framework and a boundary between what can be termed as politics and what therefore can be excluded or discounted.

However, it is equally unhelpful to provide a definition that portrays all activities as involving politics and being political. It might be argued that within a UK context there is an increasing acceptance of a broad definition of politics, where the personal is political and where all human relationships are perceived to be struggles for power; such a definition would be regarded with a great deal of scepticism and worry in Czechoslovakia, Hungary and Poland. In these countries over the last 40 years individuals have actually lived within the context of the political and have therefore found no escape from the public gaze or surveillance by the State. A definition that seeks therefore to embrace all human activities as being political implies that human beings occupy only the public sphere, and that there is no separation between public and private; this implies there are no boundaries between what people decide to do collectively and what they decide to do as individuals. Within this all-embracing public sphere there is no room for the individual, or for individual privacy, individual rights and the choice of whether or not to be involved in the public and the political.

The view that 'all is political' creates problems for the existence of civil society and the possibilities for individuals to make decisions which do not involve the political process. Daily consumer trans-actions, private investment decisions, decisions about lifestyles and personal aspirations have all to be located within the private sphere and the sphere of civil society in a modern democratic community. The failed coup in the Soviet Union in 1991, the Czechoslovakian 'Velvet Revolution' of October 1989 and the revolutions in the former GDR, Hungary and Poland confirm the existence of civil society – that is, the existence of a sphere that is separate from the political and which at times provides resistance to the political sphere. Indeed, what these revolutions confirmed was a revolt against a regime that denied the existence of civil society, the existence of private lives, and the possibility that human beings, given the choice, want the security of their private lives protected against public institutions:

Communism was overthrown by life, by thought, by human dignity ... I favour a political system based on the citizen and recognition of fundamental civil and human rights in their universal validity, equally applied, that is, no member of a single race, a single nation, a single sex or a single religion may be endowed with basic rights that are any different from anyone else's. In other words, I favour what is called a civil society.

(Havel 1992: 7, 31)

The study of politics tends to follow two broad traditions; the first perceives politics as a process, whilst the second emphasises that the study of politics is related to a specific arena, forum or institution. Within the first category 'process' tends to reflect a broad approach to the study of politics, whilst in contrast the institutional approach is likely to be narrow. However, it is possible to bring together the process and the institutional approach, so that the study of public expenditure, for example, would involve the institutional approach and also the view that the institutions of government, bureaucracy, interest groups and political parties are involved in a process since they seek to change and therefore reflect the changes in the wider social context.

The starting point of this text is based on two arguments. First, it is accepted that politics is a process of struggle for power and that therefore within this context most human relations involve power relations and so are political. But there is a need to separate the study of micro politics from macro. There is a need to separate relationships within families and households, which are political because they reflect gender struggles, from the macro study of politics, which involves conflicts between different groups and individuals on issues of resources which can only be resolved through the process of political choice. The argument that 'all is political' broadens the study of politics to such an extent that other areas of study, including economics and sociology, become redundant. The tools and concepts which these disciplines offer are simultaneously undermined and any competing perspectives and disciplines are discounted. This study accepts the view that there are other concepts to be utilised in the study of public expenditure but that there is a specific political dimension which also deals with the subject.

The second dimension to the study of politics is related to the question of the process that is concerned with organising the distribution of resources and how the political process is utilised as one method which deals with the question of resource allocation. Asking the question 'how could the individual become satisfied in a dissatisfied society', Heller and Feher (1988) have argued that the individual is more likely to discover self-determination through personal relationships that are founded on symmetrical reciprocity, mutual respect and common cause. Within this context, therefore, access to the political process has to be seen as being the mechanism that provides the possibility of self-determination and individual freedom rather than the means to the imposition upon others of our view of a good society. Political activity should therefore be a process which enables the individual. Individuals continue to have wants and needs which cannot possibly be satiated; satisfaction thus depends on a process of self-determination within the context in which people find themselves:

> We are thrown by the accident of birth into the present, into our world, into the dissatisfied society. The world has become a 'context', the context for our indeterminate possibilities. Self-determination is not context-free; indeed coping with its context is its intrinsic feature . . . we can be satisfied with our lives even if we cannot satisfy all our needs provided that we succeed in transforming our contingency into self determination.
>
> (Heller and Feher 1988: 29)

Heller and Feher have pointed to the dangers of voters choosing between their personal rights in exchange for welfare rights and have suggested that no individual has the right to trade off rights which are seen as inalienable and therefore not to be negotiated for welfare rights. Political rights, that is the rights of the political citizen, have to be kept separate from social rights or social citizenship.

This study perceives the concept of politics to be both a means and an end in the way people organise themselves. Politics can be perceived to be the best means of resolving conflicts, and it is always for the better for people to resolve their differences through argument and compromise than through the use of force. The emergence of modern political parties has provided a means of reflecting competing perspectives and attitudes. The political market-place has contributed to the resolution of conflict by offering individuals a range of choices between different visions and priorities, with political parties often acting as the suppliers of policies and voters acting as the consumers trading off policy against costs. The political process within the context of democratic governments is perceived to be the legitimate means for allocating resources.

However, whilst politics might have the potential to resolve conflicts it cannot be assumed that the political process will always benefit the individual. Politics has often been used as the means for coercing certain groups of people, for transferring power and resources in such a way that benefits certain interest groups, and also for encouraging prejudice and discrimination against specific individuals, especially

those who are defined as foreigners by specific communities. Very often
the political process has been the means, therefore, for legitimising the
tyranny of majorities against minorities and has also been the vehicle
for legitimising the process of exclusion and inclusion for the conferring
and taking away of rights. There are many occasions where political
parties have used the ideology of nationalism as the route to power.

Politics has therefore also been a threatening experience, because it
is by nature an arbitrary process with no rules and procedures for
guarding individual rights where the rights of individuals are seen as
being related to the wider social context. It is against this background
that individuals concerned with democracy and human rights have
argued for the need for a written constitution to make the rights of the
individual inalienable, where the powers of government are decentralised, with appropriate checks and balances, and where the conduct
of policy is guided within the context of written rules. According to this
approach the major concern is to limit the role of politics as the means
of allocating power and resources. It for this reason that some market
liberal thinkers have pointed out that the political process is more
unjust and arbitrary in the allocation of resources than the economic
market-place. Within the economic market-place the individual is
treated as the sovereign consumer willing to pay a price in exchange for
goods and services, in contrast to the political market-place, where the
aim is to influence the political process to gain access to politicians and
those who have resources. Within the political market-place those who
have ready access to the political process are more likely to be better
served than those who are not involved. The political market-place is
therefore more likely to discriminate in favour of groups who are seen
as important in sustaining the incumbent political party in government. In contrast, those voters who are not perceived to be a threat to
the party in government are therefore more likely to be ignored and
marginalised. Individual voters are not of equal value in the political
market-place. In the economic market-place, those who are willing to
pay a price have to be treated as equal consumers.

In seeking to provide a 'politics' of public expenditure, the central
concern has been to construct an argument that shows that the
decisions which governments make on the allocation of resources will
always involve choice. There is nothing inevitable in the policy-
making process. Governments always have a series of policy options to
choose from, and although they do not have complete autonomy,
governments do have sufficient room to make policy decisions founded
on choice rather than being dictated by external factors that are seen to

be outside the control of government. Furthermore, it must be emphasised that these policy options do not carry a common weighting or have a similar status; policy-makers themselves are equally involved in a process of selective perception, which means that they are more likely to select policies which are more proximate to the ideology of their party, more likely to involve political arithmetic and political calculation, and also to involve political judgement. Whilst political parties have visions, politicians are also pragmatic in negotiations; their visions have to coincide with the preferences of the voters. Politicians have to win electoral support to put their visions in place, which in turn means that not all policy options would be judged as feasible if these policies were perceived to be politically costly to the Government, which in turn is likely to lead to inertia. Irrespective of the strong market liberal case to abolish mortgage tax relief neither the Conservative Party, with its commitment to a market-orientated economy, nor the Labour Party, in pursuance of a more equitable housing policy, are likely to phase out this subsidy. The political cost is too high, since 70 per cent of the UK population are home owners.

POLITICS AND PUBLIC EXPENDITURE

Decisions on public expenditure are likely to involve a series of processes including:

(a) a process of selective perception in terms of the extent to which certain expenditure decisions correspond with the ideology of the party;

(b) a process of political calculation where the government decides the likely outcome of an expenditure decision on the electorate and judges the electoral cost of increasing public expenditure or reducing the burden of taxation. Increasing education or health expenditure might not reap the same degree of political benefit as reducing taxation since the effects of the latter are more immediately visible. In contrast, reducing expenditure on health or education might not be politically costly at least in the short term. It is only if these services are neglected in the long term that public concern is likely to increase.

(c) a process of political judgement based on the nearness of an election – as the time for an election gets nearer governments are less likely to make decisions which injure any part of the electorate, so no government is likely to increase taxes or reduce expenditure during an election year. Instead it is more likely to increase expenditure, but on visible programmes – that is, on programmes which have a high rate of political benefit, such as increases in pensions or child benefit.

Although it is useful to suggest that there is a relationship between party political ideology and the process of policy choices, it would be misleading to assume that there exists a consistent party ideology. Ideology within a political party should not be perceived to be a coherent set of ideas and beliefs; rather, it tends to represent a compromised agreement between competing value systems. Political parties are uneasy alliances of members with competing ideologies who sometimes also form dissenting factions within a party. The Campaign Group of MPs within the Labour Party and the No Turning Back Group inside the Conservative Party are two contemporary factions representing the views of radical socialists in the Labour Party and radical market liberals in the Conservative Party. Although factions such as the Bevanites, Revisionists and Militant Tendency have always been easier to identify because of the nature of debate at the Labour Party Conference, the Conservative Party also has the Bow Group, the Monday Club and Centre Forward, each representing a different interpretation of Conservative values. Over the last 40 years disagreements between market liberals and One Nation Conservatives have continued to persist inside the Conservative Party as much as those between the social democrats and radical socialists within the Labour Party.

It is difficult to sustain a view that political parties have identifiable political ideologies; instead, it is more likely that the principles and priorities represent compromises and negotiation between different factions. Market liberal purists including Hayek and Seldon have, for example, criticised the Thatcher Government for not promoting a market liberal agenda, because these market economists had assumed that the Conservative Party had adopted a coherent strategy founded on market principles. Equally, commentators such as Miliband have criticised Labour governments for abandoning their socialist principles. Commentators who criticise governments and political parties for not adhering to some coherent set of principles fail to recognise that political parties want to become the incumbent government. Political parties seek to provide a leadership of ideas to the electorate, but must also reflect the values of the electorate they seek to represent. And because by nature political parties reflect alliances of values and ideas, political party ideologies tend to reflect a series of compromises between factions rather than adherence to one set of coherent values. Within this context it is therefore essential for any discussion of public expenditure to take into account the presence of competing views within political parties and the process of compromise between competing factions.

The study of the politics of public expenditure must therefore involve the following dimensions:

(a) an understanding of party politics that includes the competing perspectives and priorities as announced in various party pro-grammes, pamphlets, policy statements and party conference reports;

(b) an awareness of the politics that reflects the tensions of views within a political party: the views which gain ascendance also become the overall views of the party and, therefore, the party's view;

(c) the recognition that there is no direct proximity between party ideology and policy choice, since political parties also take into consideration the trade-off between compromising ideology with political judgement;

(d) the realisation that the proximity of elections also means that political parties are involved in political arithmetic, that is, in ensuring that they are able to thread together an electoral majority, sometimes also using the process of fine tuning by targeting specific policies on marginal constituents who are seen as crucial to the electoral success of the party.

The concept of a politics of public expenditure emphasises the concept of choice. Governments are continuously making decisions about what to produce, how to produce, and for whom. They make decisions on production allocation and distribution of resources. Within the UK context 40 per cent of national resources are being directed through government, which means that governments do have a major influence on people's daily lives. Decisions on whether to uprate pensions in line with inflation or earnings have a major impact on the lives of the elderly; decisions to prioritise resources on education and health have a similar effect. The concept of politics therefore implies a choice between a series of competing policy options of how to prioritise resources.

Although external events do restrict the options available to a government, in responding to these immediate events, even in the short term, that government always has a series of choices, whilst in the longer term external events become less restrictive and therefore increase the autonomy of government. Although governments might come under extreme pressures in the short term to reduce expenditure programmes to satisfy external financial markets, they have a series of options available of which programmes to reduce and which programmes to protect. Public expenditure represents the input of policy and the degree of commitment by government to the policy process in terms of prioritising resources. The decision to prioritise one expenditure programme usually means an opportunity cost in terms of less resources made available to other programmes.

This process also represents political choice, because there are aspects of certain expenditure programmes which can be switched on and off at very short notice, especially expenditure on capital projects. Governments might be constrained during their first year in office by the political priorities of their predecessors, but these constraints can be loosened provided that the government has the political will to challenge the political priorities of its predecessors. The Labour Government of 1974 made housing and health its priority on taking office. It found little opposition from the civil service in increasing housing subsidies during its first year in office because it (the Government) argued that these were its political priorities. The Conservative Government of 1979 also made commitments to spend more on defence and law and order whilst the housing programme took the brunt of the reductions in government expenditure plans.

Professor Richard Rose (1989) has produced a detailed study of expenditures by programme for the period 1946–85 as they appear in the Appropriation Accounts for the use of the Comptroller and Auditor General. Rose comes to the conclusion that much of public expenditure by programme can be explained through inertia, in the sense that expenditure programmes tend to reinforce a view of high durability. Rose argues that a total of 99 programmes, which make up 84 per cent of all expenditure programmes, have continued since the years of the 1945 Labour Government. These programmes make up over 99 per cent of total expenditure. Since 1945, 19 programmes have been terminated, which equates with 1 per cent of total expenditure. The reforming Labour Government of 1945 'inherited' 118 expenditure programmes at a total cost of £99 billion in sterling's 1985 value. In six years the Attlee Government introduced 24 new programmes, yet the impact of these programmes has been, after four decades, to increase expenditure by £7.5 billion. In contrast, the Thatcher Government despite its commitment to rolling back the frontiers of government, continued to spend £120 billion on inherited programmes, whilst between 1979 and 1985 it managed to save £2.1 billion.

However, whilst programmes are durable, the issue of political choice in public expenditure cannot be resolved in relation to whether programmes are launched or terminated, but whether expenditure on existing programmes is increased, reduced or held stationary. The issue of choice does not depend on the question of, for example, whether expenditure on health is terminated, but whether expenditure on health is increased and by how much. Rose argues that in 1946 total expenditure on the 188 programmes totalled £28.8 billion in 1985 prices. By 1985 the 99 programmes that had been continuously in effect had increased in cost three times, to £98.3 billion:

> The inheritance of public policy is the cumulative sum of many actions taken by many governments, each carried forward by the force of political inertia. The greater the momentum behind a programme the harder it is to slow down, re-direct or stop it.
>
> (Rose 1989: 38)

The nature of politics, according to Rose, is that politicians are concerned about short-term choices, thus ignoring long-term effects. The concern of the politician is to be elected and to be perceived as doing something now – that is, essentially, the nature of politics within a democracy. However, in making decisions about the short term, politicians are making choices that are political, since they are still involved in making decisions about resources which are finite; this means that resources are prioritised even if these resources represent 'marginal additions' to an existing programme. The additional margin over a number of years implies a large increase. As Rose (1989) points out, compounding an average growth rate of 6.8 per cent does not produce so dramatic a change, at least in the short term, but over a decade the expenditure doubles; it trebles in 16 years, and increases by 453 per cent after 25 years.

DEFINING PUBLIC EXPENDITURE

The debate over public expenditure during the 1970s and mid-1980s was characterised by predictions of governments going bankrupt (Rose and Peters 1979), of pluralist stagnation (Beer 1982) and of fiscal crisis (O'Connor 1973). Common to all these forecasts was a concern with the rate of growth and the size of UK public expenditure in relation to the national economy. Other accounts equally emphasised that other countries did have larger public sectors and, furthermore, that these countries experienced faster rates in the growth of their public expenditures without any indication of adverse effects being evident between economic performance and the size of the public sector (OECD 1978,1983; Newton and Karran 1985; Klein and O'Higgins 1985).

These contrasting perspectives reinforce the view suggested by Shapiro that:

> All stories and accounts, no matter how much their style might protest innocence, contain a mythic level – that is they have a job to do, a perspective to promote. a kind of world to affirm or deny. Seemingly neutral accounts of activities deliver, by dint of their grammatical and rhetorical structures, implicit political arguments.
>
> (Shapiro 1984: 2)

The concept of public expenditure is therefore, like other political concepts, a contestable terrain, to be occupied by changing and competing definitions, where those who seek to do the defining represent a vested interest and where those who gain the ascendancy will also reflect a specific political ideology and therefore offer a specific series of policy choices.

Definitions of public expenditure are mainly influenced by either a macro or micro perspective of what constitutes public expenditure. The macro perspective tends to perceive public expenditure as one aggregate in the national economic accounts that is likely to impact on the macro economy, including issues of inflation, unemployment and interest rates. In contrast, the micro perspective concentrates on individual expenditure programmes and the implications of changes in expenditure and policy outputs. However, as Heclo and Wildavsky (1982) have argued:

> The present and growing danger is that macro-analysis of the economy is tending to overwhelm the micro-analysis of policies . . . Up till now the macro tail has wagged the micro dog; it is time that both acquired a place up front where the barking and gnashing of teeth take place.
>
> (Heclo and Wildavksy 1982: 383)

These authors have pointed out that decisions on public expenditure in the UK have continued to be the product of struggles between the

Treasury and the spending departments. The Treasury tends to give priority to the macro economic implications of expenditure decisions, whilst spending departments emphasise the policy commitments contained in their budgets. In the expenditure cycle it has been the macro analysts and the Treasury view that have continued to have the ascendancy in the battle for the definition of what constitutes public expenditure. The axiom is, as far as the Treasury is concerned, that whatever the Government spends must be contained in the definition of public expenditure, since the Government has to raise the revenue either through taxation or borrowing to meet that expenditure. The Treasury therefore tends to treat all public expenditure as an aggregate, with no attempt to evaluate the differential effects of different expenditure programmes on the economy. It therefore tends to treat capital expenditure programmes in the same way as current expenditures.

The job of Treasury ministers, especially the Financial Secretary to the Treasury, is to reach an agreement in a series of bilateral discussions with spending departments on the spending limits for each department. The effective financial secretaries earn their creditability with the Chancellor of the Exchequer when they are able to show that they have been able to keep the bids of spending ministers within the planned target allotted to public expenditure, irrespective of what happened to expenditure programmes in the course of those dis-cussions. Spending departments are allowed a budget; the effectiveness of the expenditure is left to the department to evaluate. The concern of the Treasury is to ensure that departments stay within their spending limits.

ANALYSING PUBLIC EXPENDITURE WITHIN THE MACRO AND MICRO PERSPECTIVES

The macro approach – the Treasury view of public expenditure

The macro perspective gives sympathy to ideas of a homogeneous public sector. It suggests that the public sector is hermetically sealed from the private sector, where the former is dependent on the prosperity of the private sector and also where the public sector is perceived to be driven by its own momentum towards continuous expansion. In contrast, the programme approach attempts to show that expenditure programmes represent historical developments in policy aimed to meet a plurality of social needs. Although macro analysts are aware of the objectives of expenditure programmes as much as micro analysts are aware of the implications of programmes at the macro level, these views are founded on different premises and assumptions. They represent political struggles, reinforcing and articulating the legitimacy of entrenched interests.

The macro approach is based on the postulate that whatever government spends it has to get from elsewhere, either through increases in taxation or government borrowing. The concern of the macro economist is to analyse the growth of public expenditure in relation to national resources, where the government decides the total for public expenditure and then allows departments to bargain within that total. The macro view suggests that decisions on public expenditure have to take into consideration the wider economic context – namely the relationships between the public and the private sector, the prospects for growth in the economy, the implications for distributing resources between the private and public sectors, and also private versus public consumption:

> The Public Expenditure Survey process is generally held to break down into three main stages. One is the assessment of resources available to the nation. Second there is the question of the broad allocation of resources between public expenditure and other uses. Finally there is the third stage which is the allocation of those resources which are earmarked for expenditure as between the different programmes.
>
> (Pliatzky 1976: 28)

Sir Leo Pliatzky has also argued that one of the major achievements of the Thatcher years was the willingness of the Government to set its policy objectives on public expenditure as a percentage of GDP:

> the public expenditure total . . . is a measure of the amount which has to be raised by revenue and public borrowing. It is also an approximate indication of the demands made by public expenditure on the output of the economy. These two factors – the requirement for taxation and borrowing and the constraints of available output – are highly relevant in answering the question of what the total of public expenditure should be.
>
> (Pliatzky 1989: 33)

This approach to public expenditure implicitly accepts the view that there are two sectors to the economy, each hermetically sealed from the other. The private sector is the sector which produces marketed goods, the other, the public sector, produces non-marketed goods. The private sector is the main generator of income and taxation on which the public sector depends. Pliatzky argues:

> The point is that only the market sector satisfied the demand for tradeable goods and services. The size of the non-market sector – that is the free or subsidised public services is governed by two things. These are, first, the market sector output of tradeable goods and services, and, second, the proportion of that output which the government is willing and able to extract by taxation and public borrowing.
>
> (Pliatzky 1989: 34)

This approach is identical to that adopted by Bacon and Eltis (1978) in their book *Britain's Economic Problem: Too Few Producers*. These authors also pointed to a two-sector economy: a marketed or private sector, and a non-marketed, which represented the public sector except for the nationalised industries, which were described as providing tradeable goods. The Oxford economists argued that the non-marketed public sector was dependent on the private marketed sector for the financing of public goods and services. Bacon and Eltis also argued that the public sector was 'crowding out' the private sector by competing for resources and finance, and had contributed to Britain's poor economic performance. The public sector competition for resources had pushed up the costs for the private sector, resulting in lower investment, higher unemployment and inflation. A large public sector deficit meant that the government was competing with the private sector for savings and therefore higher interests, thus contributing to a disincentive to invest, and was also competing with the private sector in employment of labour, thus pushing up labour costs.

The micro approach – a programme perspective

In contrast, the programme or micro approach implies that decisions on public expenditure are determined by factors related to an individual programme. The programme approach points out that the resources of government are directed to meet specific programme purposes, such as the provision of education, health and a postal service. Public expenditure within programmes reflects the commitment of government to a specific expenditure programme, which implies less resources being directed to other programmes. Within the programme approach, therefore, influences such as demography, the costs of providing a service, ease of access and quality of output are seen as being among the determinants in the growth of social security, health, education or social services expenditures.

These are described as demand-led expenditures, where once access has been decided, government has little autonomy in altering the structure of an expenditure programme except by seeking to alter the legal framework which defines the area of expenditure. The programme approach also emphasises the relationships between expenditure 'inputs' and policy 'outputs'. The government expenditure plans for education for the years 1992–3 provide examples of the level of resources being allocated to education and policy outputs in terms of the number of students staying on at school beyond the age of 16, the number of successes at GCSE, the number of successes at 'A' levels, and also student participation ratios in both further and higher education.

The macro approach is favoured by those who see public expenditure primarily as an area of concern in terms of how it is to be financed, the implications for government revenue, borrowing and financial markets. It reflects, for example, the thinking implicit in the Medium Term Financial Strategy (MTFS) as constructed and pursued by Conservative governments since 1980. The MTFS outlined the 'pathways' for national income, public expenditure and its percentage of the former, the total for government revenue, and figures for the Public Sector Borrowing Requirement (PSBR) and the money supply. The MTFS implicitly suggested that public expenditure had helped in 'crowding out' the private sector, in that growth in the economy was perceived to be dependent on the commitment of government to restrain the growth of public expenditure. Second, the MTFS also acknowledged the view that government borrowing was highly correlated with changes in the money supply and therefore inflation, which in turn implied that a policy to reduce inflation required a policy to control the money supply, government borrowing and public expenditure:

> The Budget is a further stage in the Government's medium term policy of reducing inflation . . . The central feature of the anti-inflation policy is the gradual reduction of monetary growth. To achieve this reduction without intolerably high interest rates public sector borrowing will be reduced.

> (HMSO 1980a: 3)

Reinforcing this relationship, Leon Brittan, then Financial Secretary to the Treasury, made the following observation:

> Let me start with two simple facts. The first is a statistic. The PSBR is at present about $4\frac{1}{2}$ per cent of total GDP – compared with an average of $2\frac{1}{2}$ per cent in the 1960s. The second is an economic relationship. That is, the PSBR and the growth in the money supply.
>
> (House of Commons 1980b: 2)

Alongside the MTFS, the Government in 1982 also decided to break with the past practices of publishing data for public expenditure in both volume and constant prices. The 1982 Expenditure White Paper therefore represented a watershed in the public expenditure survey, in that details on expenditure were from now on to be published using only volume prices. This decision corresponded with the Government's overall economic strategy of controlling inflation by controlling the money supply and therefore restraining public expenditure. Expressing public expenditure in volume terms therefore reinforced the Government's major concern of showing public expenditure as a cost which had to be financed by taxes and borrowing that were expressed in volume terms and not at constant prices. Sir Anthony Rawlinson, when Second Permanent Secretary to the Treasury, confirmed this view:

> This change to full cash planning is fundamentally a change of policy rather than of technique. What has changed from the way in which the Survey subsequently developed is that resources against which expenditure is to be planned and which primarily constrain it are now seen as financial. This is consistent with current economic conditions and with the Government's strategy. It is cash expenditure which should be considered in relation to and made consistent with the Government's objectives for taxation, the borrowing requirement and the money supply.
>
> (HMSO 1983a: 81)

However, this continued concern with public expenditure as an aggregate has also meant that governments have paid insufficient attention to the process of the effectiveness and efficiency of individual expenditure programmes. Heclo and Wildavsky described the process as:

brutalisation by aggregation [where] all expenditures are treated as
being interchangeable – where a missile, a motorway or a hospital
amount to the same thing.

(Heclo and Wildavsky 1982: 77)

The ascendancy of a macro perspective suggests that public expenditure decisions are not the product of any rational analysis of what
public expenditure programmes seek to achieve, but that expenditure
decisions are often the product of a series of bilateral negotiations
between Treasury ministers and spending departments, usually
achieved in the climate of short-term pressures and influences.

Financial Secretaries to the Treasury are involved in a continuous
process of negotiating bilateral deals with spending ministers, where
the brief for the Financial Secretary is simple. The brief is to make sure
that spending ministers adhere to the global spending targets set out by
the Treasury in the Public Expenditure White Paper (published in
January) and which have to be revised during the Autumn Statement
in November.

A different approach would be to ask what public expenditure
within individual expenditure programmes seeks to achieve. This has
been called the programme approach (Rose 1984b). It emphasises the
need to study individual expenditure programmes and the factors
which influence these programmes, where the concern is to explain
changes in an expenditure programme in relation to the legislation and
public policy that are enshrined within an expenditure budget. The
programme approach is therefore concerned with both the inputs as
expressed in public expenditure terms, and also the policy outputs that
indicate which objectives have been achieved for a certain level of
expenditure.

Whilst the macro approach is concerned with evaluating the
implications for public expenditure in cash terms, the micro or
programme approach is concerned with evaluating expenditure in real
terms, that is, by taking into account the real value of inputs, which
means that changes in the rate of inflation must be taken into
consideration. Those involved in the provision of services are concerned with the level of finance that allows them to deliver a service to
the public. They are therefore concerned with the question of whether
their service is receiving new revenues that allow them to expand a
service, or whether they are receiving the same level of finance, or less,
especially when government estimates have tended to underestimate
the rate of inflation, thus creating underfunded expenditure programmes.

Over the past decade there have been various initiatives within the Treasury and spending departments to evaluate the effectiveness and efficiency of expenditure programmes. The Financial Management Initiative and Value for Money represent two mechanisms which the Government has introduced within spending departments, yet both are seen as being weak proxies for the market-place, where prices are set between consumers and suppliers. The absence of markets within the public sector means that the suppliers, namely the professionals and the bureaucracy, are still seen as setting the prices as monopoly suppliers.

Privatisation can be viewed as the mechanism which seeks to break up the monopoly position of the bureaucracy and the public sector professionals. Compelling local authorities to move towards competitive tendering for their maintenance and cleaning services is seen as the attempt to break local authority monopoly. The sale of utilities, including British Gas, British Telecom, electricity and water, is also seen as being compatible with the government approach to breaking the process of ownership and control, and therefore of introducing more consumer rights and consumer choice. The Education Reform Act, 1988 seeks not only to break the monopoly of the local authority as an education provider, but also the monopoly of the teaching profession by introducing 'opt-out' schools and local management of schools. Finally, the Health Service reforms are also seen by the Government as an attempt to introduce internal markets to the NHS by creating competition between Hospital Trusts, as providers of health care, and the doctors and health authorities, who purchase health care on behalf of their patients.

The two perspectives outlined here reflect the debate over whether it is public expenditure (macro) which determines the programme approach (micro), or whether it is the micro which determines the macro. Or, to put it another way, does macro policy determine the changes in expenditure programmes or does public expenditure reflect the needs which arise from individual programmes? Being clear about the distinction between these approaches is important because they represent different explanations of which factors can be considered to impinge on changes in public expenditure.

According to the macro perspective, policy changes are explained by referring to the wider economic and political context in which expenditure decisions are made. Macro analysts point to economic events and a government's economic policies (that seek to respond to these events), arguing that policies on public expenditure are inextricably linked with economic policy.

In contrast, the programme approach tends to point to influences such as demographic changes, which determine the size of an expenditure programme, and argues instead that most expenditure programmes are demand determined. The social security programme, for example, is influenced by both the number of elderly people claiming pensions and the rate of unemployment. Health expenditure is also perceived to be demand determined, again highly influenced by the number of elderly people. According to this approach the autonomy of government is limited, in that a government cannot start from a zero budget but, rather, has to take as given the costs of a programme.

THE PROBLEM OF MEASUREMENT

This section expands on the proposition that there is no single correct way to measure the size of the public sector, and looks at the implications of the macro and micro analyses in measuring public expenditure. Within a macro frame of reference there is no problem in measuring public expenditure; all government activities need to be financed and are therefore by definition public expenditures. In contrast, at the programme level, there would be a debate as to what should or should not be encompassed by the definition of public expenditure. This includes, for example, a debate on how to treat lendings to the nationalised industries, or transfer payments.

Sir Richard Clarke (1973) has pointed out that public expenditure between 1952 and 1971 had expanded from 41.3 per cent of GDP (factor costs) in 1959 to 50.8 per cent in 1971. The author went on to suggest that:

> the balance [had] tilted over when the interests of the public as consumers of public services came to be regarded as politically more important than their interests as taxpayers.

> (Clarke 1973: 142)

This quotation supports the view that within the macro approach the size of public expenditure is measured as a ratio of GDP, since it is assumed that the expansion of the public sector always means a shift of resources away from the private sector. Roy Jenkins, whilst Home Secretary, warned that public expenditure had become a threat to individual freedom:

> I do not think that you can push public expenditure significantly above 60 per cent and maintain the values of a plural society with

adequate freedom of choice. We are here close to one of the frontiers of social democracy.

(R. Jenkins, speech at Anglesey Labour Party, 23 January 1976)

Although it has not been possible to show how Mr Jenkins arrived at this measure (Heald 1983), it can be argued that its deployment contributed to the Labour Government's decision to embark on policies aimed at cancelling the planned growth in public expenditure without too much dissent on the Government benches and in the wider labour movement.

However, that Labour administration was involved in constructing a departure from past definitions and measurements of public expenditure. It seems that the Treasury was influenced by the OECD's approach (Pliatzky 1982), which implicitly questioned the correctness of the United Kingdom definition of a public sector activity. Whilst the UK Treasury assumed that the finances of the nationalised industries were part of public expenditure, the OECD's view was that:

> The stand taken is that what is of most interest is to identify separately that expenditure which will sooner or later have to be covered by taxation, it is in effect expenditure decided by non-market criteria.
>
> (OECD 1978: 11)

Second, it would seem that whilst the Treasury was working within this spirit of reform it accepted a second change to its measurements. In future the ratio of public expenditure was to be expressed as a percentage of GDP at market prices and not factor costs. This was at least measuring like with like, since public expenditure included indirect taxation whilst the previous GDP at factor costs did not. Pliatzky explains the consequences of these changes as follows:

> the alarming 60 per cent figure was brought down by the new treatment of the nationalised industries and debt interest to an expenditure/GDP ratio of $51\frac{1}{2}$ per cent of GDP at factor cost; by putting GDP on the basis of market prices, the ratio was further brought down to just under 46 per cent.
>
> (Pliatzky 1982: 166)

The acceptance of re-evaluating and re-defining public expenditure raises three issues. First, why had the British Treasury previously favoured a system of accounting which brought the lending to the nationalised industries under Treasury control? Presumably it was because the Treasury wanted to maintain some control over the activities of the nationalised industries but it had, nevertheless, also contributed to a discourse which encouraged a view that the public sector was too large. Second, why did the Treasury accept the reforms at this time? Again, the argument seems to be that it was a calculation by the Labour Cabinet as much as the Treasury, in the hope that by massaging the expenditure figures there would be less panic in the financial markets. Finally, it would seem that whilst Pliatzky argued from a macro approach he was equally willing to reduce the size of public expenditure. According to the new definitions, Pliatzky has shown that public expenditure in 1959 was 33.4 per cent (GDP market prices), rising to 37.5 per cent in 1971 and to 43.1 per cent by 1980.

The second problem in defining public expenditure is related to whether all public expenditure should be treated in a homogeneous manner, and whether all government activities should be assumed to be exhaustive expenditure. This question is directed at the assumption that public expenditure represents a resources reallocation from the private to the public sector with no attempt to evaluate the correctness of such an approach. The author (Mullard 1987) has argued that public expenditure has to be disaggregated into the capital, current and transfer components of the expenditure programme. This is important because it can then be asked whether the transfer component of an expenditure programme should represent a resource reallocation to the public sector. Transfer payments on social security, education grants, subsidies on transport and housing, agriculture and the nationalised industries have the common characteristic of increasing the demand potential of their recipients by either giving the recipient a direct cash benefit or by indirectly reducing the price of a commodity. The effect of transfers, therefore, must be a reallocation of income between different income groups, a process which is carried out by the public sector, rather than being an activity carried out on behalf of the public sector.

CHANGES IN PUBLIC EXPENDITURE: THE HISTORICAL CONTEXT

The study of public expenditure utilised in this text continues the process adopted by the author in previous publications (Mullard 1987, 1990). These studies have usually addressed the following concerns:

(a)   The provision of an analysis of public expenditure as a total whilst seeking to provide a measurement which takes into account the rate of inflation which influences changes within this total. The argument has been that using one deflator like the GDP to account for inflation was not sufficient and therefore what was needed was to apply various deflators. Within this context, therefore, the following expenditure programmes have been selected and then disaggregated by economic category:

1. Law and Order	Current Expenditure
2. Defence	Current Expenditure
3. Education	Current, Capital and Transfers
4. Health	Current and Capital Expenditure
5. Environment	Current and Capital Expenditure
6. Roads	Current, Capital and Transfers
7. Trade and Industry	Current and Transfers
8. Social Security	Transfer Payments
9. Housing	Capital and Transfers
10. Personal Social Services	Current and Transfers

The study involves research into ten major expenditure programmes. In contrast the Public Expenditure White Papers tend to itemise public expenditure within fourteen expenditure sub-divisions. The expenditure programmes chosen constitute approximately 90 per cent of total expenditure. The breakdown by economic category means that, within capital expenditure by expenditure programme, constituting over 97 per cent of total capital expenditure, current expenditure can be equated with 87 per cent of total current expenditure, and that transfers, grants and subsidies make up 85 per cent of expenditure within this category.

(b) The make-up of the total for public expenditure depends on the constituent parts – that is, the individual expenditure programmes – whilst in turn each expenditure programme needs to be disaggregated by economic category. It is these changes within the factors which influence changes within a programme, and therefore changes within the aggregates for total expenditure.

(c) The attempt to understand the micro changes within an

Table 1.1 Expenditure by programme 1962–90 disaggregated by appropriate GDP deflators

Year	Defence	Law	Education	Health	Environment	Roads	Transport	Housing	Social Security	Total
1962	8.02	1.04	4.85	4.25	1.80	2.12	0.26	1.75	7.32	32.9
1964	7.33	1.08	4.96	4.22	1.88	2.10	0.25	2.10	7.53	32.4
1966	7.48	1.22	5.32	4.75	2.04	2.02	0.37	2.17	6.00	31.4
1968	6.58	1.19	5.18	4.52	1.77	2.06	1.37	2.30	6.92	32.4
1970	5.70	1.32	5.38	4.58	1.81	2.05	1.27	2.06	6.72	31.3
1972	5.38	1.34	5.61	4.59	1.90	1.81	1.51	1.63	7.30	31.5
1974	5.16	1.43	5.54	4.87	1.75	2.28	1.68	2.95	7.27	33.8
1976	4.99	1.48	5.70	4.90	1.57	1.86	1.17	2.97	8.02	33.3
1978	4.84	1.46	5.37	4.91	1.39	1.59	1.38	2.32	8.92	32.5
1979	4.86	1.49	5.03	4.75	1.42	1.57	1.36	2.17	9.22	32.1
1981	5.17	1.74	5.35	5.35	1.35	1.67	1.55	1.45	10.9	34.9
1982	5.28	1.74	5.16	5.13	1.40	1.79	1.46	1.01	11.5	34.8
1983	5.19	1.72	5.09	5.28	1.44	1.70	1.54	1.65	11.1	35.1
1984	5.28	1.71	5.23	5.19	1.28	1.50	0.99	1.73	11.5	34.9
1985	5.07	1.63	4.89	5.02	1.24	1.47	1.01	1.36	11.4	33.4
1986	4.82	1.65	4.99	4.93	0.52	1.32	0.98	1.36	11.5	32.6
1987	4.33	1.62	4.84	4.82	0.52	1.21	0.69	1.35	10.9	30.9
1988	3.97	1.58	4.62	4.69	0.51	1.10	0.80	0.91	10.2	28.8
1989	3.84	1.61	4.55	4.72	0.54	1.16	0.95	0.74	9.8	28.2
1990	3.72	1.64	4.46	4.61	0.48	1.27	1.01	0.66	9.7	27.8

expenditure programme distinguishes the approach of this study in contrast to other, more macro, approaches. Furthermore, it is the micro changes that reflect and emphasise the concept of political choice.

Trends in public expenditure since 1962

During the period 1962–90 the trend in total for public expenditure would indicate that expenditure on programmes as related to this study had been held constant at about 32 per cent of GDP. Expenditure seemed to grow to about 34 per cent in 1974 and 1975 but then started to fall to around 30 per cent until the early 1980s, when expenditure again resumed an expansionary trend (Table 1.1). However, since 1985 the trend has been in continuous decline with expenditure falling sharply to 27.8 per cent in 1990 (Figure 1.1). The study of the year-on-year annualised differences confirms the extent to which government has managed to bring expenditure under control, especially after 1984 when there has been no real additional increase except in 1982 and 1990 (Figure 1.2).

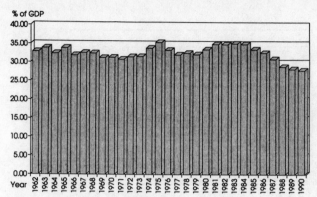

Figure 1.1 Total expenditure of 10 major expenditure programmes 1962–90 at constant prices

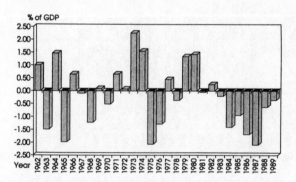

Figure 1.2 Total expenditure, year-on-year changes 1962–90

Explaining the changes by programme

Defence expenditure

The level of expenditure as a percentage of GDP continued to decline throughout the period from a peak of 8 per cent of GDP in 1962 to under 4 per cent in 1990 (Figure 1.3). Irrespective of the Government, therefore, defence expenditure has taken a declining share of national

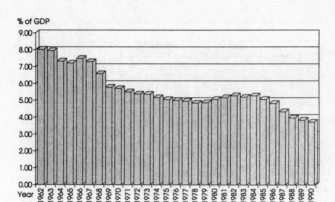

Figure 1.3 Defence expenditure 1962–90

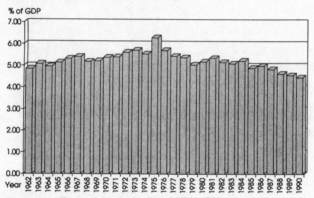

Figure 1.4 Education expenditure 1962–90

income, thus acting as an enabling factor for other programmes to be expanded.

Education expenditure

The education programme has been disaggregated by economic component. At an aggregate level education expenditure was being expanded between 1962 and 1975 from under 4.9 per cent of GDP in 1962 to reach a peak of over 6 per cent in 1975. From 1976 to 1984 education expenditure returned to a level of 5 per cent of GDP, but then continued to decline further to 4.5 per cent in 1990 (Figure 1.4). The disaggregation by economic component shows that when total expenditure had been expanding during the 1960s and early 1970s capital expenditure had also been expanding. In contrast, as educa-

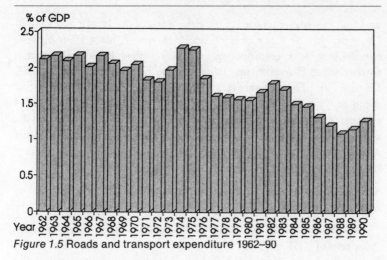

Figure 1.5 Roads and transport expenditure 1962–90

tion expenditure as a total was being brought under control after 1975, capital expenditure declined very steeply from £2 billion to £700 million, this figure being allotted to school buildings and repairs. The level of expenditure remained at £700 million during the 1980s.

In contrast, current expenditure was also growing during the 1970s, but the rate of growth seemed to peak and remain stable. Current expenditure in real terms increased from £6 billion in 1962 to £14 billion in 1975. The relative stability in current expenditure indicates the degree to which both Labour and Conservative Governments had managed to control the wage costs in education.

Roads and transport

Road expenditure peaked during the years 1974 and 1975, growing from 2 per cent of GDP during the 1960s to 2.4 per cent in 1974. After 1975 expenditure declined sharply to 1.5 per cent of GDP in 1982 and 1.2 per cent by 1989 (Figure 1.5). The analysis by economic category confirms the extent to which capital expenditure had taken the brunt of the reductions, although since 1985 capital expenditure has again been expanded. Grants and subsidies to transport again reached a peak during the years of the Labour Government between 1975 and 1976, but subsidies have been continuously reduced during the 1980s.

Social housing

The analysis of expenditure on housing confirms that expenditure was expanded during the 1960s from 1.5 per cent of GDP to over 2 per cent, and that this was expanded during the years of the Heath and Labour Governments to 3 per cent of GDP. However, after 1976 housing expenditure was continuously reduced under both Labour and Conservative Governments, falling to 0.4 per cent of GDP by 1990 (Figure 1.6). The disaggregation by economic category confirms the rapid decline in capital expenditure from a peak of £5 billion in 1974 to about £500 million in 1982 with a slight recovery to £1 billion in the late 1980s. Grants and subsidies also peaked at about £4 billion in the mid-1970s but the sale of council housing and the increases in rents meant that subsidies had fallen to just over £1 billion by 1990.

Environment expenditure

Expenditure was held at a stable level with mild fluctuation at around 2 per cent of GDP until 1976 but, again, it seems that this followed the trend for other expenditures, declining during the 1980s to below the level attained in the 1960s to around 1 per cent of GDP, and by 1990 to 0.5 per cent of GDP (Figure 1.7).

Law and order

In contrast to the other expenditure programmes, expenditure on law and order continued to be expanded from the mid-1970s so that expenditure increased from about 1 per cent of GDP during the 1960s to 1.5 per cent of GDP during the 1980s (Figure 1.8, p. 30).

Trade and industry

Expenditure expanded from under 0.4 per cent of GDP during the early 1960s to 1.5 per cent in the 1970s as the Government expanded expenditure on various employment projects and also on grants to industries. However, during the 1980s expenditure declined to around 1 per cent of GDP (Figure 1.9, p. 31). The study of expenditure on grants and subsidies confirms the extent to which government policy has changed on employment and on grants to industry.

Health expenditure

The study of health expenditure confirms the relative stability of the financing of health. Expenditure started at about 4 per cent of GDP during the 1960s and expanded to a new plateau of 5 per cent of GDP

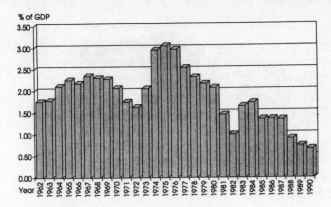

Figure 1.6 Housing expenditure 1962–90

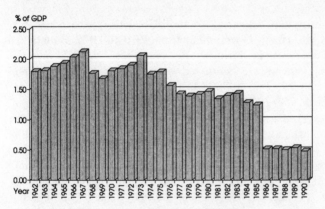

Figure 1.7 Environment expenditure 1962–90

during the 1970s and 1980s (Figure 1.10, p. 31). The analysis by economic category confirms the continuous expansion in current expenditure, which again reflects the rising costs of health care and also the willingness of governments to meet these costs. Furthermore, the stability of capital expenditure, when contrasted to the housing, roads and environment programmes that were drastically reduced, again points to the priority given to health expenditure whilst other programmes were experiencing retrenchment and reductions.

The detailed study by expenditure programme between 1962 and 1990 would suggest that the approach adopted by both Labour and Conservative Governments tended to follow very similar patterns. Expenditure on all programmes was expanded during the years of the

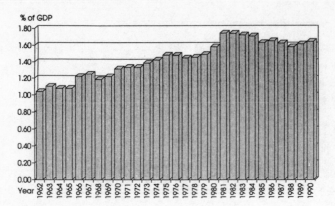

Figure 1.8 Law and order expenditure 1962–90

Labour Governments between 1964 and 1970. This approach was also adopted by the Heath Government from 1970 to 1974. Equally it could be pointed out that during the first two years of the 1974 Labour Government expenditure continued to be expanded. This trend reached a watershed in 1976, when all expenditure programmes seemed to peak; after 1976 all programmes experienced reductions and constraint except for the law and order programme, and health.

Education expenditure was reduced from 5 per cent of GDP to 4.5 per cent in 1990, with capital expenditure being reduced drastically. This approach is applicable to the housing programme, roads and environment, where most of the reductions seemed to fall on the capital component. The Labour Government in 1976 achieved most of its reductions by constraining capital expenditure – a policy that was pursued by the Thatcher Government during the early 1980s. However, despite the expansion of current expenditure it would seem that in the longer term the Government has again managed to restrain the growth of current expenditure during the 1980s.

The study of the year-on-year changes raises three questions. First, how can the stability/fluctuation between expenditure programmes be explained? Studies by Clarke (1968), Rose (1984c) and Judge (1982a) would suggest that the post-war period was characterised largely by a bipartisan approach and by continuity of expenditure programmes. Commitment to expansion in expenditures on health, education, defence and law and order continued under Labour and Conservative Governments. Judge explains the growth of public expenditure as follows:

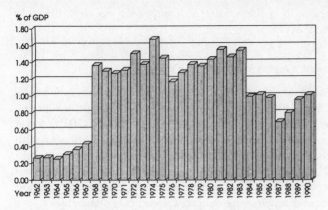

Figure 1.9 Trade and industry expenditure 1962–90

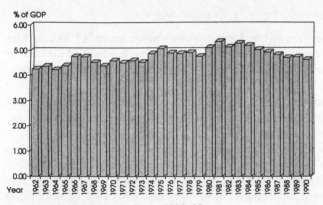

Figure 1.10 Health expenditure 1962–90

There are no significant differences between the records of Labour and Conservative governments at the level of aggregate expenditures. In fact there seems to have been a steady acceleration in the rate of growth under both parties.

(Judge 1982a: 29)

The second question is related to whether or not there is commonalty between the programmes and their groupings. One area of commonalty is related to the economic component within an expenditure programme. Programmes with a high ratio of capital expenditure, and these include housing, roads and environment, can be described as being more likely to experience change; in contrast, expenditure programmes with a high current component are less likely to experience change.

Programmes with a high current expenditure component

The education, health, defence and law and order programmes all contain a high level of current expenditure. At current prices, expenditure on education expanded by 1.20 per cent of GDP (market prices), compared with 0.33 per cent at constant prices; health increased to 1.92 per cent of GDP compared with 0.90 per cent, whilst defence fell by 1.10 per cent of GDP at current prices, but 2.99 per cent at constant prices. This would suggest that when measured in constant prices these programmes experienced a slower rate of increase.

Programmes with a high capital/transfer component

The housing, roads and environment programmes all have a high capital component. Expenditure on housing fell by 0.13 per cent at current prices compared with 0.26 per cent at constant prices, whilst expenditure on roads fell by 0.05 per cent at current prices and 0.21 per cent at constant prices. Programmes with a high capital component therefore tend to experience a higher rate of reduction when measured at constant prices.

The social security programme, agriculture and the nationalised industries all have transfer/subsidy as their highest component. Social security expanded by 5.45 per cent at current prices compared with 5.84 per cent at constant prices; agriculture fell by 0.71 per cent at current prices and 0.64 per cent at constant prices, and the nationalised industries fell by 1.62 per cent at current prices and 2.01 per cent at constant prices. These results substantiate the view that demand-led expenditures tend to retain their real value.

AN ATTEMPT TO MEASURE PUBLIC EXPENDITURE USING APPROPRIATE PRICE DEFLATORS

In this section two ways of looking at the growth in public expenditure are outlined, one expressed in value (i.e. at current prices), the other in volume or real terms (i.e. at constant 1985 prices). This is a well-tried method but the concern here has been to provide a departure from past practice. The most frequent practice has been to deflate the monetary value by a single deflator, usually the GDP price deflator. In this

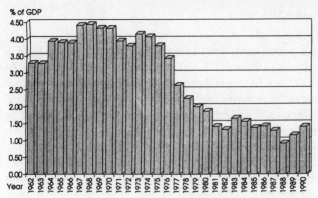

Figure 1.11 Total capital expenditure 1962–90 at constant prices

section the aim has been to show that the capital, current and transfer components within an expenditure programme should be deflated by their appropriate price deflators before a single value for an expenditure programme at constant prices can emerge. This practice is adopted in this section and the data recorded here have been utilised throughout the study.

Capital expenditure

Here the objective has been to look at capital expenditure both as a total and by programme at current and constant prices, using the capital formation deflator to calculate the latter. At current prices total capital expenditure was 3.1 per cent of GDP (market prices) in 1962 but by 1990 this had fallen to 1.4 per cent of GDP (Figure 1.11). When capital expenditure is deflated by its price deflator (GFDCF deflator), then the ratio taken by capital expenditure in 1962 was 3.3 per cent of GDP falling to 1.4 per cent in 1990. The analysis at constant price terms and in monetary values suggests that these were not significantly different.

The breakdown by programme also confirms only small differences in the measure at current and constant prices. Housing at current prices fell by 0.9 per cent of GDP, whilst at constant prices the reduction was also 0.9 per cent; education was also reduced by 0.38 per cent of GDP at current prices and 0.40 per cent at constant prices. In health, roads and environment there are no differences between the two measures.

Current expenditure

At current prices total current expenditure grew from 14.8 per cent of GDP (market prices) in 1962 to 18 per cent in 1983, but then started to fall every year after 1985 to 15.3 per cent in 1990 (Table 1.3, p. 36). In contrast total current expenditure deflated by the public sector consumption deflator continued to decline as a percentage of GDP after 1966, when this reached a peak of 19.7 per cent (Figure 1.12, p. 37). Current expenditure in real terms has continued to decline from 18 per cent in 1968 to 17.6 per cent in 1978; it started to rise again during the first years of the Thatcher Government to 18 per cent, but after 1985 the Conservative Government seemed to regain control and expenditure continued to fall from 15.7 per cent in 1987 to 14.5 per cent in 1990 (Table 1.4, p. 37).

This means that when measuring the growth of total expenditure there are significant differences when it is measured in current or constant prices. Using a monetary value, it would seem that current expenditure was always on a rising trend; this is not so when it is measured at constant prices. The measure at current prices would suggest that the Government had a problem of controlling the rate of growth in current expenditure, whilst the measure at constant prices would suggest that the Government was in control.

The breakdown by programme confirms this variance. Within the defence programme, the level of reduction shows a fall of 1.10 per cent of GDP (market prices) at current prices, and 2.99 per cent at constant prices. In law and order expenditure expanded by 1.72 per cent at current prices compared to 0.63 per cent at constant prices. In education there was an increase of 1.21 per cent at current prices and 0.31 per cent at constant prices; and in health an increase of 1.82 per cent at current prices compared to 0.80 per cent at constant prices.

Transfers and subsidies

The study of Table 1.5 (p. 38) confirms that at constant prices, using the consumer price deflator, expenditure increased from 11 per cent of GDP in 1962 to 11.9 per cent in 1990. Within the overall trend, however, there has been a steep increase in transfers during the 1980s, from 11 per cent of GDP to over 15 per cent – the increases being associated with the increases in unemployment and the expansion of the social security programme. Since 1987 expenditure on transfers has declined to 12 per cent of GDP, again reflecting the changes in unemployment. Unemployment increased from 1.4 million in 1979 to

Table 1.2 Capital expenditure 1962–90 by expenditure programme in real terms

Year	Housing	Education	Health	Roads	Environment	Total
1962	1.19	0.60	0.20	0.64	0.66	3.29
1963	1.24	0.54	0.20	0.66	0.65	3.29
1964	1.58	0.58	0.24	0.79	0.75	3.94
1965	1.62	0.51	0.27	0.76	0.74	3.90
1966	1.71	0.48	0.27	0.75	0.69	3.90
1967	1.89	0.59	0.32	0.89	0.73	4.42
1968	1.80	0.62	0.33	0.93	0.76	4.44
1969	1.71	0.59	0.29	1.00	0.73	4.32
1970	1.48	0.60	0.30	1.13	0.81	4.32
1971	1.17	0.64	0.32	0.96	0.86	3.95
1972	1.02	0.68	0.35	0.89	0.85	3.79
1973	1.25	0.71	0.35	0.90	0.95	4.16
1974	1.78	0.58	0.31	0.76	0.64	4.07
1975	1.77	0.50	0.32	0.76	0.46	3.81
1976	1.61	0.46	0.31	0.63	0.42	3.43
1977	1.24	0.34	0.25	0.48	0.32	2.63
1978	0.99	0.26	0.23	0.45	0.30	2.23
1979	0.76	0.23	0.24	0.43	0.33	1.99
1980	0.61	0.24	0.24	0.42	0.35	1.86
1981	0.23	0.21	0.26	0.40	0.31	1.41
1982	−0.01	0.18	0.29	0.51	0.35	1.32
1983	0.37	0.18	0.28	0.51	0.31	1.65
1984	0.47	0.19	0.29	0.49	0.12	1.56
1985	0.33	0.18	0.28	0.48	0.10	1.37
1986	0.41	0.17	0.28	0.47	0.09	1.42
1987	0.36	0.17	0.24	0.44	0.08	1.29
1988	0.05	0.13	0.21	0.45	0.08	0.92
1989	0.12	0.17	0.25	0.51	0.10	1.15
1990	0.28	0.19	0.27	0.62	0.04	1.40

3.3 million in 1983. The levels of unemployment declined after 1987, when the rate fell from 3 million to 1.7 million in 1990.

The breakdown by programme shows that the trade and industry programme increased by 0.45 per cent of GDP at current prices and 0.47 per cent of GDP at constant prices, roads between 0.16 per cent at current prices and 0.19 per cent at constant prices, and that agriculture fell by 0.18 per cent of GDP at current prices and 0.13 per cent of GDP at constant prices. The study by programme also indicates small divergences between the two sets of measurements.

In disaggregating these programmes by economic component and then comparing the changes at current prices and constant prices it

Table 1.3 Current expenditure by programme 1962–90 in cash terms

Year	Defence	Law	Education	Health	Environment	Roads	Trade	Total
1962	6.30	0.82	2.82	3.18	0.89	0.66	0.21	14.88
1963	6.07	0.84	2.90	3.18	0.89	0.70	0.21	14.79
1964	5.72	0.84	2.81	3.11	0.89	0.65	0.20	14.22
1965	5.75	0.86	2.96	3.28	0.95	0.66	0.25	14.71
1966	5.65	0.93	3.12	3.39	1.02	0.66	0.28	15.05
1967	5.76	0.99	3.23	3.50	1.11	0.68	0.34	15.61
1968	5.44	0.98	3.12	3.46	0.84	0.62	0.61	15.07
1969	4.83	1.02	3.18	3.41	0.79	0.59	0.65	14.47
1970	4.74	1.09	3.30	3.56	0.83	0.59	0.65	14.76
1971	4.72	1.15	3.36	3.59	0.85	0.61	0.71	14.99
1972	4.72	1.17	3.55	3.72	0.92	0.58	0.71	15.37
1973	4.66	1.20	3.58	3.62	0.97	0.63	0.64	15.30
1974	4.85	1.34	3.82	4.28	1.04	0.65	0.64	16.62
1975	4.89	1.44	4.71	4.60	1.28	0.71	0.69	18.32
1976	4.97	1.47	4.29	4.57	1.14	0.65	0.70	17.79
1977	4.76	1.39	4.01	4.44	1.07	0.63	0.66	16.96
1978	4.58	1.38	3.96	4.44	1.04	0.63	0.69	16.72
1979	4.61	1.41	3.76	4.28	1.04	0.62	0.63	16.35
1980	4.97	1.55	3.92	4.77	1.10	0.62	0.64	17.57
1981	5.01	1.69	4.05	4.93	1.01	0.69	0.49	17.87
1982	5.22	1.72	4.01	4.79	1.04	0.70	0.45	17.93
1983	5.20	1.72	4.03	5.00	1.13	0.64	0.46	18.18
1984	5.29	1.71	4.18	4.91	1.16	0.53	0.42	18.20
1985	5.04	1.62	3.86	4.71	1.14	0.51	0.42	17.30
1986	4.86	1.66	4.06	4.68	0.43	0.49	0.43	16.61
1987	4.44	1.66	4.00	4.69	0.45	0.49	0.36	16.09
1988	3.98	1.59	3.75	4.50	0.43	0.43	0.42	15.10
1989	3.86	1.62	3.51	4.50	0.44	0.46	0.41	14.80
1990	3.94	1.74	3.58	4.59	0.47	0.46	0.55	15.33

becomes apparent that any explanation of dynamics within public expenditure has to include the study of programmes and of changes within programmes. The current expenditure component measured in monetary values and at constant prices reveals that current expenditures grew faster than when measured at constant prices, which in turn points to the need to consider the process of inflation within this component. On the capital and transfer components there is less variance between the two measurements.

Furthermore, claims made by governments that they have increased expenditure in 'real terms' are usually based on the use of a single price deflator. This means that programmes with a high current component, such as education and health, might have hidden reductions in real

Table 1.4 Current expenditure 1962–90 by expenditure programme in real terms

Year	Defence	Law	Education	Health	Environment	Roads	Trade	Total
1962	8.02	1.04	3.59	4.04	1.13	0.84	0.26	18.92
1964	7.33	1.08	3.59	3.98	1.14	0.83	0.25	18.20
1966	7.48	1.22	4.12	4.49	1.35	0.88	0.37	19.91
1968	6.58	1.19	3.78	4.19	1.01	0.75	0.73	18.23
1970	5.70	1.32	3.98	4.28	1.00	0.71	0.79	17.78
1972	5.38	1.34	4.04	4.24	1.05	0.66	0.80	17.51
1973	5.36	1.39	4.13	4.17	1.12	0.72	0.73	17.62
1974	5.16	1.43	4.07	4.56	1.11	0.70	0.69	17.72
1975	5.05	1.48	4.86	4.76	1.33	0.74	0.72	18.94
1976	4.99	1.48	4.31	4.59	1.14	0.65	0.70	17.86
1977	4.96	1.45	4.18	4.62	1.12	0.66	0.68	17.67
1978	4.84	1.46	4.18	4.68	1.10	0.66	0.72	17.64
1979	4.86	1.49	3.97	4.51	1.10	0.66	0.66	17.25
1980	5.06	1.58	4.00	4.87	1.12	0.63	0.65	17.91
1981	5.17	1.74	4.17	5.09	1.04	0.72	0.50	18.43
1982	5.28	1.74	4.06	4.84	1.05	0.71	0.46	18.14
1983	5.19	1.72	4.03	5.00	1.13	0.64	0.46	18.17
1984	5.28	1.71	4.17	4.90	1.16	0.52	0.42	18.16
1985	5.07	1.63	3.89	4.74	1.15	0.51	0.42	17.41
1986	4.82	1.65	4.02	4.65	0.43	0.49	0.43	16.49
1987	4.33	1.62	3.91	4.58	0.44	0.48	0.35	15.71
1988	3.97	1.58	3.73	4.48	0.43	0.43	0.42	15.04
1989	3.84	1.61	3.49	4.47	0.43	0.45	0.39	14.68
1990	3.72	1.64	3.39	4.34	0.44	0.44	0.52	14.49

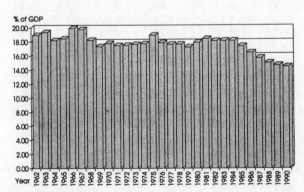

Figure 1.12 Total current expenditure 1962–90 at constant prices

terms despite the view that these expenditures could have experienced an increase in expenditure.

Table 1.5 Grants, subsidies and transfer payments 1962–90 by expenditure programme in real terms

Year	Trade	Roads	Agriculture	Education	Housing	Social Security	Total
1962	0.00	0.64	1.46	0.67	0.56	7.32	10.65
1963	0.00	0.59	1.26	0.76	0.54	8.09	11.24
1964	0.00	0.48	0.93	0.79	0.52	7.53	10.25
1965	0.00	0.58	0.88	0.92	0.63	8.49	11.50
1966	0.00	0.40	0.51	0.71	0.46	6.00	8.08
1967	0.00	0.43	0.56	0.72	0.46	6.20	8.37
1968	0.64	0.38	0.56	0.78	0.50	6.92	9.78
1969	0.52	0.26	0.49	0.80	0.56	6.93	9.56
1970	0.49	0.21	0.43	0.80	0.58	6.72	9.23
1971	0.48	0.16	0.50	0.84	0.58	6.82	9.38
1972	0.70	0.26	0.41	0.89	0.60	7.30	10.16
1973	0.65	0.36	0.37	0.87	0.81	6.73	9.79
1974	0.99	0.82	0.88	0.88	1.18	7.27	12.02
1975	0.74	0.77	1.23	0.91	1.29	7.68	12.62
1976	0.46	0.58	0.64	0.93	1.36	8.02	11.99
1977	0.60	0.47	0.36	0.91	1.30	8.09	11.73
1978	0.65	0.48	0.29	0.92	1.33	8.92	12.59
1979	0.70	0.47	0.25	0.83	1.41	9.22	12.88
1980	0.78	0.50	0.30	0.94	1.46	9.69	13.67
1981	1.05	0.55	0.34	0.96	1.22	10.91	15.03
1982	1.01	0.58	0.32	0.91	1.02	11.54	15.38
1983	1.08	0.56	0.41	0.89	1.28	11.06	15.27
1984	0.57	0.49	0.45	0.86	1.27	11.52	15.18
1985	0.59	0.48	0.39	0.82	1.03	11.39	14.70
1986	0.55	0.37	0.45	0.80	0.95	11.52	14.64
1987	0.34	0.29	0.52	0.76	0.99	10.97	13.87
1988	0.38	0.22	0.45	0.76	0.86	10.16	12.83
1989	0.56	0.19	0.29	0.90	0.62	9.76	12.32
1990	0.49	0.21	0.30	0.89	0.38	9.65	11.92

A detailed study of ten expenditure programmes for the period 1962–90 would indicate that the levels of public expenditure between 1962 and 1973 were stable at about 32 per cent of GDP. This stability was followed by a period of growth during the years 1974–6, when expenditure reached 34 per cent of GDP, but was then held at a new plateau of 34 per cent, until the early 1980s. However, since 1984 the trend has been continuously downward, so that since 1988 expenditure has fallen below its 1962 level. Total expenditure in 1990 was 27.8 per cent of GDP, in contrast to 33 per cent of GDP in 1962.

Underlying these periods of stability, growth and restraint at total levels were dynamics both at the programme level and within the study

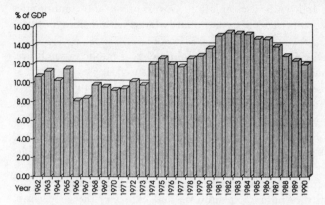

Figure 1.13 Total transfers 1962–90 at constant prices

by economic component that seemed to be producing different trends. Capital expenditure has, for example, continued to decline sharply since the mid-1970s, when it had reached a peak of 4 per cent of GDP. By 1990 this had fallen to 1.4 per cent of GDP. Within capital expenditure the fastest area of decline was the housing programme, which was being steadily reduced from 1974. Expenditure declined from 1.6 per cent of GDP in 1975 to 0.3 per cent in 1990.

Current expenditure, by contrast, experienced stability between 1962 and 1984, taking some 18 per cent of GDP. However, since 1986 current expenditure has fallen steadily; by 1990 it was below its 1962 level. Current expenditure in 1990 represented some 14.5 per cent of GDP, in contrast to the 1962 figure of 19 per cent.

CONCLUSIONS

The concern of this chapter has been to introduce the concepts of politics and political choice and how they can be applied to the study of public expenditure. It was argued that the study of the concept of political choice implies a process of indeterminacy, in the sense that explanations of changes in public expenditure have to be located within a specific context and climate. The politics of public expenditure points to a series of decisions concerning the allocation of resources through the mechanism of government as being policy outcomes that could well have been different. The study of the political dimension describes a process of continuing reflection and re-evaluation, since the emphasis is placed on political choice, political judgement and political calculation. Governments and communities in modern democracies are continuously faced with making political decisions.

In introducing the themes of defining what is public expenditure, and how public expenditure should be measured, it was argued that the processes of definition and measurement continually involve political choice, in the sense that those who succeed in defining and measuring also create a framework for what is possible and what is excluded. This chapter has attempted to outline two perspectives which seek to occupy the contestable terrain of what is public expenditure.

The macro perspective places the emphasis on a 'holistic' view of what constitutes public expenditure, and expresses the concerns of those who seek to budget for the public sector and therefore live within a world view that 'what government spends it has to get'. It aims to reflect the UK Treasury aphorism that 'finance must determine expenditure, not expenditure finance'. The problem is that although this view seems to carry the authoritative stamp of realism it does in fact conceal significant judgements which in the final resort are political judgements. The macro approach corresponds with the view that public expenditure evolves its own momentum towards inexorable growth, and that the major aims of governments should be to control that growth. Political parties and communities within the context of a democracy tend to create continuing pressures towards expansion, and it is the central objective of Chancellors and Treasury ministers to keep expenditure under control.

The programme approach, in contrast, is concerned first with showing that the changes within the total are the expression of fluctuations within individual programmes, where programmes are defined by the objectives they aim to meet. The programme approach seeks to evaluate the impact of expenditure on policy and to evaluate the relationships between policy inputs (public expenditure) and policy outputs. The programme approach is therefore concerned with measuring the quality of public service in relation to a specific budget. It is therefore concerned with the consumers of that service, and seeks to ask who benefits and who loses when there are changes in public expenditure plans and allocations. The centrality of these approaches is that each is put forward as a political argument to legitimise a specific way of interpreting the world.

In addition, the concern of this chapter has also been to discuss the competing methods that are utilised to measure the growth of public expenditure. In 1973 Sir Richard Clarke claimed that public expenditure had reached a peak of over 50 per cent of GDP (factor costs) and argued that the balance had shifted towards public consumption (Clarke 1973). This was followed by further alarm in 1976 when Roy Jenkins argued that expenditure had reached 60 per cent and was now threatening democracy and individual freedom (Jenkins 1976). In contrast, Pliatzky (1982) was able to argue that the ratio in 1982 was 46 per cent of GDP (market prices). Within the definition adopted in this study, public expenditure in 1982 was 36 per cent of GDP (market prices) at current prices, and 35 per cent of GDP (market prices) at 1985 constant prices. In 1990, total expenditure fell to 28 per cent of GDP.

Within this study there has been an attempt to provide a method of measuring public expenditure by utilising the programme approach. The studies by expenditure programme disaggregated by economic category and then deflated by the appropriate price deflators provide an indicator of the factors that influenced changes at the programme level. This approach confirms that whilst expenditure did expand during the 1970s to levels which were above those of the 1960s, the rate of growth was halted at the higher levels in the early 1980s and then was reduced continuously, so that by 1990 the levels of expenditure were below those of the 1960s. The major constraining factor has been the capital component in all expenditure programmes, except for the health service. There have been large reductions in the housing capital programme, school buildings, roads and infrastructure expenditure over the past two decades.

In addition to the reductions in the capital programme, governments have also managed to bring current expenditure under control, which means that they have succeeded in restricting the rate of wage increases in the public sector, including health and education.

The following chapters are concerned with linking the process of change in public expenditure during the 1970s and 1980s to the continued changes in the relationships between the events which acted as constraints on the options available to government, as well as with seeking to understand the autonomy of government. Governments, like individuals, are involved in a continuous process of negotiation and compromise between events that tend to restrict choice, and the need to behave as autonomous individuals. Governments are equally restricted by events that are beyond their immediate influence, yet they seek to promote their own political choices and the choices of those who put them in office.

Chapter 2

Explaining public expenditure

INTRODUCTION

The study of the politics of public expenditure requires an ability to analyse a series of tensions and conflicts in the context of the policy-making process. First, there is a need to explore the meaning of politics within the specific context of public expenditure decisions. This means making transparent the boundaries between political choice and constraint, and between events and the autonomy of government. For example, the decision by the UK Government in the Autumn Statement of November 1992 to make growth their major concern represented both a decision that reflected the Government's response to external events and the fact that this decision implied an element of political choice. Equally, the decision to leave the ERM was neither inevitable nor did the Government have complete choice in making that decision.

Second, there is a need to understand the processes of constraints that put limits on politics and choice. One example of constraint is that of demographic changes and how forecasts of changes in population structure are likely to influence government policy. However, whilst recognising the presence of such constraints, governments are involved in the process of selection between different policy options in the allocation of resources, that is, between competing claims and the influence of vested interest groups. The political changes which governments make to expenditure programmes in the short term tend to involve making choices which are related to the margins of the programmes without necessarily seeking any fundamental shift. The political decision of whether to uprate pensions in line with inflation or with earnings might have only a minor impact on the total costs of pensions; nevertheless, such a marginal decision will have long-term effects on the cost of such programmes. So whilst pensions represent a demand-related programme in the sense that the programme is effected by the number of elderly people and by longevity, the decisions to increase pensions, to target higher pensions to the over-80s, or to change the rules on redundancy are all political decisions that involve political choice.

Finally, exploring explanations of changes in public expenditure requires the use of concepts and models which are interdisciplinary in nature. Public expenditure decisions reflect political choice, and have an impact on economic policy as well as providing resources for social and public policies. This implies the use of concepts which are derived from theoretical models as applied, for example, to market liberalism and the concepts of rational individualism, and also to theories of the state and capitalism. Yet whilst these concepts are useful in drawing a wider canvas there is a life in politics which unfolds as a day-to-day process. Politics implies that responses to external events are not necessarily predetermined but are somehow open to political choice, political judgement and political calculation. There is therefore a need to balance explanations that are derivative of theoretical models with an attempt to see politics as an unfolding process.

The concern of this chapter is to reflect on these two levels of analysis: that of providing an explanation that takes consideration of the tensions between constraints and autonomy; and an approach that combines the study of concepts with the study of the day-to-day political process. The following sections seek to explore a series of concepts and how these have been used as 'tools' to explain the dynamics of public expenditure. It will be argued that explanations of public expenditure can be located within four major political 'languages'. These 'languages' are categorised as follows:

(a) public choice theory;
(b) theories of pluralism;
(c) theories of capitalism;
(d) theories of bureaucracy.

The theory of public choice is closely associated with the language of liberalism and with concepts that are derived from market economics. First, theories of public choice have utilised the concept of rational individualism and have applied the concept of rationality to explore the relationship between voters and government and the implications for the overspending state in the context of a democratic society.

Second, there are concepts that are associated with theories of pluralism and the impact of functional groups on public expenditure. Third, there are concepts which seek to emphasise the context and climate in which decisions are made, including the concepts of capitalist society and the location of public expenditure in the context of capitalist democracies. This theoretical perspective is founded on Marxist concepts of exploitation and alienation in the context of the capitalist state, where public expenditure is either perceived as meeting the needs of a capitalist economy or reflecting the conflicts of class interests and their influence on the state. Fourth, there are those concepts which are associated with the study of bureaucracy, public sector professionals and public sector organisations, and how these impinge on public expenditure.

THE THEORY OF PUBLIC CHOICE

The 'home domain' of public choice theory utilises the concepts of rational individualism, choice and markets as developed by market liberal economists and political theorists. The market liberal perceives the rational individual as being at the centre of the economic and political market-place:

> Voters and customers are essentially the same people. Mr Smith buys and votes, he is the same man in the supermarket and in the voting booth. There is no strong reason to believe his behaviour is radically different in the two environments. We assume that, in both, he will choose the produce or candidate he thinks is the best bargain for him.
>
> (Tullock 1976: 4)

The concept of self-interest emphasises that the individual is a rational agent with rational expectations who is capable of making choices between a variety of options, and that rationality is influenced by the individual's natural and technical competencies. The rational individual continuously seeks information and the knowledge with which to make decisions that further individual welfare and well-being. This means that since individuals are rational, they make decisions on the knowledge that is at their disposal, and that, as the information changes, individuals are also likely to change their decisions. Market liberalism accepts that all individuals know what is best for them.

The market represents a method that brings a measure of spontaneity into transactions between the consumer and the supplier of goods through the price mechanism. Prices are decided through consumers gathering information of different prices and suppliers seeking information about potential demand. The consumer is described as being the price-maker in a competitive market environment where there are no barriers to entry for suppliers. In importing the market equilibrium model to the study of the political process, the emphasis is put on the individual as the consumer of goods in the political market. The individual in the political market seeks to maximise well-being through higher levels of public expenditure at the least possible cost, and the supplier of public goods as represented by the Government seeks to meet consumer demand, but also promises minimum costs.

Within the context of market liberalism, democracy represents the price mechanism which allows for competition between political parties and their attempts to persuade voters to select and vote for their product as outlined in the party manifesto. However, public choice theorists have tended to come to different conclusions in explaining the relationships between the Government as the supplier of goods and services and the individual voter as the consumer.

First, there are those who argue that, although the consumer is rational, the consumer is likely to underestimate the value of public goods and overestimate the costs, thus leading to an underspending on public goods. According to this approach, governments are likely to underspend on public services because these are less valued by consumers when contrasted to the more visible benefits of personal taxation. It is this thesis that suggests that in the midst of private affluence there will be public squalor. In contrast, there are market liberals who suggest that one major consequence of democracy has been that of government overload and fiscal crisis.

Downs and the underspending state

The link between the economic and the political market is the maximising individual pursuing personal welfare and well-being as the consumer of goods and services. Both consumers and producers meet in the market-place where prices are determined through the process of auction. In the political market the maximising individual is the voter and the supplier is the political party seeking to become the government. The electoral process represents an auction for peoples' votes where parties, through their manifestos, seek to provide a series of services for a price. The election results reflect the services people want and the price they are willing to pay. Downs (1957) has utilised the concept of maximisation to explain the public expenditure process and has come to the following conclusions:

> Because the government in our model wishes to maximise [its] political support, it carries out those acts of spending which gain the most votes by means of those acts of financing which lose the fewest votes.
>
> (Downs 1957: 52)

According to this approach, therefore, the primary aim of the political party is to win the next election, to continue to be the incumbent government or to replace the party in government. In contrast, voters seek to improve their welfare at the least cost to themselves in terms of personal taxation. Political parties and voters meet in the political market-place where parties try to outbid each other in making promises, whilst voters examine the agendas of the parties. Downs has argued that goods supplied in the political market tend to be valued differently by the consumer/voter than goods purchased in the economic market. In the latter sphere goods are purchased on a quid pro quo basis in contrast to political goods, which are financed through taxation, and where the consumer tends to underestimate the cost of such goods. Public goods tend to be one step removed from the consumer:

> the electorate is chronically ignorant of the cost and benefits of many actual and potential government policies. It is ignorant because of the cost of obtaining information as to the benefits received from government policy . . . [and] the remoteness of government expenditure coupled with the visibility of taxation produce a budget which is too small to finance higher spending.
>
> (Downs 1965: 541)

Within a Downsian framework, therefore, the consequences for public expenditure are twofold:

The problem of private affluence and public squalor

Within a democracy governments are likely to give higher priority to private consumption than to public consumption. Since taxation is highly visible governments are reluctant to make pledges for increased public consumption or for increased taxation to finance these services.

This is therefore likely to result in private affluence and public squalor, with more income being directed at private consumption often at the cost of public goods.

Voters are likely to judge governments according to private consumption since living standards are measured in terms of personal affluence. Freedom and citizenship become equated with consumerism, often at the cost of goods which are public goods but which are not necessarily seen to contribute to the quality of life. The motor car is equated with personal freedom even if this results in more road building and air pollution. The feasibility of introducing a carbon tax depends on whether the Government has the political will to trade votes for the wider public interest. The defeat of the Government in Holland in 1991 reflects the tensions between the concerns for the environment and the political will to meet the costs.

The problem of short-termism and political expediency

Governments are only likely to increase spending on public services in a climate of growth in the economy. Growth acts as the 'enabling' factor, making possible increases in both private and public consumption. Increases in tax revenues can finance public services without governments having to decide to increase the rate of taxation. In contrast, as the economy stagnates or enters a period of recession the pressures build on government to constrain public expenditure but also to reduce taxation as a means of protecting personal consumption.

Since public goods are not directly visible to the voter the Government can reduce expenditure on certain goods without incurring an immediate political cost. Reducing expenditure on capital projects such as the building of a new hospital or school is not seen as a reduction in the quality of a service, at least in the short term. Only in the long term if these projects continue to be postponed and the deterioration of the service becomes more immediately visible is the Government likely to come under electoral pressure and public services to become an issue of political concern.

It is only under these specific conditions that political parties will therefore seek to outbid each other in making pledges to provide higher public services. The issue for Downs is that these conditions for expansion happen less frequently than those on which the success of government depends in improving private affluence.

The economic consequences of democracy

The overspending state

In contrast to Downs, other public choice theorists have argued that the democratic process has actually contributed to fiscal overload, ungovernability and the illegitimacy of the state (Rose and Peters 1979; Brittan 1977; Birch 1984). Rather than public expenditure being controlled through the democratic process, democracy itself was likely to generate excessive expectations of government. The process of democracy and political parties outbidding each other in the political market-place encouraged voters to overestimate the potential of the Government, whilst rival political parties fostered expectations in their zeal to become the incumbent government:

> Democratic political practice is best regarded neither as a method of popular participation in government nor as a means of putting into effect the people's will but mainly as a competition for power by means of votes among competing teams . . . subject to endemic and growing weaknesses . . . [and] the generation of excessive expectations among voters by the processes of political competition and the disruptive effects arising from the pursuit of self interest by rival coercive groups.
>
> (Brittan 1977: 266)

In accordance with this perspective the state is not constrained by the level of taxation people are willing to pay. Instead the experience has been one of increased tax burdens and government's willingness to use public sector borrowing to finance a continuing expansion of government. To explain how governments manage to increase public expenditure and also taxation Peacock and Wiseman (1961) pointed to the effect of war and changes in public expenditure and voter expectations. These authors argued that wars represented a cataclysmic event which in turn would result in a displacement effect in the level of taxation which the electorate would see as tolerable. Voters are willing to pay more taxes as their contribution to their nation's effort in times of danger to the nation. Peacock and Wiseman suggest that, since the aim of government is to expand its activities, it uses the period after a war to utilise the new revenues, which hitherto had been devoted to the war effort, on other areas of public provision. Taxation is not reduced to its pre-war levels, instead:

> Public expenditure in Britain can be described as a series of mountain ranges with peaks of increasing heights separated by plateaux . . . the major peaks occur in periods covered by war.
>
> (Peacock and Wiseman 1961: 25)

Because political parties seek to outbid each other in their attempt to win the next election they are also likely to increase voter expectations of what governments can achieve, thus leading to an overload of the democratic process. The democratic process becomes the means through which strategic groups aim to influence the political process, thereby ensuring that their members are at the front of the queue when the state allocates resources. At this stage government no longer serves the interest of the individual but acts in a manner similar to the medieval king who becomes dependent on the feudal barons in the delivery of resources to specific functional groups, namely the professionals, the bureaucracy and groups involved in receiving direct subsidies from the government:

> In the redistributive state, government has become what it was in the Middle Ages – an inscrutable power above the people, to be lobbied, petitioned, and propitiated for the favours it can dispense . . . Sovereign powers, the power to tax in particular, come to be shared with private groups. Eventually the question of who governs must arise.
>
> (Tumlir 1984: 19)

The effects of the electoral business cycles

The electoral business cycle approach builds on the theme that political parties are primarily concerned with maximising their votes. However, since the incumbent government seeks to retain office, it is also tempted to manipulate the electoral cycle to ensure it remains in power. According to this model, the suggestion is that during an election year the Government would tend to utilise the levers of public expenditure to reflate the economy or to provide direct benefits to targeted voters as part of the Government's electoral arithmetic. However, since such an attempt means increases in public expenditure and increases in borrowing to finance that expenditure, the problem of inflation then becomes a major concern after the election.

According to the electoral cycle model decisions on specific expenditure programmes are more likely to be targeted during an election year, with the aim of increasing the visibility of those who gain from expenditure decisions. Hence it is likely that governments would increase pensions prior to an election since such a decision would be welcomed by both the pensioners as an interest group and the wider electorate, who would perceive the Government to be 'caring'. Spending ministers responsible for expenditure programmes that are of major concern to the electorate are also likely to be more successful in making additional bids during an election year, and thus recover ground lost when other expenditures had been a priority for the Government.

The Autumn Statement of November 1991 outlined by the Chancellor of the Exchequer, Norman Lamont, represented a good example of the relationship between public expenditure decisions and the electoral cycle. At one level the Autumn Statement confirmed that the Government was willing to use public expenditure as a fiscal instrument to move the UK out of recession before the next election, which in itself represented a major break in macro economic policy since 1979. Second, the Chancellor also accepted a planned PSBR of between £20 billion and £50 billion for the next three years, which also meant a major shift from the Chancellorship of Nigel Lawson, when the budget had not only been balanced but the Government was actually paying back some of the national debt. The Government also seemed to break with the previous commitment of reducing public expenditure as a ratio of GDP; instead, the Autumn Statement proposed stability between growth in the economy and growth in public expenditure. The aim over the next five years was that public expenditure in the UK would stabilise at about 41 per cent of GDP. Third, the Autumn Statement also reflected the targeting of new expenditures. More resources were to be directed to areas of popular expenditure, including health and education. The question of whether or not John Major won the April 1992 election because the foundations had been laid during the autumn of 1991 still needs to be confirmed, but there can be no doubt that the Government was able to fight the election on the pledges for public expenditure which had been outlined in the Autumn Statement.

The first and major problem with the business cycle approach as an explanation is that it assumes there is fiscal illusion and fiscal drag where the real value of money is eroded because of inflation, and voters become less aware of the real costs of public goods. It also assumes that politicians have sufficient autonomy to manipulate the economic cycle. This raises the question of why there should be asymmetry of information available to the voters and the politicians. In addition, it could be asked, why do politicians not manipulate the economy in such a way that would continuously achieve high levels of growth and prosperity?

The second criticism is that the political business cycle is presented as a model with independent predictive variables, suggesting that there is a stable relationship between changes in macro economic variables and government popularity. This raises the question of why, despite high levels of unemployment in Britain between 1979 and 1982, the Conservative Party won the 1983 and also the 1987 election? Furthermore, rather than expanding the economy as the theory would predict, all governments have tended to reduce public expenditure during an election year – a view also echoed in the work of Alt and Chrystal (1979, 1983):

> We are unable to accept that policy was determined on the basis of a myopic electorate . . . we strongly contest that there is any effect upon government expenditure of election business cycles, popularity and ideology – in short we conclude that the political business cycle is not something that the economic profession in the United Kingdom should take seriously.
>
> (Alt and Chrystal 1979: 11, 19)

Third, the approach implies that politicians react passively to priorities which are set by the electorate. There is, therefore, no attempt made to build into the model either the ability of the Government to influence perceptions, and thereby the potential ability to change the terrain of the political agenda, or the possibility of ideological differences between the political parties.

Do parties matter?

The view that public expenditure financed through a progressive tax system results in more income equality has led some theorists to argue that differences in public expenditure can be explained in terms of which political party has been the incumbent government. Tufte (1978) and Castles(1982) have sought to construct images of parties and attempted to explain changes in public expenditure in relation to party government. Images were constructed on the expectations that parties of the Right were more likely to prefer to reduce taxation rather than increase public expenditure whilst in contrast, parties of the Left were described as being more interventionist, less trusting of the market place and more likely to increase public expenditure as the means to increasing employment and re-distribute income. Tufte (1978) argues that

> Political parties differ on what they consider as desirable economic policy. Parties of the Right favour low rates of tax, oppose income equalisation and trade higher unemployment for less inflation . . . Parties of the Left favour income equalisation, lower unemployment and larger government budgets.
>
> (Tufte 1978: 197)

Studies of party images and the expectations of out-turn on public expenditure have tended to provide conflicting results. Castles' (1982) study of the OECD area suggests that there is a relationship between changes in expenditure and government. This study has been substantiated by Taylor (1983) but questioned by Alt and Chrystal (1977) and Rose (1984c), who have tended to argue that in the UK political parties have not made any difference to the trends in public expenditure. According to this view public expenditure has continued to grow irrespective of which party has been in government. Under both Labour and Conservative Governments expenditure has continued to move in an upward direction:

> What parties say is not what parties do, hence the need to distinguish between rhetoric and reality. Rhetoric has its place in securing the support of activists within the party and in swaying the opinions of voters.
>
> (Rose 1984c: xiii)

There is a need, according to Rose, to separate the appearances of what political parties claim they stand for and the reality of actual policy out-turns.

The tax backlash

One of the implications that can be derived from the explanations outlined above is that the visibility of taxation cannot be assumed to act as a budget constraint on government expenditure. The cost of information does not necessarily lead to a reluctant voter but, rather, to the lack of a budget constraint among voters (Brittan 1977), thus creating a bias which leads to the continuous expansion of public expenditure. Indeed, Rose and Peters (1979) would argue that this process has led to the continuous growth in both public expenditure and in the level of taxation. This has resulted in reductions in take home pay, dissatisfaction and indifference to the Government:

In a politically bankrupt society, individuals do not doubt government's claim to rule . . . But they are not prepared to do voluntarily what government asks. The tacit premise of the indifferent citizen becomes 'exclude the government'. One immediate way to demonstrate indifference is by avoiding and evading taxes. This effectively increases the take home pay of individuals, whilst simultaneously making it harder for the government to meet the cost of public policy.

(Rose and Peters 1979: 34)

These authors seem to be suggesting that public expenditure has not been expanded with the consent of the voter, but that the voter has been encouraged to overestimate the benefits of a public good without realising the costs. Such an approach attracts the same criticism as that applied to electoral business cycle pluralists, namely that these authors also accept the axiom of the maximising individual, where the concept of rational choice is limited to private consumption. Again, myopia seems to be confined to public expenditure. Indeed, it could be asked whether this is a reflection of pluralist theorists and their preference for a more market liberal approach to government and an antipathy to public expenditure.

THEORIES OF PLURALISM

The pluralist perspective suggests that the process of democracy is not limited to the relationship between individual voters and government, but recognises the possibility that the individual, in pursuing self-interest, would join with others of similar interests. The aim of the group is that of the individual, that is, to influence the political process. The access and potential influence of groups on the political process depends on the degree of power which these groups can exert. Pluralists would not claim that there is equality of influence or equality of access to resources between interest groups but, rather, what is central is that no one group is described as being sovereign, which means that, despite inequality, no one group would be always dominant. Power in this sense is fragmented and dispersed.

Theories of pluralism differ from public choice theories in that the process of democratic government shifts from the centrality of elections and parliament to the concept of functional democracy, where government has to negotiate with strategic economic groups whose influence is greater than that of the individual voter. Within this context public expenditure is seen as reflecting the willingness of government to provide subsidies and grants which benefit vested interest groups but not necessarily the public interest. A typical example would at present be the willingness of governments in Europe and the US to continue to subsidise their agriculture at the cost of world trade, the price to consumers and the cost to Third World countries.

The acceptance by pluralists that there are two forms of political actors – the individual and functional groups – carries with it likely areas of conflict. First, there is the likelihood of conflict which arises around the individual who votes for a particular government and the possibility that sectionalist interests could subvert the priorities of that government. Second, if it is accepted that certain groups do have better access to government, it must also be recognised that some groups are more likely to have their demands met than others.

How then does pluralism resolve the problem of conflicting interests? Pluralists answer this question by providing a specific theory of the State. The State is described as an arbiter seeking to resolve conflicts of competing claims by giving priority to what is perceived to be the public interest. To do this, pluralists assume that there is a public interest which is defined by the State. Furthermore, they assume that there is consensus as to what defines the public interest. Within the pluralist perspective, therefore, there seems to be also some functionalist assertions as to the nature of the State, mainly that its task is to identify need and to respond accordingly. Alford and Friedland (1985) point to similarities in the work of Dahl and Parsons and their reliance on the existence of shared value systems:

> In the pluralist perspective, democratic participation with a consensus political culture leads to a governable state. Situational participation must occur within a functioning consensus. The tension between participation and consensus is mediated by the party system and by governmental leadership socialised to balance between group demands and public interest.
>
> (Alford and Friedland 1985: 9)

The pluralist perspective encompasses a diversity of explanations for the changes in public expenditure – explanations which often seem to be inconsistent and which also conflict in predicting outcomes. At one level the growth of expenditure is described as being the product of democratic government and of individuals pursuing self-interest. In contrast, however, there are pluralists who would equally argue that the process of democracy subverts the primacy of the individual. Hence 'big government' is explained in terms of profligate government and sectionalist interests. This approach is inconsistent in the sense that it seeks to imbue individuals, in the economic market, with rationality but does not extend this to the political market. It is an approach which assumes that the private goods market is an environment of perfect competition whilst the public sector is assumed to be dominated by monopoly groups.

THEORIES OF CAPITALISM

In contrast to the centrality of the individual in pluralism, the 'home domain' of the class perspective is the capitalist economy (McLennan 1984; Jessop 1977, 1983). According to this approach any explanation of public expenditure must be located at two levels of analysis: first, within the context of the needs of capitalism, where the political process and the concept of political choice have little or no role in explaining public expenditure decisions; and second, in relation to the dynamics of class conflicts and class interests; this approach locates the Government in the social relations of class forces. Both interpretations represent separate traditions within a Marxist perspective, which can be identified with Determinist and Voluntary Marxism:

> the tension can be categorised as between voluntaryism and determinism . . . voluntaryism is a view of society as a network of human meanings . . . determinism is a view of society conceived like a thing, a facticity; coercive controlling and moulding individual members.
>
> (Gouldner 1980: 25)

Theories of the capitalist state

The identification of the State as the capitalist state in Marxist theory provides the framework for understanding the role of public expenditure in the context of a capitalist economy. Theories of the capitalist state aim to show that public expenditure is utilised by the State to ensure the maintenance and continuity of a capitalist economy. Public expenditure on health and education is explained in terms of producing a healthier and better educated labour force, which is perceived as essential to the success of a capitalist economy. Expenditures on the infrastructure, including roads and telecommunications, contribute more directly to the profitability of private enterprise as the Government takes over the cost of these essential services. Within this context the economy is divided into two major sectors: the productive and the unproductive. The former is defined as providing the surplus which allows for the existence of the latter. Accordingly, the public sector is described as belonging to the unproductive sector (Yaffe 1978; Fine and Harris 1979), since state activities are not perceived to generate surplus value. According to this approach, therefore, public expenditure represents an attempt to channel resources, including benefits for the unemployed and pensions for the elderly, from the productive sector of the economy to the non-productive public sector as a means of maintaining political stability:

> state expenditure does not produce surplus value – goods that the state buys are acquired with already produced surplus value. The profits acquired by the individual capitalist producing for the state come to him out of a re-distribution of the already produced surplus value.
>
> (Yaffe 1978: 218)

Although Offe (1984) argues that public expenditure is directed at the crisis of surplus value he introduces the concept of de-commodification to explain how the process of increased state expenditure removes human labour from the process of commodity exchange. Because the State provides public services, pensions, health, housing and education become socialised and separated from the discipline of the market place. So, whilst the State seeks to reassert surplus value it creates new problems of disincentives to work and invest. Thus Offe notes:

> we wish to argue that since the mid 1960s the increasingly dominant and exclusive strategy of the capitalist state is to solve the problem of the obsolescence of the commodity form by politically creating conditions for subjects to function as commodities.
>
> (Offe 1984: 124)

Explanations of public expenditure as derived from the theory of the capitalist state lead to two types of interpretation:

(a) that all expenditures are functional to the needs of capitalism either by contributing to the process of accumulation and growth or by increasing the legitimacy of the State within socially disenfranchised groups;

(b) that public expenditure does not avert crisis because all public expenditures depend on the use of existing surplus value. The State is not capable of producing surplus value.

The theory of class

The cohesive State

In defining the State as a factor that is part of class relationships, the level of analysis shifts from the theory of the capitalist state to the view that the State is 'political', in the sense that governments represent competing class interests. According to this approach decisions on public expenditure represent two types of outcomes: first, that public expenditure is the means of reconciling class conflict, with the State acting as a neutral mediator providing services which act in the public interest; and second, that public expenditures represent the changing boundaries in class relations.

According to the cohesive approach to public expenditure

> The capitalist state plays an organic role in organising the political unity of the bourgeois and constituting it as the politically dominant class . . . this can only become possible because of the relative autonomy of the state from the various fractions, components and specific interests of the capitalist class.
>
> (Poulantzas 1980: 125–7)

The State as an arena of political dominance

Within this category, the State becomes a terrain where classes are involved in tactics and strategies to maintain, improve or secure their class position. The emphasis is put on political organisation and the ability of classes to mobilise resources. Relating this approach to public expenditure, Gough (1979, 1983) has concentrated on what he sees to be the contradictory qualities of a capitalist society, namely:

> the simultaneous tendencies to develop the power of individuals to exert social control over the blind play of market forces and tendencies to repress and control people, to adopt them to the requirements of the capitalist economy.
>
> (Gough 1979: 12)

Gough accepts that there are central imperatives which are essential for the continuation of a capitalist economy. However, he repudiates any form of functional relationship between such imperatives and the expansion of public spending:

one implication that could be drawn is that the mode of production generates certain functional requirements in the field of welfare policy which the state or some other body outside the economy must necessarily perform. This is emphatically not the position taken here. It does not follow that the state will necessarily perform these functions.

(Gough 1979: 37)

Gough identifies four factors which contribute to the growth in public expenditure: demographic pressures; the demand for improved services; the rising costs of the public sector; and new social needs. However, these are not sufficient to explain the growth in public expenditure. These pressures need to be put into the wider economic context that takes into consideration the level of economic activity and trade union influence, since it is within this environment that the social wage is negotiated. The growth of public expenditure represents the ability of the working class to win concessions:

the welfare state is the vector of two sets of political forces: 'pressure from below' and 'reforms from above'. The first refers to the myriad ways in which class movements . . . demand social reforms to protect or extend their interests. 'Reforms from above' refers to the various ways in which the state seeks to implement social reforms which will serve in the longer term economic, social and political interests of capital.

(Gough 1983: 157–8)

Whilst it would seem that Gough wants to introduce a political variable by suggesting that what happens to public expenditure is neither inevitable nor predictable, and that governments make deliberate choices, this point is not developed. He recognises the implication of what he is saying and notes that if he continues along this path then his perspective stops being Marxist and starts to become pluralist:

class conflict alone however will not suffice, if this were all we would be back with a Marxist variant of pluralist theories . . . there are imperatives created by the capitalist industrialisation process and there are functions to be performed which cannot be carried out by individual business firms.

(Gough 1979: 62)

The above quotation expresses very neatly a major contradiction within a Voluntaristic Marxist theory that seeks to give primacy to class struggle and yet not appear to be falling into a pluralist view of the State. In contrast, whilst Determinist Marxists continue to explain the State within the context of a capitalist economy, their study of class struggle has to be subordinated to the continuity of that mode of production, in spite of class antagonisms. Having started with good intentions, Gough also seems to fall into a functional explanation:

> paradoxically it would appear that labour indirectly aids the long term accumulation of capital and strengthens capitalist relations by struggling for its own interests within the state.
>
> (Gough 1979: 55)

There are four areas of criticism which need to be directed at the class perspective:

(a) The identification of the productive and unproductive sectors is not dissimilar to the marketed and non-marketed sectors identified by Bacon and Eltis (1978). It is an argument which assumes that doctors, teachers and social workers are non-productive because they are not directly involved in production of goods which are directed to export markets.

(b) Some Marxists have tended to argue that public expenditure is a functional response to various forms of capitalist crisis. It is a weak form of explanation because it does not explain the variety of responses that are available and, furthermore, assumes the State to be an all-knowing and omnipotent state.

(c) Explaining public expenditure as being integrative promptly raises the following questions: When does expenditure stop being so? When can public expenditure be explained as not being in the interest of a class? The cohesive state approach also relies on the assumption that the State *does* know what the interest of capital as a whole ought to be even if particular capitalists do not.

(d) Finally, there is the more particular criticism directed at the analysis, provided by Mandel (1980) and others, who seem to be in agreement with those monetarist economists who seek to confirm the existence of crisis by providing a link between increases in the money supply and inflation. Since the empirical evidence on such a relationship is inconclusive it might be feasible to point out that Mandel's diagnosis could also be erroneous.

THEORIES OF BUREAUCRACY

Theories of bureaucracy compete with public choice theory, pluralism and classicism in that the 'home domain' of this perspective is the organisation. The universal concepts to be derived from this approach include a theory of elites and oligarchy and their impact both on the democratic process and decisions on public expenditure. There are three areas of analysis which can be identified within theories of bureaucracy. First, there is the study of public sector professionals, their coherence in terms of shared ethics and monopoly of knowledge, and their ability to influence public expenditure because of their monopoly of certain skills. This includes the study of the behaviour of professionals, including doctors and teachers, local authority officers and civil servants, and their impact on their respective budgets. Second, there is the study of the bureaucracy itself where civil servants are described as being budget maximisers. Third, there is the analysis of public sector employees and the influence of public sector trade union wage demands and the relationship between wages and the cost of public services.

The influence of professionals

The study of professionals is associated with organisations, the study of structures, and how such structures are related to achieving the goals and objectives of these organisations. Organisations are defined as institutions with identifiable goals, which have formal rules and procedures that govern the behaviour of their members. These elements are seen as essential for the existence and continuity of the organisation. Organisations are defined as rational institutions seeking to maximise their own interests.

Defining organisations as being rational, however, raises the issue of who defines that rationality. Within organisations, leaders have the capacity to establish structures that perpetuate the autonomy of leaders. It is a context in which knowledge is the source of power. Professionals are seen as having a knowledge estate that enables them to define the demand and supply of services.

The prospect that knowledge is a source of power suggests that those who define themselves as the experts are able to use their knowledge estate to increase their influence on government. Government becomes dependent on professional groups for their expert advice. The implication of this, in explaining public expenditure, is that such changes are influenced by professionals who are able to structure the organisation to their own liking and are able to define its goals.

Professionals are likely to influence public expenditure in two ways. First, by political advertising of their specialism; and second, by pointing to the gap between what the profession could achieve and the amount of resources which are available (Judge and Hampson 1980):

> Political advertising can be defined as the promotion of a particular product, idea or issue through the provision of publicly available information by politicians, bureaucrats, producers or ordinary citizens who have the intention of altering or sustaining the supply of policies by the government.
>
> (Judge and Hampson 1980: 70)

Furthermore, Hood and Wright (1981) have pointed to how professionals have tended to use what they call the 'bleeding stump' approach if a service seems to have its resources threatened. The bleeding stump strategy ensures that when resources are threatened the professionals reduce the area of provision that is most visible, which directly and immediately affects clients. This advertises the plight of the service with the hope of increasing the unpopularity of a government decision:

> Whenever spending cuts are in prospect, fantasy statements variously and picturesquely known as 'sore thumbs' and 'bleeding stumps' will be produced, exaggerating the potentially disastrous effects of proposed cuts or suggesting that cuts will have to be made in areas which are least likely to be accepted.
>
> (Hood and Wright 1981: 163)

The campaign by the British Medical Association against the Government proposals for reforming the Health Service between 1989 and 1991 can be perceived as a good example of political advertising by the medical profession against the health service reforms. The BMA launched a poster campaign in London and other major cities and also produced leaflets that were made available in doctors' surgeries. Leaders of the BMA also gave evidence to the Health Service Committee. In the meantime, the financial crisis of the new hospital trusts at Guy's and Bradford Infirmary were used as the bleeding stump strategy to signal to the Government that the reforms were not likely to benefit the Health Service.

Second, professionals are likely to influence the growth of the public sector through the cost element. This, I have pointed out, is likely if the professionals are capable of becoming a monopoly in the delivery of a service by being able to influence the numbers entering the service and also by being able to define what is needed. Maynard (1980) has estimated that, within the NHS, the number of physicians entering the service exceeded government estimates by 4,500 in 1970 and by 2,300 in 1975, whilst Culyer and Wright (1978) have suggested that:

> properties of demand and supply are highly attenuated if not wholly destroyed by the role of the physician. As an agent for his clients he largely determines both what shall be demanded and what shall be supplied.
>
> (Culyer and Wright 1978: 10)

The influence of civil servants

The concepts of rational individualism and monopoly of knowledge have also been utilised to explain the impact of civil servants on government growth. The starting point is that civil servants act in their own self-interest as rational agents, where self-interest is defined as the willingness of bureaucrats continuously to maximise their budgets. Various studies have sought to show that civil servants do proliferate increases in public expenditure (Breton 1974; Niskanen 1971; Borcherding 1977; Dunleavy 1991):

> my hypothesis implies that it is through the maximisation of the budget that bureaucrats are able to achieve the highest possible income and prestige consistent with the constraints to which they are subjected.
>
> (Breton 1974: 162)

According to Breton, bureaucrats are budget maximisers since higher budgets imply more staff, which in turn means redefining responsibilities, and encouraging redeployment, promotion and prestige for some. It is, therefore, in the interest of spending departments to research the needs of their client groups and to articulate these needs in new expenditures and expanded budgets.

Borcherding (1977) has argued that he has been able to calculate the contribution made by the bureaucracy to public expenditure. He suggests that he can show that influences such as demographic changes, which he categorises as democratic, could be separated from non-democratic influences, namely the bureaucracy. In so doing, Borcherding suggests that:

> The exact effect on costs of the gradual monopoly-bureaucratisation over the century is difficult to assess. Earlier I assumed that government services were as productively rendered as services in the private sector. The evidence does not suggest this, but

instead the Bureaucratic Rule of Two seems to be more appropriate. This increase would then explain about one eighth of the total budget growth over the period – not an insignificant portion.

(Borcherding 1977: 62)

The question which arises here is whether the model of the budget maximising bureaucrat applies to the United Kingdom. Studies by Heclo and Wildavsky (1982), Pliatzky (1982), Castle (1980), Barnett (1982) and Dunleavy (1991) all seem to suggest that the budget/utility theory of bureaucracy does not apply to the United Kingdom and that what emerges as crucial in Britain is the relationship between the Treasury and Spending Departments. Heclo and Wildavsky (1981) have described the civil service as a community and Whitehall as village life with shared norms and mores, reinforced by the constant transfers between departments and the Treasury. The Treasury cannot possibly investigate all expenditure items, but instead adopts the practice where:

> The small numbers at the centre means that the co-operation of operating departments is essential. 'There are so few people that there's no chance of the Treasury taking over things' a high official explained. 'It is utterly dependent on the departments to do most of what has to be done.'

(Heclo and Wildavsky 1982: 7)

Finance officers and Treasury civil servants are not hermetically sealed departments; they meet formally and informally, always seeking to keep each other informed. The loyalty of the departmental permanent secretary is not just to the department but to the civil service. Departments do not act as pure budget maximisers but aim instead to work with the Treasury. The Treasury is informed of policy changes, especially if this means new expenditure, which gives the opportunity for Treasury civil servants to get their ministers better prepared. According to Heclo and Wildavsky, the UK civil service has to be viewed differently from that of the United States:

> Life at the top in Britain may not be warm-hearted chumminess but it does demonstrate a coherence and continuity unknown in the United States. If co-ordination means the degree to which different participants take each other into account then British political administration is extraordinarily well co-ordinated.

(Heclo and Wildavsky 1982: 9)

Whether or not it is appropriate to perceive the UK civil service as budget maximisers is questioned further by more recent events in the

British political process. The concern of the second Thatcher Government was the programme of privatisation of public sector utilities including gas, water and electricity but also compelling civil service departments to become cost centres with decentralised budgets. Privatisation has meant a shift from the ethics of public service to the ethics of markets and consumer-orientated services. This has meant reductions in the responsibilities of some government departments and also within local government. The question which arises is: why has privatisation been allowed to go on with what seems to be little opposition from civil servants, and how could this be compatible with a budget maximising model of the civil service?

Furthermore, work by Hood, Huby and Dunsire (1984) has shown that the increase in expenditure between 1971 to 1982 was not correlated with changes in civil service manpower. During the period, the number of civil servants fell from 700,000 to 652,000, in contrast to an increase in expenditure of 36 per cent. The authors conclude:

> These results might be interpreted in two ways. First they might be read as a special case – the product of one administrative culture . . . Alternatively – and more interestingly – these results might be read as indicating some general weaknesses of the budget/utility approach to bureaucracy.
>
> (Hood, Huby and Dunsire 1984: 177)

Rather than try to construct a model of bureaucratic influence, Heclo and Wildavsky (1982) and Rose (1984a) have argued that bureaucratic influence ought to be perceived as inertia which is inbuilt into expenditure programmes and the expenditure process. Pointing to this process, Heclo and Wildavsky suggest that the Public Expenditure Survey Committee (PESC), as a method of providing a survey of expenditure and the planning of resources, has led to an inbuilt bias towards higher levels of expenditures. The forward planning in the PESC involved making assumptions about economic growth and the level of taxation that would be available. Very often these assessments were optimistic and yet, despite the errors of projections, governments did not change their expenditure plans:

> By the end of 1975 public spending in Britain was widely regarded as being out of control. The PESC system that we had called the most thorough and the most sophisticated was soon labelled as the chief culprit. What we had seen to be part of the solution to control

public spending after 1967 had apparently become part of the problem.

(Heclo and Wildavsky 1982: xii)

The existence of inertia implies that ministers, in planning their expenditure, do not commence negotiations with a zero budget. They are not able to change expenditures on an annual basis. Expenditure on pensions cannot suddenly be changed, whilst some forward planning is required in education and health. These are historic commitments which are often left as unquestioned ongoing policies:

> In theory, a new government could seek to repeal or alter the established commitments of government. But in practice there is little political incentive, for most established programmes create clients who expect these programmes to continue . . . The expectations of voters are institutionalised with government by politicians, bureaucrats and ministers responsible . . . So strong are the established commitments of government that government budgets start from the premise that most revenue is committed.
>
> (Rose 1984a: 49)

The influence of public sector trade unions

The third aspect of bureaucracy seeks to show how public sector employees contribute towards the expansion of public expenditure. This takes into consideration the impact of wage bargainers in the public sector and their ability to influence the government as the employer in the bargaining process. Bain (1984) has shown that public sector trade unionism continued to expand after the Second World War from 3.3 million in 1948, or 70 per cent density, to 5.2 million in 1979, or 82.4 per cent density. The expansion of trade unionism has been accompanied by the ability of public sector unions to maintain wage relativities between the public and private sector. Furthermore, recent research has suggested that after 1974 it was the public sector that had become the wage leader in collective bargaining (Dean 1981).

The impact of wage costs on public expenditure is measured through the concept of the relative price effect (RPE). The RPE indicates the changes in cost of the public sector in relation to the overall cost changes in the economy. The presence of the RPE depends on two assertions, both outlined by Baumol (1967). First, whilst costs in the private sector can be offset by increases in productivity, such increases cannot be offset in the public sector. The RPE assumes that increases in wages in the public sector are not offset by increases in productivity since the public sector belongs to the non-marketed sector of the economy. Second, pay relativities in the public and private sectors are described as stable, which means that if wages in both sectors are rising at the same rate, then the cost of the public sector will always be moving faster.

Research by Judge (1982b) has suggested that the RPE contributed around 25 per cent to the cost in health spending between 1949 and 1977. Maddison (1984) has shown that prices in the public sector for the periods 1950 to 1973 and 1973 to 1980 increased by 6.1 per cent and 17.9 per cent. This contrasted with private sector increases of 4.3 per cent and 15.5 per cent respectively. In previous studies this author (Mullard 1987, 1990) has suggested that the view that the RPE had wholly contributed to the growth of public expenditure could not be sustained. Nevertheless, the evidence derived suggests that the RPE was positive and had added to the growth of public expenditure after 1968.

Concepts derived from theories of bureaucracy differ from those derived from individualism, pluralism and Marxism because the concepts of elites, oligarchy and knowledge estates all subordinate the link between governments and voters to the ability of elites in organisations to distort the political process. Whilst market liberals, pluralists and Marxists tend to assume that politicians have the autonomy to make changes because of voter or class pressure, the perspective of the bureaucracy points to the increased dependence of governments on strategic groups. Public expenditure changes reflect the influence and impact of organisations because of the knowledge estate of professionals, the inbuilt inertia of the expenditure process and the ability of public sector trade unions to maintain wage relativities with their counterparts in the private sector. In this sense the dynamics of public expenditure are not attributed to claims made upon government by voters but, rather, reflect the effect of those who work within the public sector and their ability to influence government. Within the framework of a theory of bureaucracy, changes in public expenditure are the product of the influence of public sector professionals and their ability to advertise claims for their particular budget, and the ability of public sector trade unions to exert pressures on government that are not related to the environment of the market-place and where expenditure programmes are expected to grow incrementally when there is an absence of methods which would allow governments and electors to evaluate the effectiveness of public expenditure inputs against policy outputs. Those who are employed in the public sector are perceived to be immune from the pressures of the market, in that as suppliers of public goods they hold a monopoly position in relation to the consumer. The level of demand does not change, irrespective of the quality of services delivered.

Chapter 3

Conservative Party politics and public expenditure
With Harry Fineberg

INTRODUCTION

Within the context of liberal democracy the presence of political parties is an essential dimension, since parties confirm political choice, and the acceptance of political differences and political priorities. Political parties reinforce the ethics of pluralism and diversity in that, first, they seek to represent different views and perceptions, and second, they provide electors with the opportunity to choose between policy alternatives. Political parties are associated with values and perceptions that seek to reflect those of the communities they seek to represent. They provide the mechanism that allows for the differences of opinion and arguments that are essential for the continuity of the democratic process.

Central to this text is the concept of political choice and the argument that seeks to emphasise that the process of decisions on public expenditure involves a political dimension. Decisions on public expenditure involve macro decisions in defining the boundaries between the private and public sectors of the economy, and issues of taxation and public finance. At the micro level, these decisions reflect competing approaches to expenditure programmes and the provision of new or additional resources for claims on health expenditure, education or railways.

Since political parties reflect competing visions they also create the opportunities for political choice to be exercised by voters, thus legitimising the process of democracy. However, it would be misleading to argue that there exists a clear relationship between political parties, government and electors. Experience reinforces the view that there is always likely to be a discrepancy between what political parties do when they become the Government and what they say in terms of ideas and objectives when they are not the Government. Policy statements have a different status to the process of policy implementation. The Conservative Party and the Government could argue that their objective is to create more opportunity and choice for the individual – to create a classless society. The question of how that opportunity and choice can be created depends, first, on the Government's definition of a classless society and, second, on the Government's willingness and ability to direct resources in such a way that opportunity and choice become the reality. If the definition of a classless society implies the removal of barriers to opportunities then the Government could argue that it seeks to produce a framework which enables the construction of a classless society. However, if the concept of enabling also involves the direction of resources to the provision of public services, the making of a classless society involves the political choice of dividing resources between private and public goods.

Furthermore, there is the problem of assuming that members of a political party share similar ideas and beliefs, when the reality is that political parties represent uneasy alliances of interests and ideas. Within both the Labour Party and the Conservative Party there were differences of opinions during the 1992 election. Within the Conservative Party were groups who wanted John Major to emphasise the continuity of principles between his leadership and that of Mrs Thatcher, whilst others wanted to argue that John Major represented a break from the market liberalism of Mrs Thatcher, and that he represented the Conservativism of One Nation. Equally, within the Labour Party there was unease about Labour's image of being a modernised social democratic party, and there were those who felt that the Labour Party was still committed to the collectivism of the post-war consensus. The durability of a political party depends both on the ability of party leaders to accommodate differences of views and opinions and, more importantly, the ability of the party to win elections and become the Government. Intra-party disputes are more likely to intensify when parties lose elections than when they form the Government.

Groupings and factions are now well established within the major political parties. Factions have very often been associated with the Labour Party as groupings divided into Left and Right, each offering very distinct and competing visions of socialism. In contrast, dissent within the Conservative Party has tended to be characterised around single issues rather than visions. The increase in the number of professional MPs within both parties, together with their willingess to

associate themselves with views and ideas rather than with pragmatism, has meant that factions have also emerged within the
Conservative Party.

The attempt to explain the relationship between politics and policy
must therefore take two issues into consideration. First, there is a need
to recognise that there are discrepancies between what parties say they
will do and what they actually do, that is, the difference between the
rhetoric of policy statements and the reality of policy outputs. It cannot
be assumed that there will be a direct correspondence between abstract
ideas and policy-making, nor can it be assumed that the making of
policy will be influenced by a coherent political ideology. Leaders of
political parties might argue that their core principles do not change,
but that these principles have to be applied to a society which is
constantly changing. Political parties have to ensure that their political
visions correspond with those of whom they seek to vote them into
government.

Second, there is the additional problem of accepting that political
parties are alliances of interests and ideas. Political parties do not
represent a single body of ideas, but rather a series of sometimes
competing and contradictory ideas with which, through an intricate
process of compromise and negotiation, they create a programme that
neither alienates nor produces internal party divisions that are likely to
harm the party's electoral opportunities.

Studies that have sought to evaluate the impact of political parties
on public expenditure have tended to conclude that different parties,
despite their rhetorical statements, tended to pursue similar policies
when they formed the Government. Utilising econometric methods to
define the meaning of politics, these models tend to suggest that
political parties do not have much success either in their attempts to
control public expenditure or in the channelling of resources to
different expenditure programmes.

This approach to politics and political parties, however, fails to
capture the dynamics of the political process and the concept of
political choice. Political parties are involved in the day-to-day process
of politics, outlining their priorities for change. By contrast, econometric models of politics are based on the benefit of hindsight and the
longer term view; it is much easier to judge governments and their
impact over the long term than to evaluate government as a day-to-
day process.

The continuing preoccupation of this text is to capture the climate of
politics as a process, where policy-making, policy implementation and

policy outcomes remain indeterminate. It is an approach which seeks to define politics as a mechanism that communities utilise to make possible their life projects. The continuous debates both within and between political parties and electors reflect the dynamics of policy-making within a democracy. Decisions on public expenditure represent that continuous process of choice. The following sections attempt to provide an outline of Conservative Party politics and the relationships between Conservative Party thinking and public expenditure policy.

CONSERVATISM AND THE CONSERVATIVE PARTY

There are two distinct interpretations of the relationships between the Conservative Party, Conservative Governments and, in particular, the financing of the public sector. First there is the approach which seeks to show that the Conservative Party underwent a profound change in its attitude towards balanced budgets and adopted a cautious approach to the public sector after the electoral defeat of 1945. This approach suggests that there was an acceptance of Keynesian interventionism in economic policy as well as a more positive attitude to welfare expenditures (Gamble 1974). Second, and in contrast, is the interpretation that seeks to point to the differences between the relationships within the Conservative Party and the constraints of winning elections and striving to become the incumbent government. This second view seeks to confirm that the Conservative Party continues to remain committed to the central theme of pragmatism – that is, a Conservative Party that continues to reject visions and a systematic approach to government.

The view that the Conservative Party has undergone a profound change suggests that the process of shifting the Party towards Keynesian economics and Beveridge had actually begun during the years of the Coalition Government and that the first Keynesian budget deficit had actually been presented by the Government in 1941. The Conservative Party is perceived as having readily accepted the principles of the Beveridge Report in 1942 and that Party policy-making was increasingly coming under the influence of pro-Keynesian interventionists, including Harold Macmillan and the Tory Reform Group. Utilising the Disraelian rhetoric of One Nation Conservatism to justify a more interventionist approach to the economy and social policy, this faction gained control over policy-making in the Conservative Party during the post-war Conservative Governments (Seldon 1981; Middlemas 1986).

Further proof of this approach was the decision not to undo most of the nationalisation and welfare measures of the 1945 Labour Government when the Conservatives returned to office in 1951. It must be pointed out that the Conservatives remained in office until 1964, which means that they had 13 years in office without seeking to change the fundamentals of the post-war consensus. A placatory attitude towards the trade unions was pursued that prioritised peaceful industrial relations at almost any cost. The 1944 commitment to full employment was accepted, and the Party sought to outdo the previous Labour Government in the number of council houses built (Seldon 1981).

The revolution in favour of market forces under Mr Heath's Government has been exaggerated, and the period 1970–4 can be described as being the most thorough experiment in Keynesian and corporatist strategies of all, including the years of previous Labour Governments. It was only in the aftermath of electoral defeat in 1974 and the election of Mrs Thatcher that a clear break with the consensus can be discerned.

THE CONSERVATIVE PARTY IN TRANSITION (1940–51)

Whilst these broad changes cannot be disputed, what is still open to interpretation is what these changes did actually represent. For instance, could a fundamental shift be discerned in the Party as a whole, or was the change imposed by the Party leadership on reluctant backbench MPs and the Conservative Party? After all, most of the Conservative MPs elected in 1945 had been in Parliament since 1935 and had therefore been associated with the policies of retrenchment and balanced budgets. These MPs had fully accepted the Treasury view that public expenditure was inflationary and bad for business profitability. In contrast, after the defeat of 1945, the Keynesians in the Party were few. A larger group had taken the view that welfare expenditure had a stabilising effect and would help to attract support for the Party at a time when it was being blamed for appeasement and military failure as well as for pre-war unemployment, bad housing and the means test.

A very significant part of the new critical atmosphere was to sweep aside inter-war political deference and to locate the Conservative Party as a core element of the old system that had failed so badly. The Conservative Party in 1940 had been in a crisis and was forced to accept a leader it did not want, Churchill, and the collectivists who rallied round him in the leadership. It also needed a strategy to lead it out of its unpopularity and to assuage popular suspicion. The careful, slow local interventionism allowed by Baldwin and Chamberlain was dismissed as wholly inadequate. In 1940 therefore the acceptance of Keynes and Beveridge were founded on reluctance and political expediency. To have stood against these ideas would have led to long-term electoral failure:

> our need [was] to convince a broad spectrum of the electorate, whose minds were scared by inter-war memories and myths, that we had an alternative policy to Socialism which was viable, efficient and humane, which would release and reward enterprise and initiative but without abandoning social justice or reverting to mass unemployment.
>
> (R. A. Butler, cited in Gamble 1974: 53)

During the 1945 election campaign, despite the acceptance of collectivist ideas, the Conservative programme reasserted an un-complicated faith in the market, which it had been argued would have undermined a commitment to full employment. The programme also made commitments to lower taxation, which in turn carried resource implications for the implementation of the new welfare programmes. The language of One Nation Conservatism that seemed to imply a wider social reform programme was always likely to be constrained by the Party adherence to market economics and the principles of individual choice and responsibility.

The Industrial Charter produced by the Conservative Party in 1947 is often cited as the major indicator of the degree to which the Party had come to accept Keynesian economics and the welfare state. In many important respects this is an accurate evaluation. Full employ-ment was accepted as the legitimate and important objective of economic policy, as were the rights to strike and to belong to a trade union. The document also contained commitments to expand the welfare state; R. A. Butler, who had been appointed to chair the industrial relations committee by the Conservative Party Conference in 1946, had produced the Charter in May 1947, and it was fully endorsed by the Party Conference that October. The Charter confirmed the ascendance of the New Conservatism:

> To those who are well versed in Conservative principle and practice the views it [The Industrial Charter] expresses will not seem particularly new or startling. To those members of the public,

however, who have been deluded by Socialist propaganda into believing that we have no policy; that we are opposed to the whole idea of planning, that we are the enemies of trade unionism, that we have no answer to unemployment and that we think of national-isation in terms of unscrambling eggs, it may come as something of a surprise.

(R. Butler, cited in Hoffman 1964: 151)

According to the late Earl of Stockton (Harold Macmillan), who had been the Conservative Housing Minister, Chancellor and Prime Minister during the 1950s and early 1960s, the Industrial Charter provided the major reason for the Conservatives' winning the election in 1951 and remaining in office until 1964:

The Industrial Charter, as it was called, proved our determination to maintain full employment, to sustain and improve the social services and to continue the strategic control of the economy . . . The principles laid down in this document guided our policies in the future Conservative Governments.

(Macmillan 1969: 303)

However, there are other aspects to this landmark report that need to be emphasised. It is not just that the Conservative Party favoured the abolition of wage and price controls and rationing. The Labour Government had in 1951 already completed its own bonfire of wartime controls. For the Conservative Party, however, the need to balance collectivism with individualism was motivated by internal party considerations as well as a calculated electoral advantage. The Party leadership could not ignore those who were committed to market liberal principles, so when the Charter was presented to the Party Conference, One Nation Conservatives and market liberals crossed swords over the document, and it was the centre right majority giving their support to the Charter that decided its acceptance. The resistance to the New Conservatism committed to the principles of Keynes and Beveridge had already been anticipated by the Charter's authors when distinctly market liberal language was utilised at various stages of the document. For example, on the issue of taxation the document stated:

there is a very definite limit to the proportion of his personal income that the citizen is prepared to allow the government to spend for him in normal times of peace. Our main objective in the matter of taxation must be to reduce government expenditure.

(Conservative Party 1947: 18)

It could be argued that these comments had been designed to placate the market liberals within the Party and that amidst the Keynesian commitments these compromises were of little consequence and certainly had little influence over the policy-making process. Alternatively it could be pointed out that in statements such as this and others that seemed to attack the political patronage of collectivism, it reflected a faction within the party whose ideas maintained a presence, however marginalised. It could also be argued that the majority of the Party had come to accept the Keynes–Beveridge programme for strategic and electoral reasons rather than out of conviction, and that market liberals always had the opportunity of arguing their case and of returning to prominence if and when the Keynes–Beveridge programme became a political liability for the Conservative Party. To this degree, therefore, the Conservative Party always contained a faction and a body of ideas that could be substituted for the dominant paradigm and also to challenge it.

Market liberal views together with traditional approaches to private property had strong roots at the local level within the Conservative Party, especially in the shires and suburbs. At the 1949 Conservative Conference resolutions were put forward favouring reductions in health and social services. Selwyn Lloyd, then a rising figure within the ranks of the Party, argued that the public sector was characterised by administrative waste and bureaucracy, and called for a reduction in public expenditure in order that taxation could be reduced:

> We must decide what level of public expenditure our economy can sustain and then we must cut down to that level. After all, that is what every family and every individual has to do.
>
> (Conservative Party 1949: 30)

Another MP, Godfrey Nicholson, speaking at the same Conference, argued:

> we are spending 40 per cent of the national real income by way of central and local taxation . . . We must tell them that we shall regard no government expenditure as sacrosanct . . . We must tell them that they may apply to the social services and to the cost of living subsidies.
>
> (Conservative Party 1949: 33)

In addition, a member of Morpeth Council asked the Party to allow local authorities to sell council housing on the grounds that the costs were becoming an excessive burden on local ratepayers:

I want to be able to relieve the ratepayers. I want now to realize a property owning democracy. I want to feel that the people of this country shall have a stake in their country.

(Conservative Party 1949: 78)

These three comments came from different levels of the Party, and it is important to evaluate the context of each separately. It is not suggested that either Selwyn Lloyd or Anthony Eden, who had also argued for the need to reduce public expenditure, were supporters of market liberal principles; on the contrary, Selwyn Lloyd was soon to be the co-author of the consensus-minded 1951 election manifesto. What is all the more important is that these key figures in the Conservative Party felt it was necessary to utilise a market liberal language for a Conservative audience that had supposedly accepted the principles of post-war collectivism. The themes of targeting welfare benefits, selling council housing, reducing waste in the public sector and curbing public expenditure that were articulated in the mid-1940s, despite the Party's shift towards the post-war settlement, seemed to continue to preoccupy the Conservative Party. The tenacious character of this language and its world view also prevented alternative discourses from taking root in the Conservative Party, such as the combination of financial orthodoxy with ideas of industrial and social partnerships, as developed by Christian Democratic Parties in Europe during the post-war period.

CONSERVATIVE GOVERNMENTS AND PUBLIC EXPENDITURE

The election campaigns of 1950 and 1951 confirmed that in certain areas of policy the Conservative Party wanted to adopt a more traditional and pre-consensus position. For example, the Conservative Shadow Minister for Labour, Maxwell Fyfe, stated that a Conservative Government would not seek to reform industrial relations, at least without prior agreement with the trade unions. The Party leadership, afraid that such a statement was likely to be misread and would rekindle suspicions within the trade unions, replaced Maxwell Fyfe with Sir Walter Monckton, an experienced conciliator who seemed to carry both the confidence of the business community and the trade unions. Sir Walter Monckton had been a co-author of the Industrial Charter and was known for his views on consensus in industrial relations. The consequence was to persuade the Conservative Party to give up their opposition to the closed shop and contracting out of the political levy.

The incident does to an extent reveal the anxiety and uncertainty within the Conservative Party which was anxious above all not to take political risks:

> differences over the extent of de-nationalisation and the future of welfare policy continued to hamper the Party up to the 1951 election despite its evident need to attract dissident Labour and floating voters. Such was the climate of uncertainty, that Central Office feared to publish the costings of Conservative health policy, the crucial decision to aim for 300,000 houses a year was only taken after a surge of enthusiasm during the Conference in 1950.
>
> (Middlemas 1986: 215–16)

The theme of the 1951 election manifesto, however, was still Churchill's call to 'set the people free', reflecting the tensions within the Conservative Party, as the manifesto declared:

> The choice is between two ways of life; between individual liberty and state domination; between concentration of ownership in the hands of the state and the extension of ownership over the widest numbers of individuals. A Conservative Government will cut all unnecessary Government expenditure, simplify the administrative machine, and prune waste and extravagance in every department.
>
> (Conservative Party 1951: 2)

The Conservative Party was faced with the dilemma of, on the one hand, having to give support to the welfare reforms of the post-war period, which implied increased expenditure on health, housing and education, and, on the other, having to indicate that it would manage the public sector better than the Labour Government. The Labour Government had to be associated with waste and unnecessary public expenditures that a Conservative Government would be able to reduce without putting the welfare state at risk. In the meantime such a declaration helped to keep the Conservative Party united, since the pledge to reduce public expenditure was likely to create the opportunities for tax reductions.

The Conservative victory of 1951 was much narrower than had been expected. This provided Churchill with the opportunity of creating a government that was conciliatory, reassuring the manual working class voter that the Conservative Party could be trusted again, and that the modern Conservative Party was no longer the Party of the inter-war years:

Churchill's insistence [was] that full employment, good industrial relations and rising working class living standards constituted the new face of Tory democracy.

(Middlemas 1986: 218)

At the centre of Churchill's strategy were good and peaceful industrial relations. Sir Walter Monckton, appointed as the new Minister of Labour, reflected Churchill's political priorities since the Government had to reassure the trade unions that it did not seek to undermine the immunities they had secured under the Trade Union Act, 1946. Nevertheless, the pursuit of reconciliation was not wholly welcomed by the Party, in that during the Conservative Conference of 1953 demands for legislation to prohibit the closed shop and for mandatory ballots in trade union elections again re-emerged and were articulated more forcefully in 1956: 'attitudes in the Party were veering against the practice of co-operation, to the point of denying that common ground existed' (Middlemas 1986: 263).

The inability of the Government to secure a long-term policy on incomes together with the increase in the number of disputes in engineering and on the railways had persuaded many within the Conservative Party that despite the Government commitment to the welfare state and full employment it was unlikely to secure the co-operation of the trade unions. The trade unions' concern was to damage the Conservative Government and to re-elect the Labour Party. In this context it became paramount for the Government that a new framework of industrial relations was required to ensure that the trade unions were brought within the ambit of the law. The Inns of Court document *A Giant's Strengths*, published in 1958, confirmed the extent to which the Conservative Party had been shifting from its voluntary approach to industrial relations.

The strategy of caution and conciliation did have implications for public expenditure. Most obviously it meant that policies pursued by the previous Labour Government, which had gained popular support, were not likely to be reversed even if they had given rise to substantial increases in public expenditure. Food subsidies, which had been introduced with rationing during the war, had survived the phasing out of rationing and in a different form were made up of grants and deficiency payments to farmers. The commitment to deficiency payments by the Conservative Government seemed to contradict its commitment to return to competition and market prices. However, such a criticism did not take into consideration the fact that the Conservative Party was also seeking to represent vested interest groups, including farmers, who obviously benefited from the government's farm policies:

> Conservative Governments were always more susceptible to pressure from the farm lobby and conscious of the importance of votes in agricultural constituencies.
>
> (Seldon 1981: 218)

In outlining its political priorities, it seemed that expenditure on public sector housing continued to be the main priority for the Government during the 1950s. The pledge to build 300,000 houses in the public sector had been outstripped in the first year as an additional 50,000 houses were added to the stock of public sector housing. This meant that the Government had to give a lower priority to increasing the capital expenditure for roads and railways and also delay the building of a new power station by the electricity board since this was likely to increase the demand for bricks that were needed for the housing programme. The building of new homes was always likely to be more politically visible and more politically important, at the least in the short term, than the building of a new power station.

> The Government's social policy was guided too often by expediency, for example, preferring housing where there were more votes to education; not pressing for rent increases sufficient to enable landlords to put their houses in good order for fear of risking electoral unpopularity, or postponing the provision of a proper financial basis for pensions for fear of upsetting the unions. Moreover, the Government made little attempt to think out a coherent and balanced social policy. The Cabinet's Social Policy Committee fell into disuse, and there was markedly little co-ordination between the Departments concerned with social policy.
>
> (Seldon 1981: 246)

The approach to expenditure programmes was guided by the three principles of political judgement, political choice and political arithmetic. The Conservative Government judged that housing was a major issue of concern, whilst in terms of political arithmetic it argued that it would increase the number of Conservative voters; in terms of political choice, housing was chosen as being of more immediate electoral advantage to the Party than investing in education, which tended to be more long term, or health, where new expenditures were less directly visible.

The subsequent achievement of the policy objective, however, depended on the ability of the Housing Minister, Harold Macmillan, to gain the backing of the Prime Minister, Churchill, in his battles with the Treasury and the Chancellor, R. A. B. Butler. It was this alliance between a spending minister and the Prime Minister that ensured housing became a priority for the Treasury and the Government – it also served as a lesson for future Chancellors of the Exchequer. Treasury ministers had to make sure in their expenditure and taxation policies that they had the support of the Prime Minister in their bi-lateral discussions with spending ministers and also in having these policies accepted by Cabinet.

In contrast to housing, other expenditure programmes seemed to be downgraded during the 1950s. Both in health and education ministers were initially rather ineffective and lightweight, unable to fight for their corner and their department budgets. On health, for example, the Government accepted the Labour Party's expenditure plans. Capital expenditure on hospitals remained static as resources were diverted to the housing programme. Lacking the personal support of the Prime Minister and with no minister within the Cabinet, the NHS continued to experience a shortage of beds and also recruitment difficulties for doctors and consultants in certain parts of the country. Even a competent Minister of Health like Ian Macleod could not overcome the problem of low electoral weighting.

Education was in a similar situation to health, having low political priority and under the charge of an education minister who was not a member of the Cabinet. The 1950s saw the beginnings of demographic change as the number of school age children began to expand whilst the Government seemed reluctant to provide the funding to meet the new demands for schools, teachers and books. Between 1951 and 1954 expenditure in real terms only increased by £87 million. There was a general reluctance to accept new initiatives for the expansion in higher education places, and proposals to establish technical colleges were rejected because of their financial implications.

On pensions and family benefits the Government adopted the same low profile as on education and health. The main concern for pensions was whether the Government would be able to fund pensions with the growing number of elderly people claiming state pensions. A proposal to raise the retirement age was abandoned because the Government wanted to avoid any confrontation with the trade unions.

Whilst on social expenditures the Government did manage to achieve a broad consensus, the financing of the nationalised industries was always likely to result in tensions and conflict between spending ministers and some Conservative MPs. With the Government committed to the restructuring of these industries, ministers found themselves defending plans to increase expenditure and borrowings for the nationalised industries, leading very often to dissent within the backbenches. Dissident MPs argued that public money was being squandered on public sector monopolies which were not the creation of a Conservative Government but were the inheritance of socialist planning. The nationalised Coal Board came under pressure from Conservative MPs arguing for increased competition policy and less dependence on coal:

> A limit on the total amount of borrowing which each industry could raise and which the Treasury could guarantee was specified in an Act of Parliament. When this limit was reached, the Minister concerned with the industry in question had to put a further Bill to Parliament in order to get increased borrowing and guarantee power. These pieces of legislation were liable to get Conservative Ministers into trouble with their own supporters, who were unreconciled anyway to the continued existence of the nationalised industries and objected in particular to giving Parliamentary approval for guarantees to finance expenditure over which Parliament had no control.
>
> (Pliatzky 1982: 22)

The picture that emerges in the early 1960s therefore is of a Conservative Party which had won three elections in succession based on policy commitments as articulated by the new Progressives. In government, the Conservative Party was able to continue to declare a Gladstonian approach to public expenditure, emphasising its priorities to eliminate waste and inefficiency in public services whilst at the same time expanding public expenditure and taxation. The Conservative Government continued to oppose the concept of universal benefits, arguing instead for a more selective approach to the system of welfare benefits – a theme that continued to dominate Conservative Party thinking during the 1960s and that was to re-emerge during the years of the Heath Government in 1970.

It is, however, also important to emphasise that public expenditure during this period of the New Conservatism was an important economic policy instrument (Mullard 1992). The commitment to full employment as outlined in the Industrial Charter of 1947 depended on the Conservative acceptance of Keynesian budgetary principles, which maintained that the Government could influence the economic cycle through fiscal policy. The extent of this commitment was best reflected in 1958 when Harold Macmillan, as Prime Minister, accepted the resignations of his entire Treasury team, including Peter Thorneycroft, Enoch Powell and Nigel Birch. The Treasury had argued that the Government should aim to reduce public expenditure by £50 million to dampen demand in the economy. Macmillan interpreted the Treasury strategy as a return to deflationary policies and unemployment, which he thought was unacceptable. Subsequently, Macmillan prompted Selwyn Lloyd and Reginald Maudling to be his Chancellors of the Exchequer where each was committed to increase public expenditure and go for growth in an attempt to escape the balance of payments constraint.

CONCLUSIONS

The Conservative Government approach to public expenditure in the post-war period was influenced by the following factors:

(a) the electoral defeat of 1945 and the process of reassessing policy with the aim of returning to office;
(b) the post-war settlement based on the twin commitments of full employment and the welfare state that contrasted to an image of a Conservative Party which had presided over unemployment and poverty;
(c) the need to minimise the tensions between those factions that were committed to market liberal principles and those that had accepted the axioms of Beveridge and Keynes.

The most urgent need after the electoral defeat of 1945 was to make the Party electable with its own distinct programme. In this sense the architects of the Conservative programme had to emphasise both continuity with the popular policies of the Attlee Government but also the need to produce an alternative vision without alienating support. In this the Conservative Party seemed to succeed by offering continuity with Labour's proposals for health and education expenditure. The Party could also claim that it would be more competent, by building more houses than the Labour Government, and also that it would seek to free people from socialist planning and controls.

The attitude to public expenditure reflects a continuing tension for the Conservative Party. The Party had to show that it was committed to the principles of the welfare state, that is, to the public provision of health, education and housing whilst at the same promising to reduce the burdens of both government and taxation. To achieve these twin aims the Conservative Party continued to argue that it agrees to reduce taxation whilst increasing resources for essential public services.

The Conservative Party has throughout the post-war period continued to argue that its approach to the welfare state stands in sharp contrast to the Labour Party. The Conservative Party has always favoured a mixed economy approach to welfare services, arguing that in areas of education and health provision there is always the opportunity for private provision. Parents are seen as having the right to purchase private education for their children whilst individuals are seen as having the right to purchase private health care. Both these rights to private provision are defined as being essential to democracy and freedom.

In addition Conservatives have always preferred a selective approach to welfare benefits in contrast to the arguments for universal benefits. Conservatives argue that government should concentrate benefits on those who are in need rather than seeking to provide widespread benefits. Within this context Conservatives favoured the introduction of better targeting of benefits for those in poverty and on low wages. Whilst Labour politicians have favoured the introduction of equal pay legislation and minimum wages, Conservatives have sought to introduce subsidies directed at families on low pay. Conservatives have criticised the concept of universalism in the provision of family allowances and, more recently, of child benefits.

A central element to Conservative philosophy is the argument for individual responsibility, i.e. that individuals should not abandon their responsibility to the Government. A Conservative vision of the citizen reveals an image of citizenship founded on the duties of the individual towards their families and society. Within a Conservative approach the citizen is a person who balances rights with responsibility, rights that the Government provides in terms of a legal framework that protects individuals' rights to property and safety, and at the same the responsibility of the individual to maintain a network of duties to the family and the Government:

> The pamphlet One Nation argued that because the Labour Government had sought in health, in insurance, in education, in housing to supply through the social services an average standard for all, it had thereby in practice failed to meet the requirements of those in greatest need ... The machinery of the welfare state was not helping the weak by its repression of the opportunities and independence of the strong ... Attention through the social services to the needs and standards of life for all members of the community

is regarded by the Conservative Party as something which ought to flow from the nature and organisation of the community itself.

(E. Powell, in Macleod and Powell 1952: 8)

The argument for selective benefits directed at those in need, as against the ethics of universal benefits, and the argument for citizens' rights through an expanded welfare state, became central to Conservative Party policy-making after 1965 when Edward Heath became leader of the Party. It shall be argued in the chapters that follow that the attempt to reduce universal benefits, such as the subsidies on school meals, and replace them with Family Income Supplement during the years of the Heath Government contributed to the Government's failure to secure an incomes policy with the trade unions. In addition, it shall also be argued that central to the politics of Thatcherism has been the continuous attempt to break with universalism and move towards a more targeted approach to public provision:

[People] are worried about a tax and social security system which, while it does not help the genuinely needy as much as they think would be right, does lead to obvious unfairness and even positively encourages dependence on the State.

(Conservative Central Office 1977: 3)

Chapter 4

The Labour Party and the politics of public expenditure

With Harry Fineberg

INTRODUCTION

The record of Labour Governments in the post-war period has been associated by their critics with economic stagnation, political paralysis and public disenchantment. Labour's commitments to an expanded role for government and increases in public expenditure are perceived to have contributed to the deterioration of the UK economy. The history of Labour Governments has been associated with policy reversals – including having to increase taxation and reduce public expenditure – because, very often, the expenditure plans of Labour Governments on taking office were judged to be unsustainable. Furthermore, it has been argued that Labour Government policies contributed to the slow economic growth that often resulted in the UK being less competitive. UK employees have sought to compensate for their tax increases through higher pay settlements, which increased further the pressures on inflation and unemployment. In the 1980s and in the early 1990s the Labour Party was perceived as being unable to change or to produce policies that were relevant. The Labour Party had become the defenders of the principles of the post-war welfare state, with an open-ended approach to big government, state intervention and higher public spending. In the aftermath of Labour's fourth successive defeat, David Willetts, once a Director of Conservative Policy Research but elected as MP during the April 1992 Election, commented that:

> For Labour, the task of integration is above all, for the state. Even after all its policy reviews, it remained the party of high spending, high taxes and more regulation, that is big government. Big government does not bring the nation together, it divides it. Interest

groups are engaged in a struggle for taxpayers' money and special favours – with the state as the battlefield.

(D. Willetts, *Financial Times*, 13 April 1992)

Labour in the 1990s is still therefore described as the party that prefers to utilise the State to create ethics of community, justice and equality. Labour seems to accept, albeit reluctantly, that markets are here to stay, and seems to acknowledge the implications of living with a market-orientated economy, but only under great sufferance. Rather than seeking to produce a policy that accommodates both the market-place and the community, Labour continues to produce policies that seem to depend on government intervention and government pro-vision of services. By implication, Labour continues to be associated with higher taxation and an expanded public sector. Labour's interpretation of socialism is therefore associated with big government and promoting the specific demands of sectionalist interest groups, namely the trade unions and public sector producer groups.

The socialism of the Labour Party reflects the Party's long-term distrust of markets, associating markets with exploitation, unem-ployment, low wages, lack of opportunity and poverty. In the meantime, trade unions are judged to have had a major influence on the policies of Labour Governments in the post-war period. Labour in government is associated with weak government, and is deemed to be dependent on trade unions in seeking to secure an incomes policy that deals with problems of inflationary pressures, of the balance of payments and of the sterling crisis. In seeking to respond to economic events Labour Governments have had to make bargains with trade unions as part of their agreement to moderate their wage demands. Such bargains have usually implied a commitment by Labour Governments to increase public expenditure to finance food subsidies, subsidies to the nationalised industries and subsidies on rents in public sector housing as part of the Government's bargain to hold down prices. However, the commitment to increase public expenditure has also meant that Labour Governments have had to increase taxation to finance these expenditures, or resort to increasing government borrowing, which in turn increases further the pressures on inflation. Furthermore, because Labour Governments have had to meet the specific demands of trade unions they have usually had to reduce their commitments to other social priorities.

Whilst critics argue that the Labour Party and Labour Governments have in the past become involved in the politics of pluralist stagnation because of their twin commitments to higher public expenditure and partnerships between government and the trade unions, Labour's argument has always been that economic prosperity depended on the willingness of government to create the sense of justice and equality which is seen as the foundations of socialism:

> It involves, in short, a large measure of economic equality – not necessarily in the sense of an identical level of pecuniary incomes, but of equality of environment, of access to education and the means of civilisation, of security and independence, and of the social consideration which equality in these matters usually carries with it.
>
> (R. H. Tawney, cited in Wright 1983: 113)

Tawney had always argued that his vision of equality was associated with providing individuals with more personal freedom rather than a commitment to generate sameness. His argument was against 'the cult of inequality' generated by inherited wealth, which in itself had been the major obstacle to individuals realising their real potential. Equality therefore implied not only the removal of unjustifiable inequalities, but also the creation of a moral climate in which individuals worked together for the good of their community:

> The socialist society envisaged is not a herd of tame, well nourished animals with wise keepers in command. It is a community of responsible men and women working together without fear in comradeship for common ends, all of whom can grow to their full stature, develop to their utmost limit the varying capacities with which nature has endowed them.
>
> (Tawney 1954: 101)

Whilst Tawney's vision of equality could generate agreement within the Labour Party, the issue of concern has always been about the means of achieving that equality. The question for the Labour Party has been whether it was possible to achieve equality within the constraints of a market economy or whether equality could only be achieved when private ownership had been eradicated. The relationships between socialism, equality and public expenditure have continued to provide different meanings for the Labour Party as it has continued to redefine and explore its commitments to the principles that constitute socialism, whilst at the same time making explicit the policy implications for public finance and personal taxation. An attempt therefore that seeks to evaluate the dynamics of socialism must also involve an attempt to evaluate the policy-making process within the Labour Party and the process of debate and argument that constitutes the formulation of Labour's approach to public expenditure.

The Labour Party has a complex structure where the policy-making process is frequently perceived to be protracted and somewhat tortuous, often resulting in a fairly untenable compromise. It reflects the tenuous relationships between the trade unions, the Parliamentary Labour Party and Labour Party Constituency Parties and the attempts by the various groupings to influence the Labour Party Conference and subsequently the Labour Party policy-making process. For example, whilst trade unions would argue that they are committed to equality, the outcomes of equality tend to have different meanings for those trade unions that tend to represent highly skilled employees in the private sector, in contrast to the trade unions that represent the interests of low-paid public sector employees. It is for this reason that Labour Governments have been unable to take for granted any commitment by the trade unions to an incomes policy since, over the longer term, trade union members tend to rebel against the equalising effects of an incomes policy.

In addition, the Labour Party continues to be hampered in its policies towards public expenditure because it seems undecided as to what it seeks to achieve through the mechanism of government intervention. At one level the Labour Party still seems to be committed to a fundamentalist interpretation of socialism that is associated with the transformation of society – that is, to replace the ethics of capitalism and the market economy with those of socialist planning:

> In the end the power of contemporary democracy must encroach upon capitalism until its last stage also has been completed . . . This is why the struggle to preserve and to extend democracy both in time and in space is likely to be the crucial feature of the politics of the second half of the twentieth century.
>
> (Strachey, cited in Wright 1983: 165)

However, the Labour Party also seeks to portray socialism as the language of priorities where public expenditure becomes the mechanism available to a society to construct a civilised capitalism through a process of income redistribution and the provision of high-quality public services:

> Socialism is a compendium of abstract principles, it is a means of giving real help to real people through better education, higher

living standards, self respect at work and joy at play and above all a sense of value as part of a living society. The central purpose of socialism is to use the power of government to ensure that private power is used in the interests of society as a whole. We shall do best if we continue to operate a mixed economy in which the operation of market forces is controlled by the government . . . The only question is where the boundary should be set in particular cases between state intervention and the market.

(D. Healey, Sara Barker Memorial Lecture, October 1979)

Whilst there might be an agreement that socialism is about equality, there continue to be tensions within the Labour Party about how that equality can be realised. During the political wilderness years of the 1950s, the arguments between the Revisionists, led by Hugh Gaitskell, and Fundamentalists, led by Aneurin Bevan, reflected the divisions between extending public ownership and increasing public expenditure as the means to achieving a classless society. In the 1990s the commitment to equality has had to be radically revised in the context of the break-up of the command economies of Eastern Europe but, more importantly, Labour has to address the aspirations of the 1990s: of a population which is attracted morally by the argument for increased welfare spending but that is also attracted to ideas of lower taxes and increased personal choice and individualism:

Labour's vision of community is an ethic in retreat inscribed in a world which is passing away . . . The way we spend our money, the way we spend our time off, even the way we travel tends towards isolation and dispersion . . . My advice is to forget community. Nobody knows what the word means any more.

(M. Ignatieff, *Observer*, 26 April 1992)

Within the context of the following sections it shall be argued that throughout the history of the Labour Party the attempt to construct different meanings of socialism has resulted in two distinct approaches to public expenditure, approaches that can be perceived to be significantly different and that are often in conflict.

THE FUNDAMENTAL COLLECTIVIST APPROACH

This approach, derived from Fabian sources, makes the critical assumption that the State (and *only* the State) can really promote the interests of the community in contrast to those of individual self-interest:

> Who is the people . . . Tom we know and Dick; and also Harry; but
> solely and separately as individuals . . . Who is their trustee, their
> guardian, their man of business, their manager, their secretary,
> even their stockholder? The Socialist is stopped dead at the
> threshold of practical action by this difficulty until he bethinks
> himself of the State as the representative and trustee of the people.
>
> (G. B. Shaw, cited in Webb *et al.* 1962: 215)

Through a reformed and democratised political system, the State may
protect the public interest by taking an increased stake in the national
economy. In so doing it is able to make enterprise accountable to the
people through Parliament. It can also ensure the efficient use of
human and material resources and avoid the waste of consumer-
orientated capitalism. Socialist planning aims to produce goods
according to basic needs rather than according to the principles of
market forces. Public ownership means the transfer of ownership from
the private sector to the community through Parliament, where the
profits can be utilised for the public good rather than private interests.

The most influential model of public ownership for the Labour Party
has been the public corporation, developed by Herbert Morrison, a
model that was utilised by the 1945–51 Labour Government:

> Morrison saw the public corporation on the model of the Post Office
> and the BBC as the best form of administration of industry,
> combining, as it did, public ownership, public accountability and
> sound business management.
>
> (Foote 1986: 179)

Managers of the new corporations were to be drawn from the industry
itself, whilst ideas of workers' control and public ownership were
explicitly rejected. The corporations would outperform their private
sector equivalents in efficiency and profitability whilst at the same time
being accountable to the democratic process.

The model of public ownership established during the period of the
Attlee Governments did have major implications for public expenditure and taxation. First, there was the immediate problem of
compensation for the former owners of the coal and steel industry but
second, and more important, was the attempt to develop a longer-term
policy of grants and subsidies towards the nationalised industries,
especially in the financing of investment projects. In this sense the
Attlee Government seemed to surrender to the Treasury view that all
forms of public expenditure had to be controlled through the Treasury,

thus denying the nationalised industries their potential to seek independent forms of finance. The nationalised industry borrowing had to be aggregated within the Government's overall plans for public expenditure, which meant that the Government had to trade off increases in subsidies to the nationalised industries against increases in expenditure on health or education.

Public ownership was regarded by the Labour Party as central to its policy objective of protecting certain industries, employment levels and the living standards of the manual working class, a group that formed the substantial majority of Labour's electoral support and that was also organised into trade unions affiliated to the Labour Party, which in turn exercised considerable influence within the policy-making process of the Party.

The politics of public ownership

1935–40

In the aftermath of the break-up of the first Labour majority government between 1929 and 1931 and the electoral defeat of 1931, the Party leadership was faced with the task of redefining the principles and policy process of the Party. In deciding what distinguished Labour from the other main parties, the commitment to public ownership became more focused. However, the evolution of public ownership was hardly systematic. The immediate programme of 1937, for example, contained a 'shopping list' of commitments, all which were enacted after 1945. The document outlined three major areas of expansion in public expenditure, including public ownership, industrial policy and increased welfare spending. The issue of whether or not an economy characterised by modest growth could sustain these expenditure commitments did not seem to figure in the debates. Ultimately the problem was to express itself in a growing tension between those collectivists for whom public ownership was the key to ending mass unemployment and poverty, and the Revisionists, who argued that nationalisation was no longer necessary.

Despite the attempt to give the Party a clearly identified domestic programme in the 1930s the public ownership list was little more than a shopping list that expanded and contracted according to the vagaries of internal party struggles:

the anticipated wealth of detailed blueprints never materialised. Such statements as did appear soon became dated. By the outbreak of war, the Party had plans for transport and electricity drawn up in 1933, a statement on coal from 1936 and statements on iron and steel from 1934 and 1935. The gas industry has always featured in Labour's plans for public ownership but no detailed statement had been prepared.

(Howell 1976: 97)

1940–45

The involvement in the wartime coalition did provide leading Labour ministers with crucial political credibility and administrative experience. Labour figures came to dominate the Cabinet Reconstruction Committee, which furthered the development of post-war policy-making. The Re-Distribution of Industry Act, 1945 had been carried through Parliament by a Labour minister in the Coalition Government, and had been part of the interventionist power assumed by that government. Labour ministers were also leading advocates of the Beveridge Report of 1942 and had sought to press their less enthusiastic Conservative colleagues to implement its conclusions. However, during the first debate on the Beveridge Report in 1943, Labour leaders could not prevent 100 of their own MPs supporting a motion that was critical of the Government's luke-warm response to the Report. Whilst the Beveridge Report was a Liberal document, founded on Liberal principles of individual rights and responsibilities, the Labour Party had become the vehicle for its implementation.

During this period Labour leaders also encountered the growing influence of Keynesian ideas inside the Treasury. The White Paper of 1944, which made government responsible for the maintenance of high levels of employment, had implications for Labour's emphasis on public ownership.

Even if the Party leadership did not seem to have grasped this implication, Aneurin Bevan, the champion of a fully socialised economy, certainly did: 'if the implications of the White Paper are sound, there is no longer any justification for this Party existing at all' (A. Bevan, cited in Howell 1976: 119).

For those who argued that public ownership was central to the socialist message and Labour's *raison d'être*, Keynesian economics had indeed become a threat. Keynesian economics sought to reform the capitalist economy and not transform it. It provided a programme for government intervention that did not include public ownership but which at the same time provided an agenda for those who wanted to 'revise' Labour's programme.

1945–51

It is probably valid to argue that the Labour Government's programme on nationalisation was implemented with the minimum of controversy in Parliament except for steel nationalisation. The Conservative Party only raised token objections at most and made no commitment to de-nationalisation. Complaints came from the Left of the Labour Party, who argued that the Government should have nationalised the banking system and other key industries, including chemicals. Labour's nationalisation programme seemed to be running out of steam by 1948 as the Government seemed to reach the end of its shopping list:

> Whilst in the next programme it will be right – and I promise you that the Executive will do it – to give proper consideration to further propositions for public ownership do not ignore the need not merely for further public ownership but for allowing ministers to con-solidate.
>
> (H. Morrison, cited in Greenleaf 1983: 474)

However, the argument for consolidation was resisted by Aneurin Bevan:

> it is so foolish for certain Labour men to preach consolidation at this stage. Before we can dream of consolidation the power relations of public and private property must be drastically altered . . . This cannot be done until effective social and economic power passes from one order of society to another.
>
> (A. Bevan, cited in Wright 1983: 183)

According to Bevan, Labour's programme of nationalisation had to be extended in order to remove the powers of private property. The achievements of the Attlee Government had only put society between the two worlds of private and public property – a Labour Government had to have the political will to extend public ownership.

The problem for the Labour Government was that its argument for nationalisation had not been associated with any socialist vision of public ownership, but rather that private owners of key industries, including coal and railways, had failed the nation because of under-investment. In contrast under a Labour Government these industries would in future serve the national interest:

> In the aftermath of war, with its thrust towards collectivism, in the new era of planning, rationalisation, and integration, that Labour

> seemed to embody, a radical transformation in the economic
> structure which was through in peaceful, almost uneventful fashion.
>
> (Morgan 1984: 109)

The nationalisation of iron and steel did, however, reveal the tensions
between planning and the market economy. The nationalisation of
iron and steel had been a last-minute addition to the Labour
programme in 1945 and it did represent a different form of nationalisation to that of the public utilities. Iron and steel represented a key
industry closely connected to other key sectors, including engineering,
which was also seen as being part of the Government's nationalisation
plan. In this sector the argument for great efficiency seemed to be more
contestable. The industry's owners, managers and workers had no
enthusiasm for public ownership, which meant that in this sector the
Government was likely to meet a different quality of resistance. The
transference of private sector monopolies to the public sector
represented a different case to that of transferring other industries that
seemed to be highly efficient and competitive.

Whilst the iron and steel industry needed reorganisation and new
capital investment, the relevance of full-scale nationalisation was
disputed by leading members of the Government, including Herbert
Morrison. These ministers argued that steel nationalisation would
encounter far greater resistance from the private employers than other
programmes of nationalisation and that it would lead to a fundamental confrontation between the House of Commons and the House
of Lords. Furthermore, the Government had by 1947 been confronted
by the major economic problem of the balance of payments and the
probable crisis of sterling. The Treasury ministers argued that the steel
nationalisation proposals would weaken further the balance of
payments problem since the Government had to increase its borrowing
to finance the new nationalisation. By 1948 Labour's nationalisation
impetus had run out of steam. The idea of a fully socialised economy
was abandoned by the Fundamentalists, including Bevan, so that the
1950 election manifesto contained no specific commitments to further
nationalisation.

Arguments for nationalisation in the 1970s

According to Morgan (1984):

> Without nationalisation above all, the morale and impetus of the
> 1945 Labour Government could not have been sustained. For most

members of the Party and the Labour Movement that was its
ultimate justification.

(Morgan 1984: 141)

Whilst still committed to the principles of public ownership and the
achievements of the Attlee Government, Labour MPs committed to
the principles of industrial democracy and seeking to continue to work
with the concepts of guild socialism as advocated by G. D. H. Cole,
had, through the 1960s and 1970s, come to the conclusion that:

> Herbert Morrison's achievement in establishing our main public
> industries was a formidable one and history will record it as such.
> But it is now equally important that the Labour Movement should
> turn its mind to the transformation of those public corporations into
> expressions of our socialist purpose. Namely, that policies and
> institutions must serve the people and not become the masters.
>
> (Benn 1979: 64)

Benn and the Institute for Workers' Control have criticised the
centralist tendencies of the socialism that had evolved in the context of
Fabian socialism, and their programme has therefore been an attempt
to provide a socialism that was more likely to be pluralistic and
democratic, by advocating the decentralising of decision-making
within public industries. Decisions would be made jointly by the
Government, trade unions and management. The missing link in this
approach has been the role of trade unions. The dominant paradigm
for UK trade unions has always been that trade unions are an essential
part of the democratic process and in fulfilling that role must act as a
permanent opposition to all governments, always protecting their
members' interests. Industrial democracy within the trade union
movement has been defined as having the right to recognition by
employers and having the right to bargain on behalf of union members
– a point that was strongly made by the TUC in its submission of
evidence to the Bullock Committee on Industrial Democracy in 1976.

Labour's social programmes

Labour's post-war programme did not just depend on public
ownership. As the successor to the wartime Coalition Government it
had inherited not only the commitment to extend the welfare state but
also to fulfil specific pledges that had been outlined in Labour's 1945
manifesto, namely, to build houses in the public sector and to establish

a free national health service. The Labour Government seemed to be carried by the wider current of reconstruction and optimism in the aftermath of the Second World War that, according to Barnet (1986), sought to build a New Jerusalem:

> Here was a vision of a garden city society filled with happy, healthy children, smiling mothers, bustling workers, serene elderly souls in the golden twilight of state pensions . . . having been equally well educated in a reformed education system, all busy in cultural pursuits other than dog racing or going to the pictures . . . For a vote for Labour was at once a vote for the New Jerusalem and a vote for the party which the electors believed could be trusted – unlike the Conservatives – to deliver it.
>
> (Barnet 1986: 11, 36)

Putting aside the vexed question of whether Labour should have given priority to social rather than economic problems, it is clear that the Labour Government had to decide which expenditure programmes would be given priority. During the election campaign Labour had placed great emphasis on housing yet, in government, Labour tended to provide additional funds for health and social security. Education and housing seemed to lose ground as the costs of the health programme continued to be underestimated and new supply bids for additional resources had to be resubmitted to the Cabinet by Aneurin Bevan:

> at a time of severe retrenchment austerity under Cripps, Morrison and other ministers complained that severe economies elsewhere, in capital investment for industry, housing, education and other areas, were not being matched by any such sacrifices on behalf of the sacred cow of the Health Service.
>
> (Morgan 1984: 161)

The housing programme suffered because the Minister for Housing, Aneurin Bevan, was also the Minister of Health. In the Cabinet, therefore, Bevan found himself winning resources for the health service at the cost of the housing programme. Labour supply was still erratic as the Government continued to deal with problems of returning soldiers to civilian life and directing labour to key industries such as the coal industry. The problems of labour supply together with Bevan's attempt to build high-quality public sector housing meant that Labour's targets on housing were not achieved during the Party's period in office – an issue that became central to the Conservative Party campaign in 1951.

Education had also taken second place to health. The main task was the implementation of the Education Act, 1944, which included the commitment to extend the school leaving age to 15 years and then to 16. This commitment carried wide resource implications, including increasing the number of teachers and school buildings. Eileen Wilkinson, the then Minister of Education, had won a significant increase in her budget during the settlement of the 1946 budget, but her demands were more strongly resisted from 1947 when the Government had moved into its austerity phase. The Government seemed to have given increased political priority to food subsidies at the cost of lower education expenditure on research and development.

The end of the Second World War did not deliver a peace dividend – which could have been channelled into social expenditures – as the Labour Government continued to meet the costs of the Empire and defence commitments. Although there had been modest reductions in 1947 and 1948, the outbreak of the Korean War led to a rapid and substantial increase in defence expenditure from 5 per cent of GDP to 10 per cent of GDP in 1951. During this period the Labour Government had also decided to create an independent British nuclear deterrent, which seemed to underline Labour's commitment to defence expenditure.

The Korean crisis put immediate financial constraints on the Labour Government in 1951. The Chancellor of the Exchequer, Hugh Gaitskell, faced with the immediate economic pressures of the balance of payments, the sterling crisis and additional demands for government expenditure, sought to reduce consumption in his budget statement as a means of dampening demand and thus the demand for imports. His strategy therefore relied on reducing public expenditure, which included reducing the plans for additional expenditure on the health service. The Chancellor also advocated a pay policy for public sector employees. As was expected, the proposals to introduce prescription, dental and spectacle charges were resisted by Harold Wilson and Aneurin Bevan in the Cabinet, each arguing that defence spending needed to be reduced instead. However, the Cabinet seemed to accept Gaitskell's budget judgement, which resulted in the resignations of both Wilson and Bevan. The irony of this crucial debate was that when the Conservatives returned to office in 1951 they quickly decided that the defence expenditure programme could not be sustained and decided to reduce the level of spending introduced by Labour.

THE SOCIALISM OF THE REVISIONISTS

Douglas Jay (1937) had already argued in *The Socialist Case* against Labour's commitment to public ownership. His view was that public ownership was not likely to create a classless society but, rather, a new class of *rentiers* similar to the leaders of the Communist Party in the Soviet Union who controlled the public utilities and passed on their wealth and privileges to their children. Jay argued that Labour had to produce a taxation system which sought to redistribute income and wealth and that this would always be the better way to achieve the egalitarian principles of socialism:

> Socialists have been mistaken in making the ownership of means of production instead of ownership of inherited property the test of socialisation ... It is not the ownership of the means of production as such, but ownership of large inherited incomes, which ought to be eliminated.
>
> (D. Jay, cited in Wright 1983: 142)

From a different point of view, Evan Durbin (1940) wanted to emphasise the inextricable links between socialism and democracy. According to Durbin, people had to be persuaded to adopt the socialist cause through the mechanism of democracy; as far as he was concerned, the pathway to socialism had to include the commitment to democracy as an end in itself as much as the commitment to equality:

> I am left with a practical problem to face. If the economic system is in urgent need of reform, and if the maintenance of democracy is an essential condition of social justice, how can the one be used to secure the other? How can expansionist and egalitarian policies be secured through the practice of the democratic method? The democratic socialist must discover such a strategy.
>
> (E. Durbin, cited in Wright 1983: 144)

The Revisionists have tended to emphasise the need to redefine socialism in the context of a changing society. The Revisionist case was eventually given intellectual coherence by Anthony Crosland in his book *The Future of Socialism* (1967), where he argued that the classical Marxist interpretation of capitalism was no longer valid. Crosland argued instead that the ownership and control of private companies had shifted to a division of interests between shareholder interests and managers, and that within the context of a managerial revolution the nationalisation of companies was no longer relevant to a Labour

Government. Governments seeking to promote equality now had alternative policy instruments to influence the economy. Generating employment and high wages could now be achieved through Keynesian techniques, whilst commitments to welfare could be expanded through a government policy aimed at generating higher levels of growth and prosperity in the economy:

> The relief of distress and the elimination of squalor is the main object of social expenditure; and a socialist is identified as one who wishes to give this an exceptional priority over other claims on resources. This is not a matter of the overall vertical equality of incomes; the arguments are humanitarian and compassionate, not egalitarian . . . This represents the first major difference between a socialist and a conservative.
>
> (Crosland 1967: 121)

The central concern of the Revisionists was the issue of equality, but rather than arguing that equality depended on ownership, Revisionists tended to argue that redistribution of income depended on the political will of government to create an environment that provided equality of access and opportunity for individuals to develop their personal capacities in the context of liberal freedoms. In contrast, Fundamentalists have continued to argue that nationalisation and social ownership should be the vehicle for achieving that equality.

CONCLUSIONS

It is within the context of this continuing debate that dilemmas and contradictions has continued to characterise Labour Governments. Labour in government have tended to construct programmes founded on ambiguity and uncertainty in an attempt to sustain a coalition of conflicting interests. Ministers committed to the Fundamentalist cause emphasised Labour's commitments to government intervention in the economy, arguing for more Parliamentary space to be given to programmes of nationalisation, subsidies to industries, planning agreements and new economic initiatives. In contrast, ministers committed to Revisionism concentrated more on social expenditure issues, arguing for a more coherent approach to income redistribution, education and health policies. Revisionist ministers also tend to be committed to a mixed economy, preferring a Keynesian approach to economic management as opposed to direct government intervention. Furthermore, Revisionists have also tended to accept the benefits of a mixed economy in welfare, seeking to provide welfare services that are orientated towards the consumer and are willing to criticise the role of professionals, which in turn seems to bring them into conflict with public sector trade unions and Fundamentalists, who continue to reaffirm their beliefs in public ownership.

The tensions between Fundamentalists and Revisionists have been reflected in Labour's approach to public expenditure. At one level there has been the problem of committing resources to further nationalisation programmes, and on another, the issue of funding the expenditure programmes of existing public corporations. Increasing resources for the public corporations in a zero sum context usually meant that whilst more financial support was channelled to the Post Office or to the electricity industry less resources were available for social programmes, including health care and education.

The commitment of resources to the nationalised industries by a Labour Government was equated with Labour's commitment to socialism. Providing funding for these industries guaranteed the employment of those who worked in these industries, which in turn was also a major concern for the trade unions. Labour Governments were therefore morally obliged to underwrite the debts of the public corporations irrespective of the service being offered to consumers. The Fundamentalist definition of socialism was confined to the producers and often ignored the aspirations of consumers or the rights of taxpayers.

Our study of the 1974–9 Labour Government shows that this period reinforced the uneasy relationship between Fundamentalists and Revisionists. The initial commitment to the Social Contract, the pledges to control prices in the nationalised industries and increased subsidies indicated the extent to which Fundamentalists had shaped the Labour programme in 1973. The launching of the National Enterprise Board (NEB) and the continued funding of British Leyland together with the plans to nationalise the ports and the aircraft industry again indicated Labour's attempts to return to the programme initiated by the Attlee Government of 1945–51.

Second, the study also confirms the tenuous relationships between the Labour Government and the trade unions. Despite Labour's claim to its special understanding with the trade unions, Labour ministers argued later that it was the Government that had done all the giving during the years of the Social Contract whilst the trade unions continued to negotiate better conditions for their members. The repeal of the Trade Union Act, 1972, the introduction of the closed shop, equal pay legislation and rights against dismissal were seen as major concessions made by Michael Foot as Minister of Employment in Labour's attempt to underpin that special understanding. Furthermore, the introduction of food subsidies, rent controls and subsidies to the nationalised industries was perceived to be Labour's attempt to create an environment of price controls that would enable trade unions to moderate their wage demands.

The Social Contract in its early phase therefore depended on the Labour Government making commitments to increase public expenditure on subsidies to industry, rents, pensions and child benefits. In contrast, the trade union response during the period 1974–5 was to ensure that the Government continued to extend its commitments; it was only the external shocks of sterling crisis and the willingness of the Labour Prime Minister together with the Chancellor to impose public expenditure cuts in early 1976 that forced the trade unions into accepting the need to provide concrete proposals on incomes policy.

It was the Labour Government that in 1976 eventually abandoned the commitment to the post-war settlement. The decision to reduce public expenditure and the acceptance that such a decision was likely to result in increased unemployment confirmed the beginnings of the departure within the Treasury from the principles of Keynesian demand management. It was therefore the Labour Government that introduced a monetarist economic strategy, announcing targets for the money supply, increasing interest rates and reducing public expenditure. Despite claims to the contrary it was the inability of the Fundamentalists to provide a coherent alternative strategy that made it possible for the Chancellor and the Prime Minister to impose the policy on their Cabinet colleagues, and it was a Revisionist, Tony Crosland, who continued to resist the demands made by the IMF on the Labour Government.

Chapter 5

The Heath Government 1970–4

INTRODUCTION

In describing the Heath Government, Sir Leo Pliatzky (1982) has suggested that there were resemblances between the Heath Government and that of Mrs Thatcher in their intentions to break with the politics of social democracy and state intervention:

> in a good many respects its [the Heath Government] philosophy anticipated the brand of politics which later came to be associated with Margaret Thatcher. There was the same commitment to restore a market economy, the same aspiration to roll back the frontiers of the public sector. This was the philosophy of Selsdon Man.
>
> (Pliatzky 1982: 98)

This chapter seeks to explore the extent to which the Heath Government was committed to break with the politics of consensus and collectivism. The study of both policy statements on public expenditure and the actual record on public expenditure would suggest that the Heath administration did not seek to break with the politics of the post-war settlement. Indeed, it shall be argued that the Heath Government did attempt to move the UK towards a more institutionalised approach to tripartite politics combined with a more active approach to Keynesian macro economic policies in order to deal with the twin problems of inflation and rising unemployment.

At one level, the record on public expenditure during the Heath years seems to be remarkable when contrasted to the commitments made by the Conservative Party. During the years of the Heath Government the rate of growth in public expenditure continued to sustain its post-war trend. Between 1970 and 1974 public expenditure increased by 5.8 per cent of GDP (market prices). This growth was mainly attributable to the increases in expenditure on housing, health, trade and industry, and social security. All these areas of expenditure reflected the political choice of the Government, the increases in expenditure on capital projects in housing and health confirmed the Government's continued commitment to Keynesian economics and the readiness of the Government to use fiscal policy to expand the economy.

The Conservative Party had, in opposition, conducted its campaign on the theme that the resources going to the public sector were already too high and that a future Conservative Government would look to 'less government but of better quality'. The Conservative Party after the 1970 victory heralded what Mr Heath was to define as the 'Quiet Revolution':

> we were returned to office to change the course of history of this nation – nothing less . . . to bring about a change so radical, a revolution so quiet and yet so total that it will have to go beyond the programme for a Parliament to which we are committed.
>
> (E. Heath, cited in Conservative Party 1970: 129)

Linking the concept of the Quiet Revolution to the Government's plans for public expenditure, the Chancellor in October 1970 declared that the aim was:

> to enable the individual to keep more of the money he earns, have greater incentive to increase his earnings and to have greater freedom in how he spends or saves his money . . . We therefore aim to be more selective in our approach to social services.
>
> (A. Barber, cited in *Hansard*, 27 October 1970, Vol. 805, Col. 37)

In providing this outline of policy statements and the contrast with the actual out-turns for public expenditure, it would seem feasible to come to the actual conclusion that the Heath Government had by 1974 failed to live up to the image that it had presented in 1970. Two types of answer have been presented to explain this apparent 'failure'. First is the explanation as presented by Holmes (1982), Bruce-Gardyne (1974) and Norton (1978). These authors believe that the Quiet Revolution was abandoned by members of the Government, although the reasons given for this departure from the original plans tend to differ. Holmes (1982) suggests that Mr Heath panicked over the level of unemployment and sought an alternative to the Quiet Revolution:

> the platform on which Mr Heath was elected in 1970 was not only repudiated but put into reverse. The Quiet Revolution was short

lived, disengagement from industry was turned into the most active interventionist policy hitherto devised . . . whilst public expenditure cuts in October 1970 foreshadowed an enormous increase in deficit spending.

(Holmes 1982: 127)

Holmes argues that the Quiet Revolution did not represent a return to nineteenth-century *laissez-faire* economics. The programme outlined in 1970 still showed a commitment to the welfare state. The intention was limited, Holmes argues, to reversing the excesses of collectivism after six years of Labour Government. Measures to be taken involved the removal of welfare subsidies on school meals and school milk, and allowed for increases in prescription charges and the introduction of rent and rate rebates. Furthermore, allowing industry to thrive without state intervention was to reflect no more than the Conservative Party's reiteration of its confidence in the private enterprise economy. Holmes implies that these commitments were not sufficiently great to constitute a break with the post-war political settlement. The reversal of these policy intentions was, therefore, not so much that they represented a qualitative break but, rather, Mr Heath's lack of commitment to market liberalism, the concept of market forces and free enterprise. Hence, Holmes describes Mr Heath as:

not being prepared to wait for private industry, and the private sector as a whole, to invest a sufficient degree to bring about economic revival. Mr Heath was not prepared to wait for unemployment to fall by workers pricing themselves back into jobs. In short Mr Heath was not prepared either ideologically or personally for the Quiet Revolution to bear fruit.

(Holmes 1982: 141)

In contrast, Norton's (1978, 1985) study of dissent within the Conservative Government aims to show that Mr Heath adopted a leadership style that allowed him to make changes in the direction of policy. Mr Heath is described as opting to choose a Cabinet of his own liking and then making decisions without consulting the Party either inside or outside Parliament:

During the period 1972 to 1974 the Government – despite its majority of 30 seats – lost no less than 6 major votes in the House of Commons. This was an expression of 'dissident' or back bench revolt by Tory MPs, their failure to gain concessions from the Government and the unpopularity of Heath's leadership.

(Norton 1978: 3)

A different perspective can be constructed from the work of Gamble (1974, 1980). He suggests that the Heath Government's adherence to the Quiet Revolution has to be considered in the context that it was a possible strategy that could arrest Britain's economic decline, meaning that the Government had not eschewed the possibility of alternative policies:

> it is important to grasp the nature of this radicalism in order to understand the reason for the several 'U' turns that were so criticised in the party . . . Such criticisms are often based on the mistaken notion that the Heath government was attempting to establish a social market economy – an attempt which was then recklessly abandoned in 1972 because the government panicked.
>
> (Gamble 1980: 36)

In Gamble's argument the Conservative Government is not assessed in terms of an ideological shift towards the social market economy, but rather as searching for a method that would arrest economic decline. Gamble, therefore, suggests that 'the Progressives still believed they could modernise the British economy and restructure British capital without altering their basic electoral strategy and the kind of consensus that existed since the War' (Gamble 1974: 123). Mr Heath is therefore not perceived as betraying his Party's programme but, rather, as leading a government that was working within the post-war political settlement, and that he:

> sought to operate within the constraints of welfare consensus – that is within the explicit recognition of the need to involve organised labour in the running of the state with new priorities for government, notably re-distributive taxation to finance social services, a large public sector and government management of the economy to maintain full employment.
>
> (Gamble 1974: 210)

Both these explanations are related to the issues outlined in Chapter 3, where it was suggested that the 1970s reflected a continuity of tension between progressives and market liberals within the Conservative Party. The policy commitments to markets, lower levels of taxation and a more selective approach to social policy would suggest that a change had taken place within Conservative Party thinking. The emphasis on individual choice seemed to indicate that market liberalism was now in ascendance within the Party. In contrast,

Gamble has suggested that during the Heath years the progressives were still in ascendancy and that the record of the Government has to be properly located within the context of constraints and events that were beyond the immediate control of the Government. Gamble argues that the Government was still working within the constraint of the post-war settlement – of being committed to welfare, full employment and an economic policy founded on the politics of consensus:

> under capitalism the function of the state has been to guarantee the best possible conditions for economic activity. In this sense the state has always exercised general control over industry . . . it is the form that has changed . . . The form of state that exists, and the politics of power that maintains it, reflects the kind of economy that exists, and the key to the organisation of the state is how it is financed.
>
> (Gamble 1974: 30)

The changes in public expenditure during the years 1970–4 need to be analysed within a framework that takes into consideration a duality of influences on government and that can be described as the influence of opinion and the influence of constraints. These categories point to the influence of Keynesian ideas (influence of ideas) and the attempt to establish tripartite structures (influence of constraints) as providing the context within which public expenditure decisions could be located.

THE GOVERNMENT'S RECORD ON PUBLIC EXPENDITURE

The study of expenditure White Papers

In the White Paper of October 1970 (HMSO 1970) the plans unfolded by the Government indicated that expenditure was planned to grow at 2.6 per cent per annum, in contrast to the outgoing Government's plans of 3 per cent per annum. To achieve this slow-down, the Government announced cuts of £300 million for the year 1971–2 and £1,600 million for the whole period to 1974–5. These intentions were further reinforced in the January 1971 White Paper (HMSO 1971a), which showed how the plans would unfold over the five-year period. Again, the Government put forward the argument for the need for more effective use of public expenditure and for the phasing out of indiscriminate subsidies. In the 1971 White Paper, the Government declared:

When the government took office last June [1970] they carried out an immediate review of public expenditure to 1974/75 to concentrate the activities of public bodies on the tasks which they alone can perform; to reduce substantially previous plans and permit taxation to be reduced. The individual can then expect to keep more of what he earns and has greater incentives to productive effort. This is the way to faster growth of the nation's resources, whilst more resources are devoted to meeting the essential needs of the public sector.

(HMSO 1971a: 5)

This approach has to be contrasted to that of the White Paper of November 1971 (HMSO 1971b), which indicated a change; the priority between January and November had shifted from one that identified areas of expenditure that could be reduced or phased out, to one of expansion:

In the period since January when the Government published their first public expenditure programmes, new needs have been identified by their continuing reviews of the longer term programmes . . . New needs have also arisen from the course of events including the rise in unemployment, particularly in the development areas, and the collapse of Rolls Royce . . . There is no question here of other needs competing for resources; only of using productive power which would otherwise be idle.

(HMSO 1971b: 5)

The November 1971 White Paper incorporated the packages of increases announced in June and October, which included mainly counter-cyclical expenditures, devised within the Treasury (Pliatzky 1982). These represented the Government's response to rising unemployment. The rate of unemployment had been rising by about 20,000 per month during 1971. However, the increases the Government announced also reflected the influence of spending departments, who were making the most of this change in mood to secure longer term expenditures. The view that the new expenditures were not just of a short-term duration was reinforced by the Select Committee:

the government seems to be over-committing itself on planned expenditures in its attempt to lower the level of unemployment. Only £300m of the £1200m proposed expenditures are being used as part of short-term demand management. The other £1bn is long-term expenditures.

(House of Commons 1973: vii)

Although the White Paper did contain short-term projects, including housing improvement grants and the building of two naval frigates, there were also increases in expenditures that were more of a long-term nature. These measures included the uprating of social security benefits and pensions, new commitments in health, education and the trade and industry programme. The study of the expenditure White Papers reinforces the view that expenditure plans, after January 1971, had resumed an expansionary trend with each expenditure White Paper (Mullard 1987).

THE GOVERNMENT'S RECORD BY PROGRAMME

Disaggregating expenditure programmes by economic component

Capital expenditure

Whilst total capital expenditure actually declined throughout the period 1970–4 from 5.33 per cent of GDP to 5 per cent, this was not so in housing, which expanded by 0.31 per cent of GDP, as did health; capital expenditure was reduced on education, roads and environment services.

Current expenditure

Current expenditure overall increased by 0.14 per cent of GDP between 1970 and 1974. As already indicated, this outcome represented the expansion in certain programmes, including personal social services where expenditure increased by 0.23 per cent of GDP, followed by health which increased by 0.21 per cent of GDP; expenditure on law and education increased too. However, during the period defence expenditure was reduced, and fell by 0.59 per cent of GDP. The growth in current expenditure confirmed the Government's longer-term expenditure commitments, which included new expenditure commitments in education, including the expansion of further and higher education, and in the care of the mentally ill and the mentally handicapped:

the last ten years have seen a major expansion of the education service, the next ten will see expansion continue as it must if education is to make its full contribution to the vitality of our society and our economy . . . in this the further education system has a vital contribution to make in ensuring that the country has a work force capable of meeting the changing needs of industry and commerce.

(HMSO 1972b: 1, 29)

In higher and further education the Government was planning for the number of students on full-time and part-time courses to grow by 335,000 by 1981. This implied an expansion in halls of residence and in the number of tutors. The plans indicated an increase in expenditure from £687 million to £1,120 million, an increase in new expenditures of 63 per cent by 1981.

The increase in current expenditure was also influenced by the relative price effect. Between 1970 and 1974, all current expenditures expanded by 2.4 per cent of GDP – the output effect increased by 0.30 per cent whilst the RPE increased by 2.1 per cent (Mullard 1987). However, the breakdown by programme again shows that the overall trend differs to that in each programme. Within programmes, including environment, law and order, education and personal social services, the output effect is consistently the larger component. In contrast, in health and defence the RPE is the larger.

The analysis of current expenditure suggests that the increases in expenditure could be attributed to 'discretionary' additional expenditures, and these included additional resources for education and the environment. In addition, however, the robust RPE would also indicate the degree to which additional expenditures in health and defence were the result of the rate of price increases and wage costs.

Transfers and subsidies

Expenditure on transfers and subsidies expanded by 1.8 per cent of GDP, and the main areas of increase were the trade and industry programme, transport, agriculture, housing and social security. The expansion of these expenditures is significant since the Government, in its original plans, had particularly singled out subsidies as the area that it would reduce. John Davies, Secretary of State at the Department of Industry, had in 1970 described the plethora of industrial subsidies as a lame duck policy. However, his department was to be involved in the rescue of Rolls-Royce and Upper Clyde Shipbuilders, in delaying the phasing out of the Regional Employment Premium, and in the expansion of development areas. Furthermore, despite these policy changes, Davies was to be replaced by Maurice Macmillan, who was described as an interventionist and was likely to depart from Davies's *laissez-faire* image. This move was applauded by *The Times*:

> the weaknesses of the DTI have resulted from an excessive commitment among some members to the political principle of disengagement. Ideological commitment in the area of industrial policy is an almost guaranteed prescription for political embarrassment, if not failure. The new team must de-emphasise a commitment to an ideology. Hopefully they are a bunch of politicians with a greater eye for industrial reality.
>
> (*The Times*, 8 April 1972)

The new industrial reality implied that the Government would not allow British industry to live within the bracing climate of the market. The suggestion seemed to be that government had to abandon such ideological commitments. Pliatzky (1982) has also argued that the change within the DTI represented a 'U'-turn by the Government.

The increased expenditures on transfers and subsidies represented a series of policy responses to a number of influences. They included a response to the increase in unemployment, as was reflected in the changes at the Department of Trade and Industry. In addition, they reflected the Government's commitment to increased pensions, housing subsidies and school meals as part of its attempt to secure a voluntary wage agreement with the trade unions.

The study of the Government's record on public expenditure confirms that the Government increased public expenditure overall. However, this analysis also points to the rejection of certain explanations. For example, it would be insufficient to argue that the Government increased public expenditure purely because of the level of unemployment and that the increases in expenditure represented demand-led expenditures. The study confirms that the increases in expenditure represented discretionary decisions and reflected the political priorities of the Government and also the Government's commitment to expenditures in areas that were of a long-term nature. The increase in programmes indicates that the Government had not concentrated the increases on capital projects. The Government provided new resources in health and social services and also in subsidies and transfers. There was no departure from welfare expenditures, since spending ministers seemed to be only too willing to expand their departmental budgets.

The policy towards public expenditure represented the Government's continued commitment to the concept of income redistribution through the public sector as part of its bargain with the trade unions to secure a policy on incomes, which the Government perceived to be the political solution to inflation. The Heath Government through its public expenditure policies sought to reaffirm the politics of consent.

EXPLAINING THE GOVERNMENT'S RECORD

In the introduction to this chapter it was pointed out that there are two interpretations of the Government's record. The first interpretation can be derived from the studies of Holmes (1982) and Norton (1985). This approach emphasises the role of political choice, the autonomy of government and the nature of the leadership style of the Prime Minister. It seeks to suggest that the expansion of public expenditure reflected, first, a series of political choices that constituted a reversal of the plans outlined in 1970 and, second, Mr Heath's lack of conviction in the Conservative programme. The second approach, as outlined in Gamble (1974), seeks to de-emphasise the concepts of autonomy and political choice and instead argues that it is the context within which the Government was operating that created the constraints and therefore influenced the policy options available to the Government. According to the Gamble thesis, the context between 1970 and 1974 still favoured a Keynesian approach to the economy and an interventionist State. In explaining the Government's record, this section seeks to provide a perspective that gives prominence both to the concept of the autonomy of government and to those elements that constrained that autonomy.

The elements of autonomy and constraint can be identified as the Keynesian influence and the Tripartite influence. The former recognises the existence of autonomy, since governments make choices of which interpretation they accept about how the economy works, whilst the latter recognises the impact of functional groups on the role of government. Governments always have a number of policy options made available to them, either internally through the civil service structure or externally through the mechanisms of independent advisers, and also through advisers that the Government might decide to import into the civil service structure. Mr Heath had, for example, established the Central Policy Review Staff (CPRS) – a think-tank of advisers that was aimed at helping the Government review the effectiveness of policy. Within the framework of policy choice the Government tends to select policies that approximate to its overall strategy.

The Keynesian influence

Within the context of this chapter the concept of Keynesianism is utilised to indicate the Government's approach to the economy. This approach is based on the view that government can influence the level of economic activity through fiscal measures, including public expenditure, and that inflation is caused by cost-push factors, including wages. In this section the concern will be to explore the question of whether the Government did continue to approach macro-economic policies within the context of Keynesian principles, which included a commitment to demand management, to deal with problems of rising unemployment, and whether it employed cost-push factors to deal with problems of inflation.

In confronting the problem of inflation, one view suggests that the Government had accepted the axioms of monetarism concerning the workings of the economy and the role of government within that context. Enoch Powell has argued that he supported the reductions announced in the 1970 Expenditure White Paper because he saw its intentions as being the way to cure inflation:

> There is a parallel between 1957 and the problems faced by this government. One is that in 1957 government spending had continued to increase and that since 1957 Britain has continued to be plagued with inflation. Since 1957 there has been a revolution in economic thinking. Policy on money supply is now at the centre of economic and public debate, the relevance of government spending to inflation has been acknowledged in theory and practice. We shall in the next few months know whether previous cycles of panic measures will be repeated.
>
> (E. Powell, *The Times*, 7 January 1971)

According to Mr Powell, therefore, the two expenditure White Papers of 1970 and 1971 had given practical acknowledgement to the monetarist theory of inflation. When the Government reversed most of the expenditure reductions in November 1971 and November 1972, Mr Powell felt that the Government had therefore abandoned its policy on inflation: 'I warn the government that inflation will accelerate again . . . the main reason is the fantastic growth in the money supply caused by the increases in public expenditure' (E. Powell, *The Times*, 9 June 1972).

Mr Powell's theme raises the question of whether the Government's original policy on public expenditure constituted an acceptance of a monetarist strategy that was subsequently abandoned. To resolve this issue we need to evaluate the debate that was conducted within the Cabinet. Reginald Maudling, in a memoir to the Cabinet, indicated that he did not agree with Mr Powell's notions about how to deal with inflation. Instead, Maudling had argued that:

> Inflation is a political problem, which traditional economics cannot cope with. Cost inflation has to be solved through strictly relevant means. The monetarist strategy is, therefore, a nonsense; the belief, that government by controlling the money supply, would cure inflation, would only lead to deflation and unemployment as powerful groups continued to expand their incomes.
>
> (Maudling 1978: 213)

Maudling's approach was also supported by another leading member of the Government. James Prior also believed that a policy directed at controlling the money supply was irrelevant to dealing with what he saw as the problem of monopolies:

> if we restrict the money supply this would destroy confidence in business and increase unemployment. Monopolies of labour and capital will still be able to extract their premiums. Those with muscle would be alright but the mass of the country will suffer.
>
> (J. Prior, cited in *Hansard*, 7 November 1972)

Furthermore, whilst the Chancellor seemed to be aware of the growth in the money supply, of which Mr Powell warned him, Mr Barber tended to suggest that the growth in public expenditure would not lead to an increase in the money supply:

> it would be inconsistent with my Budget judgement to restrict the growth of the money supply – so as to reduce demand below the level needed. But equally the money supply must not be so plentiful as to produce an additional boost to demand beyond that intention . . . nor must it accommodate any further to the rise in costs and prices.
>
> (A. Barber, *Hansard*, 27 March 1972)

In a subsequent speech at the Mansion House, however, the Chancellor seemed to be voicing Mr Powell's fears. In this speech the Chancellor found it necessary to respond to the Bank of England's Quarterly Bulletin, which had shown that the rate of increase in the money supply during 1972 was in excess of 13.3 per cent: 'I am not confident that we have done enough to ensure that monetary

expansion will moderate to the desired extent in the coming months'
(A. Barber, Mansion House Speech, cited in *The Times*, 23 October
1972).

It would seem that, whilst the Chancellor was aware of certain
monetarist arguments, the policies the Cabinet pursued did not adhere
to monetarist prescriptions. The policy throughout the period was
aimed at holding down costs. The solution to inflationary pressures was
not sought in a monetarist doctrine of controlling the money supply or
producing monetary targets, but through a process of gaining control
over wage demands. Whilst it would be true to comment that the
strategy of incomes policy or the prices and incomes boards had been
eschewed in 1970, nevertheless the Government sought to control
wage costs through the strategy of de-escalation of wage settlements in
the public sector with the hope that the private sector would follow.

Furthermore, it was in 1971, when the policy of de-escalation was
proving to be ineffective in dealing with the dual problems of inflation
and rising unemployment, that the Government adopted a more direct
and Keynesian strategy. Whilst the policy of de-escalation had some
success in public sector settlements, in pay negotiations with the miners
and the power workers, the Government found it had to concede
higher levels of settlement than it desired. In the private sector wage
settlements continued to rise, irrespective of what was happening in the
public sector.

It was against this economic background that the Government
decided to construct a policy that was similar to that of the previous
administration, a policy aimed at prices and wages. Hence, the
Government negotiated an agreement with the retailers' consortium to
hold down prices to 5 per cent per annum, whilst on its own part it
declared to hold down prices in the nationalised industries. In the
meantime the Government also started discussions with the trade
unions to explore ways of agreeing a voluntary incomes policy.

The conclusion that can be drawn here is that leading members of
the Cabinet were aware that they had to make a choice between two
strategies – the first being the strategy advocated by Enoch Powell.
This entailed the reduction of public expenditure and the control of
credit expansion and interest rates to deal with the problem of
inflation, whilst allowing the market to determine the price of labour
and the level of employment. The second strategy, articulated by
Reginald Maudling, implied that inflation was caused by functional
groups and that to deal with the rise in prices the Government had to

recognise that it was obliged to resolve inflation by consent. It seems that the Government accepted the latter:

> if the choice is to resume economic expansion with an incomes policy to reduce wage inflation or to restrain wage inflation by accepting the unemployment of 1 million people, Mr Heath will have the vast majority of the people and Conservative MPs behind him to reject unemployment. It is an inhumane attitude of mind which says unemployment does not matter. Fortunately for us this is rare in British politics.
>
> (*The Times*, 5 March 1971)

Holmes (1985a) has suggested that rising inflation and rising unemployment provided Mr Heath with the opportunity to change Government policy to one of intervention, although other options were available at the time. It would seem that Holmes is arguing with the benefit of hindsight when he suggests that the Government need not have panicked about the rise of unemployment, and that Mr Heath should have waited for workers to price themselves back into the market. Holmes is assuming that such a political agenda actually existed. It is hoped that the detailed study in this chapter shows that, within the environment of the early 1970s, a political agenda that rested on the discipline of the market place was perceived as being too politically costly and therefore not sustainable.

The influence of Tripartitism

In this section it shall be pointed out that the adoption of a Keynesian approach to the economy necessitated the Government's recognising the need to seek the consent of other spheres of influence within the economy (Keegan and Pennant Rea 1979). This implied a process of trade-off between government objectives and the priorities of functional groups, which included the trade unions. Fishbein (1984) has pointed out that the negotiations between the trade unions and the Government had become wide-ranging during 1972, with Mr Heath calling on the trade unions to become co-partners in the running of the economy and the TUC submitting their own proposals on economic policy. The success of these negotiations depended on the extent to which the Government was prepared to concede to trade union proposals on new public expenditures. These demands included pensions, the elimination of poverty through tax allowances and the holding down of housing and food costs. The talks broke down because the Government was unwilling to meet some of these proposals, namely to hold down rents and the price of school meals.

The study of some of the actors and observers involved in these discussions seems to substantiate Fishbein's thesis. From the Government side, Mr Heath's interpretation suggests that the Government's commitment to 5 per cent growth in the economy and to increased pensions had been part of the TUC negotiating position to which the Government had acceded:

> looking at the policy items of the last 18 months for which the TUC has pressed, such as increases in pensions and reflationary measures, the government have made all these concessions; it is therefore right that we should expect some sort of response from the trade unions.
>
> (E. Heath, cited in *The Times*, 1 March 1972)

It also seems that senior civil servants were aware that the negotiations included the Government having to make concessions in other areas of public expenditure that were also seen as important by the trade unions. This included the Government reversing its intentions to increase rents in the public sector and to phase out the school meals subsidy. Both actions would have increased costs for trade union members, which raised the question of whether this was compatible with asking trade unions to moderate their wage demands. This is how Mr Baldwin, Permanent Secretary to the Treasury, interpreted the negotiations:

> At the end of October 1972 the Tripartite talks were still in progress. We at the Treasury had to consider the possible outcomes in so far as they affected public expenditure and in various forms had to decide the level of the contingency reserve. Increases in education expenditure such as school meals and nationalised industries pricing led us to increase the reserve by £200m.
>
> (P. Baldwin, cited in *House of Commons* 1973: 2)

The trade union position was also made clear by Vic Feather of the TUC who was present at the talks, and Jack Jones, then leader of the Transport and General Workers Union and a member of the TUC General Council. Vic Feather announced that in talking with the Government the trade unions were seeking a settlement which was not just about wages, but that 'we [the TUC] are ready to talk with the government on pay and prices but only on the basis of a delicate balance of policies concerning rents, taxes, industrial policy and employment' (V. Feather, cited in *The Times*, 12 June 1972).

Although Jack Jones also pointed to the important issue of income redistribution, he seemed to want the Government to go further and concede on areas that he felt were of an ideological nature: 'the terms for a deal are simple . . . the government has to adopt socialist interventionist policies of freezing rents, house prices, prices in shops and a limitation on dividends and profits' (J. Jones, cited in *The Times*, 10 October 1972).

Some of the demands made by the trade union side must have been perceived to be too politically costly for the Government. There were certain policies, such as taxation, dividends, rent increases and school meals subsidies, that were of a political nature, and on these the Government could not concede:

> the TUC's price for sitting down to talk about incomes seems to be saying that to get agreement there have to be further talks about other policies. Recent policy is seen as socially divisive . . . such a bargain for incomes policy is too politically costly. The government was elected democratically to curb inflation.
>
> (R. Butt, 'The political price of the TUC',
> *The Times*, 2 March 1972)

The talks between the Government and the trade unions did break down in November 1972. Fishbein (1984) argues that the reason for the breakdown was the lack of what the trade unions saw as important concessions to their demands in relation to wage moderation: 'The absence of a "guarantee" on food prices, the government's refusal to foresake the planned rent increases; all of these raised the possibility that prices would rise considerably faster' (Fishbein 1984: 104).

This approach also seems to confirm the view that the trade unions had attached a high priority to public expenditure and that the failure of the Government to meet their demands led to the breakdown in the talks. Fishbein goes on:

> the talks clearly suggested a fairly substantial price would have to be paid for trade union acceptance of wage restraint. If the Heath government, which from 1972 onwards was the most 'left wing' Conservative government that Britain has ever had or probably ever will have, was unwilling to pay that price, it is not highly likely that a future Conservative government would be willing to do so.
>
> (Fishbein 1984: 105)

CONCLUSIONS

It would seem that the breakdown of the talks refutes the suggestion that Britain had moved towards corporatist politics and that a more appropriate term to use would be Tripartitism (Jessop 1979). Tripartitism represents a hybrid of parliamentarism and corporatism that gives prominence to the role of the strong state, strong enough to recognise and to contain the influence of functional groups. According to this approach the pay negotiations broke down because the Government was not willing to surrender its parliamentary role.

This leads to the further question of how to weight the influence of trade unions. At one level it could be argued that the years of the Heath Government represented the continued acceptance by the Government that trade unions were one of the estates of the realm with which government had to bargain. The trade unions felt that their position was strong and that the Government's commitments to growth and to reducing unemployment were not sufficient to entice them to negotiate a voluntary incomes policy. The trade unions wanted the Government to make concessions on social issues.

The trade unions seemed to influence public expenditure in three areas. First, they contributed to growth through their opposition to incomes policy thus leading to the presence of an adverse relative price effect. Second, their influence could be associated with changes in capital expenditure. This area of expenditure partially confirmed the Government's commitment to reverse the trend in the rise of unemployment, and was part of the trade union negotiated position. However, this commitment to growth was also encouraged by business interest including the Institute of Directors, the CBI and some economists who later all became associated with monetarism: 'we are faced with the greatest economic opportunity that we have ever had in the last fifteen years – we have continued expansion – let us be thankful for it. We have been calling for it for several years' (R. Ball and R. C. O. Matthews, *The Times*, 14 May 1973).

Third, the growth in public expenditure on health, education, trade and industry, subsidies to agriculture and commuters could be described as confirmation that the Government was still working within the welfare consensus:

> Conservative leaders have generally been content to give support to the priorities of the prevailing consensus on the pragmatic grounds that such a consensus reflects the balance of forces and interests within the state which define the limits of the politically practicable.
>
> (Gamble 1979a: 42)

In conclusion, between 1970 and 1974 public expenditure continued on an expansionary trend. The theme of this chapter suggests that expenditure continued to grow because the Heath Government had continued to work within the political agenda of the post-war period. If the Government had wanted to be successful in reversing this trend it would have had to seek a more radical alternative. This chapter suggests that the strategy of the Quiet Revolution was not the break with the past as outlined by Holmes (1985a) and Bruce-Gardyne (1974), but rather a search for a method that would reverse Britain's economic decline. In the meantime, public expenditure was not abandoned as the measure that could influence employment, nor was the notion of public sector provision of goods and services. These parameters represented more of a continuity with the past than a radical departure.

Chapter 6

The Labour Governments 1974–9

INTRODUCTION

In this chapter the concern will be to explain the Labour Government's record on public expenditure during the period 1974–9. It will be argued that there is a need to explain how and why the Government managed to secure three years of voluntary incomes restraint whilst at the same time was also able to reduce the levels of public expenditure. These policies have to be contrasted to the years 1970–4, when the Heath Government, in its attempt to reduce unemployment, sought a partnership with the trade unions which eventually led to the Government recognising certain trade union demands for expanding public expenditure. This chapter asks whether the strategies of the Labour Government marked a departure from the commitments to full employment and an expanding welfare state that had been the foundations of government policy in the post-war period.

Goldman (1976) has argued that the Labour Government's expenditure White Paper of January 1976 was symbolic in that it represented the departure from the assumed world of continuous growth in public expenditure:

> I think it would be hard to deny that the White Paper of 1976 does represent a major shift in government policy and an attempt to reverse the trend to an even higher level of public expenditure . . . I am a congenital optimist and I think that it could be that the White Paper does reflect a genuine and major change in policy . . . which could well mark a **watershed** in our political and economic history.
>
> (Goldman 1976: 40)

According to this thesis 1976 is perceived as being the watershed for public expenditure. The assumptions about the social and economic influences of public expenditure within the context of a mixed economy seemed to be questioned by the Labour Government. The Labour Government had announced reductions in public expenditure despite the forecasts for unemployment and despite Labour's election pledges to improve the quality of public services. The taken-for-granted assumption that public expenditure commitments could continue to expand without taking into consideration the implications for increases in taxation and inflation were firmly put on to the political agenda by the Labour Government. It was Tony Crosland who pointed out that when increases in public expenditure have to be financed by increases in taxation it was likely to result in increases in inflation, because workers will tend to compensate for their high taxes through higher wage demands.

In the previous chapter it was argued that the growth of expenditure during the period 1970–4 could be attributable to the Heath Government's acceptance of the post-war settlement. This represented the administration's recognition that it could influence the level of employment, whilst the problem of higher inflation needed the consent of strategically located groups to control costs. Thus, within this context the implication of Goldman's suggestion is that the Labour Government after 1976 had made the break with the politics of the post-war period. According to this approach, the Labour Government adopted a strategy that indicated that the era of trade-off between incomes policies and expansion of public expenditure was over. The implicit political agenda after 1976 was that trade unions had to accept the permanency of incomes policy to reduce labour costs since this was the only solution to reducing unemployment. In addition the Government made clear that it would aim for continuous reductions in public expenditure to control inflation, even if this meant lowering standards in public welfare and increasing unemployment.

A comparison of policy commitments made by the Labour Party during 1973 with the plans for expenditure outlined in 1974 and 1975 confirms that the expansion of public expenditure was central to the Labour Government. In 1973 (Labour Party 1973) the Labour Party declared that its policy objectives were the curbing of inflation, and a commitment to economic growth and to the redistribution of income. The reduction of inflation was to be achieved by the Government's controlling prices on energy, food and housing, which in turn, it was hoped, would lead to moderate wage settlements. Second, increased growth was to be achieved through more planning and direct intervention in the economy. This would include new commitments on nationalisation and the setting up of organisations such as the National Enterprise Board (NEB). Third, the Government was to work for a more equal and just society through increased expenditure on health, education, housing and cash benefits. The Labour Party also pointed out that:

> As the cost of our commitments will be building up over a period of years, we can look to the growth of the economy to meet the main parts of the costs. Also we shall make no attempt to conceal the fact that necessary improvements in cash benefits and social services may mean some increase in taxation.
>
> (Labour Party 1973: 8)

However, from July 1975, the Labour Government was involved in a series of 'cuts' packages. These resulted in expenditure falling below the level the Government had inherited in 1974. In 1974, the public expenditure ratio to GDP (market prices) was 42.2 per cent, rising to 44.6 per cent in 1975 and then continuously falling for each subsequent year. It declined to its lowest level of 38 per cent in 1977 and then rose to 39.4 per cent in 1979. By 1979 public expenditure had fallen by 6.5 per cent below the 1974 level.

This chapter is, therefore, concerned with two questions. First, why did the Labour Government seem to depart from its original commitments? Second, did this constitute a break with the politics of the post-war settlement, or did it represent a short-term tactical response to a specific context, as implied by Keegan (1984):

> Callaghan was therefore trying to appease the markets by telling them what they wanted to hear. He was also trying to frighten the Labour Party and his fellow cabinet ministers. In other words the speech was more a tactical move than a full and serious reappraisal of policy.
>
> (Keegan 1984: 90)

In considering these questions, the following sections seek to provide an analysis of the Government's record on public expenditure and to provide some explanations for the shifts in policy. The aim will be to provide a framework for understanding the extent to which the shifts in policy were determined by events that seemed to be beyond the immediate control of the Government and the extent to which the changes in policy represented political choice. The aim of this chapter is therefore to provide an explanation that seeks to combine the constraints and the autonomy of government. The concern is to explain constraints as a series of events that, at least in the short term, could be judged as being beyond the immediate control of the Government, and which elements of choice and autonomy were available to the Government.

THE LABOUR GOVERNMENT'S RECORD 1974–9

The study of expenditure White Papers

The theme of political choice included the Labour Party's commitment to an expanded public sector that was embodied within the expenditure White Paper of January 1975 (HMSO 1975). The White Paper indicated that the Government was planning for an increase in expenditure of 2 per cent per annum and declared that

> the composition of public expenditure has been modified to reflect the importance this government attaches to certain key social programmes in the pursuit of economic objectives . . . additional spending will be made on social security, housing and subsidies.
>
> (HMSO 1975: 2)

The recognition that the Labour Government intended to signal its political priorities had been confirmed by a senior civil servant, Mr P. Baldwin, CB, Deputy Secretary, Public Sector Group at the Treasury, in his response to the Treasury Select Committee, where he argued: 'The incoming government said in effect two things: We are the new government – we have our view of priorities and certain items are to be given priority' (House of Commons 1975b: 3).

On taking office, therefore, the Labour Government had made explicit that its political commitments would be reflected in changes in expenditure priorities. The Labour Government therefore made commitments to expand expenditure on housing subsidies, pensions and subsidies to the nationalised industries. All these commitments had been central to the Social Contract agreed between the trade unions and the Labour Party prior to the 1974 election. The trade unions wanted a Labour Government to control prices as a means of controlling inflation, and that implied increases in subsidies to housing and to the nationalised industries.

The 1975 White Paper represented the Government commitment to continuous growth in public expenditure over the next five years. However, the study of public expenditure plans for the period 1975–9

(Mullard 1987) confirms that from the 1976 expenditure White Paper these intentions were being revised downwards. Indeed, whilst in 1975 the Government was planning 'growth', the 1976 White Paper and subsequent White Papers indicated policies of expenditure control and reductions. The index for aggregate expenditure suggests, therefore, that there was a shift from the original plans of 1975 – a shift from the outlined objective of growth to a pattern of restraint.

The out-turns of expenditure by programme

The study by expenditure programme for the period confirms the trends outlined in the expenditure plans (Mullard 1987). The breakdown by expenditure programme is as follows.

Housing

Between 1974 and 1979 the housing programme failed to maintain its ratio both in terms of GDP and as part of total expenditure. In 1974 expenditure on housing stood at 5 per cent of GDP, but by 1979 this had fallen to 3.3 per cent – a reduction of 34 per cent. In 1975 the Government had declared that new expenditure was being made available in housing, 'to achieve a much larger programme of new house building and acquisition of new dwellings . . . increased expenditure is needed to bear the major part of the cost of capital' (HMSO 1975: 71). In addition, the Government had intended to hold down rents as part of its bargain with the trade unions; price rises were to be curbed in return for restraint in wage demands:

> The decision to freeze local authority rents meant cutting these rents in real terms – in the hope that this would help to persuade the trade unions to moderate their wage claims. The money paid out as a result would more accurately be described as an anti-inflation subsidy.
>
> (Klein 1975: 3)

The two-pronged policy, set out in 1975, of increasing housing capital expenditure and increasing the subsidy on council rent was, therefore, not sustained, as is shown by the out-turns for housing expenditure. The housing policy document of 1979 clearly indicates that the Government had shifted its priorities:

> the government's objectives are: to provide a decent home for every family at a price within their means; that implies a more selective

and discerning approach to housing policy; it means a more effective method of tackling need.

(HMSO 1979a: 94)

The language of this statement was not far removed from that of the previous Conservative Government's White Paper – *A Fair Deal for Housing* (HMSO 1971c) – where the administration had declared its housing objectives:

(a) to provide a decent home for every family at a price within their means;
(b) to provide a fairer choice between owning a home and renting one;
(c) to exercise fairness between one citizen and another in giving and receiving help towards housing rents.

The Labour Government reduced expenditure on the capital component; this fell from 1.9 per cent of GDP in 1974 to 0.8 per cent of GDP in 1979. In contrast the commitment made to the trade unions to hold down the rate of rent increases in the public sector seemed to be upheld as the transfer component on housing expanded from 1.2 per cent in 1974 to 1.4 per cent of GDP by 1979.

The Government's response to controlling public expenditure was therefore to reduce capital expenditure, which meant that less housing was now being built in the public sector, whilst at the same time being able to hold down rent increases for existing tenants by increasing subsidies to local authorities.

Education

As a percentage of GDP education expenditure expanded between 1974 and 1976 – increasing from 5.9 per cent of GDP in 1974 to 6.7 per cent in 1975 – but fell to 6.2 per cent in 1976 and continued to fall for the rest of the period, reaching 5.4 per cent in 1979. Between 1974 and 1979 expenditure on education capital fell by 61 per cent from 0.6 per cent of GDP (market prices) in 1974 to 0.2 per cent in 1979, whilst current expenditure experienced a smaller reduction from 3.9 per cent of GDP in 1974 to 3.8 per cent of GDP in 1979. In education, therefore, the Government succeeded in reducing expenditure on school buildings, gaining some control in the rate of growth in current expenditure and reducing grants to students.

Blackstone (1980) has argued that the Labour Government policy towards education during that period was influenced by forecasts of changes in the school population and the influence of such changes in the thinking at Whitehall. Falling school rolls seemed to offer justification for restraint in the education budget:

> the important background factor of a declining birth rate has dramatic consequences for the number of children at school. The school population in England and Wales is likely to fall from 9.1 million in 1977 to about 7.3 million in 1986. The decline in the primary school population began during the Labour Government. The impact of this change was considerable in that all planning and future expenditure plans were affected by it. In the competition for extra resources within Whitehall, education began to be treated as a relatively low priority, particularly because of these demographic changes.
>
> (Blackstone 1980: 232)

Rather than taking the opportunity to reduce class sizes, the Government seemed to be using the decline in pupil numbers to control education expenditure and to argue that education expenditure was now of a lower priority to the Government. The reductions in the capital programme were of similar magnitude to those in the housing capital programme. The Government seemed to be using the reductions in capital expenditure as its major weapon in bringing public expenditure under control.

Health

Expenditure on health followed the same pattern as that of education. Health expenditure was expanded during the earlier part of the period, growing from 4.3 per cent of GDP in 1974 to 4.9 per cent of GDP in 1975. However, expenditure fell to 4.6 per cent in 1979, which was still above the 1974 level. Health expenditure also increased as a percentage of total expenditure, from 11 per cent to 11.8 per cent. The Government was able to hold down the health budget partly through reductions in capital expenditure, which fell from 0.3 per cent of GDP in 1974 to 0.26 per cent in 1979, and partly through the attainment of nil growth in current expenditure.

Social security

The social security programme represented the Labour Government's commitment to 'eliminate poverty wherever it exists and to achieve

greater economic equality in income, wealth and living standards'
(Labour Party 1974).

Between 1974 and 1979, social security was the fastest area of
growth. Expenditure grew from 8.3 per cent of GDP in 1974 to 9.8 per
cent in 1979, an increase of 18 per cent over the 1974 level; as a
percentage of total expenditure it grew from 19.6 per cent to 24.7 per
cent, an increase of 26 per cent. The growth can be attributed to the
pledge to increase pensions and short-term benefits in line with
earnings or the rate of inflation, and to demand-led factors such as the
growing numbers of elderly people and the increase in the level of
unemployment. Taking these factors into account, however, Piachaud
(1980) points out that:

> social security expenditure increased during Labour's period in
> office in real terms, as a proportion of public expenditure and as a
> proportion of GDP . . . a record which cannot be a source of
> complacency or of pride but it need not be a source of shame.
>
> (Piachaud 1980: 173–85)

Trade and industry

The trade and industry programme reflected the Government's
uncertainty in its employment policies. The programme was expanded
in 1974 and 1975, and fell back in 1976 and 1977. Overall, the
programme was increased from 2.4 per cent of GDP in 1974 to 2.5 per
cent of GDP in 1979. This uncertainty was due to the Government's
policies concerning economic regeneration. On the one hand the
Government had macro policies, including the NEB and nationalisation, as the pivot of its employment and industrial strategy, whilst
on the other, the increasing levels of unemployment seemed to lead to a
series of short-term micro labour market-orientated responses. These
included new expenditures on Regional Development Grants, the
Regional Employment Premium, the Youth Employment Subsidy
and the setting up of the Manpower Services Commission. The
problem for the Government was that in announcing measures
directed at improving the labour market, this approach seemed to
imply that its macro policies were not achieving their desired
objectives.

The record on expenditure by economic category

The study of public expenditure disaggregated by economic category
within programmes confirms that the Government sought to achieve

reductions in expenditure by reducing the plans for capital expenditure. Furthermore, this analysis confirms the extent to which wage restraint in the public sector had also contributed to stabilising the growth in current expenditure.

Capital expenditure

By 1979 total capital expenditure had fallen by 2.5 per cent of GDP. The main area of reduction was the housing programme, which fell by 1.1 per cent, followed by education (-0.39 per cent), roads (-0.36 per cent) and the environment (-0.35 per cent). In comparison, the health programme was safeguarded in that it fell by only 0.08 per cent. The slight fall in the health programme, compared to other capital expenditures, might be explained in terms of the time taken to build a hospital and the relative inability of the Government to 'turn off' such an expenditure in comparison to other capital projects.

Current expenditure

The total for current expenditure fell by 0.25 per cent of GDP. The major area of reduction was the defence programme, which fell by 0.24 per cent of GDP, whilst the study also confirms that the only area of expansion was in Personal Social Services (PSS). In explaining the changes in current expenditure the author (Mullard 1987) has suggested that during the period the effect of the RPE on current expenditure had been negative and, therefore, favourable in the sense that the RPE did not contribute to an increase in current expenditure. The inflation rate in the public sector had been slowed down because of the effects of the Social Contract.

Transfers and subsidies

Expenditures on subsidies and transfers increased from 12.7 per cent of GDP in 1974 to 14.4 per cent in 1979. The largest area of increase was the social security programme, which was expanded by 1.9 per cent. Other areas of expansion were net lendings to the nationalised industries, which increased by 0.8 per cent, and the continued expenditure on housing subsidies. In the meantime some price controls that were central to Labour's policies on inflation were phased out; these included subsidies to agriculture, employment and transport.

EXPLAINING THE GOVERNMENT'S RECORD

In the previous section the focus was on how the Government achieved its reductions in public expenditure. In this section the aim will be to provide some answers to the questions how and why the Labour Government decided to embark on a policy of limiting and reducing the rate of growth in public expenditure when this meant making decisions to reduce resources on programmes that had been central to the Government's approach to the Social Contract. In seeking to provide such an explanation it shall be argued that there is a need to study the record of government as a biography and, therefore, as a process of continuous negotiation between events and autonomy. Events in this context are perceived as constraining factors; for example, the economic context tends to act as a constraint on the autonomy of government. However, governments do not just respond in a vacuum; they have their political priorities and their political preferences in choosing between policy options. In the following sections it shall be argued that explanations of the Labour Government's record can be located within the twin concepts of autonomy and events.

The concept of autonomy in this context suggests that the reductions in public expenditure reflected a process of political choice and implies that the Government 'could have done otherwise'. In accordance with this approach, the emphasis is located in the absence of political will in the Labour Government to give priority to its political commitments to rechannel resources to expenditure programmes that were perceived as essential to Labour's vision of a more just and egalitarian Britain.

In contrast, the concept of events suggests that governments have to live within a world of constraints and forces that are beyond their immediate control, at least in the short term. Within the context of events governments tend to respond to exogenous factors, which are often unforeseen and unpredictable. Governments often find themselves responding to events by producing policies that aim to deal with short-term effects rather than long-term causes. Explanations that are located within the category of events tend to picture the Government as the person in a boat blown by winds and currents that are more powerful than the endeavours of the individual. The analogy is often borrowed to describe governments as 'steering the ship of state' and being 'blown off course' by shocks they could neither foresee nor counter.

The concept of autonomy and political choice

Within this perspective are included the views of Hodgson (1981), Whiteley (1983) and Miliband (1983). These authors suggest that the Labour Government was elected on a radical programme in 1974, and that the programme was abandoned unilaterally and deliberately by the leaders of that Labour Government. These authors' starting point is that Labour's programme (Labour Party 1973) reflected a change in power relations within the different factions of the Labour Party whilst in opposition. It is an argument that seeks to confirm the ascendancy of a radical socialist faction within the Labour Party after the election defeat of 1970; as Hatfield (1978) suggests: '18 June 1970 not only saw the downfall of the Labour Government: for the Labour Party it signalled the erosion of the reformist social democratic hegemony over the formulation of policy' (Hatfield 1978: 3).

Labour's record in government between 1964 and 1970 was judged by the new radicals as confirming the weakness of a Labour Government committed to the programme influenced by the political priorities of social democracy. Labour in 1964 had abandoned any commitment to further nationalisation and had instead adopted a programme that sought to modernise the British economy within the framework of creating a 'white heat of technology'. The crisis of sterling and the pressures of devaluation had further weakened Labour's resolve to increase the levels of public expenditure on health and education, which in turn had led to disillusionment within an electorate that had given Labour a 98-seat majority during the election of 1966. The defeat of 1970 therefore seemed to confirm that Labour needed to return to the principles of radical change.

Hodgson (1981) supports Hatfield's thesis in so far as he sees the Labour Party in opposition paying more attention to the supply side of the economy. This, he argues, could be contrasted with the Crosland tradition that had previously dominated Labour's thinking, where emphasis was put on the consumption side of the economy. Crosland (1967) had argued that the programme of nationalisation was no longer necessary to the achievement of socialism and that the Labour Party had to make public expenditure the mechanism for the redistribution of income:

> The right way, in the field of social expenditure, is a generous, imaginative, long-term programme of social investment which will make our state schools and hospitals and all the services that go with them, the equal in quality of the best which private wealth can buy.
>
> (Crosland 1967: 88)

Hodgson's argument is that after 1970 the Labour Party had come to realise that the Crosland approach had only looked at one side of the economy, and that was concerned with the proceeds of production, which by implication meant that production itself could be left to the private sector. Interestingly, Hodgson's view had been articulated earlier by Mr J. MacKintosh, a Labour MP, on the intellectual 'right' of the Party:

> The real weakness of Crosland was that he did not realise that the balance between the public and private sectors in a mixed economy cannot be left to natural forces . . . It was too superficial in that it did not realise the need for an underpinning of economic theory.
>
> (MacKintosh 1978, in Marquand 1982: 230–2)

Hodgson (1981), therefore, maintains that in 1974 the Labour Party and the Labour Government had an economic theory and a strategy to underpin their programme of an expanded public sector, which some members of the Government abandoned because they chose to do so:

> the election of February 1974 took place in unique circumstances. Labour had a sophisticated and radical programme and an aroused working class ready to follow its lead. The Parliamentary leadership along with the majority of the Parliamentary party were right wing and anti-socialist, this ensured that the opportunity was squandered.
>
> (Hodgson 1981: 89)

Whiteley (1983) has also argued in a similar vein. He believes that Labour's programme (Labour Party 1973) was a radical programme that was abandoned by the leadership of the Party: 'Labour's programme 1973 was the most radical re-statement of Party policy since the war. In office these proposals were quickly abandoned . . . after 1976 the Party in government assumed policies of economic management by deflation' (Whiteley 1983: 3).

This author's evidence is what he sees as the multiplicity of crises that continued to persist and that became more apparent after the 1979 electoral defeat. He blames the electoral, membership and ideological crises on Labour Governments that have consistently abandoned Labour's pledges:

> The main thesis of this book is that these interrelated crises all have a common origin in the failure of the Labour Party, particularly in office to achieve its goals. Failures of policy performance are at the heart of the crises of the Labour Party.
>
> (Whiteley 1983: 1)

Finally, Miliband (1983) has also put the experience of the 1974 Government into its longer historical context. He maintains that the leaders of Labour Governments have always ignored the commitments made by the Labour Party:

> The pattern has been absolutely consistent: from the very beginning of the Labour Party's history, its leaders have assumed the role of dedicated and indefatigable crusaders against what they judged to be ill informed, stupid, electorally damaging and in any case unattainable.
>
> (Miliband 1983: 68)

Within the context of autonomy and political choice it is therefore argued that Labour's 1973 programme did indeed represent a radical departure and that the leaders of the 1974 Government had continued to perpetuate the Labour Party's historic betrayal of the electorate. The reductions in public expenditure after 1976 combined with the increases in the levels of unemployment confirmed the extent to which those who were not committed to Labour's programme – within both the Labour Government and the trade unions – took the opportunity to abandon Labour's radical agenda and replace it with a series of policies that were reminiscent of those pursued during the previous Labour administration.

The concept of events

Within this perspective are those explanations implying that the Labour Government's plans to increase expenditure had to be reversed because of external events and shocks that seemed, at least in the short term, to be beyond the immediate control of the Government. Within this context the Government is perceived as responding to these events and that these events acted as a major constraint on the political choices and options available to the Government. Coates (1980) explains the record of the Labour Government as follows: 'What defeated the Labour Government was the fact that the World economy was a capitalist one subject to its own laws of development, its own contradictions and points of internal tension' (Coates 1980: 161).

The concept of events seems to lead to two types of argument. First, that the Government was responding to factors that were outside its control but that were of a short-term nature and, therefore, required a tactical response. Such events included the crises of sterling in 1975 and 1976, and the oil price shock of 1973, both of which had direct implications on the Government's expenditure plans. Second, long-term adjustment explanations suggest in different ways that the size and growth of public expenditure was central to Britain's economic problems. The arrest of economic decline, according to these arguments, depended on governments embarking on a strategy aimed permanently to reduce the level of public expenditure. Long-term adjustment explanations include the thesis of resource crowding out, the problems of the no-growth state and the influence of monetarism on government policy.

Short-term shocks

The sterling crises of 1975 and 1976

Pollard (1982) has argued that the history of UK economic management confirms the view of a Treasury preoccupied with responses to the short-term crises of sterling and the balance of payments. In each of the seventeen crises of the post-war period the response has been the same, that of fiscal deflation, and stricter controls over hire purchase or higher interest rates, or both. The Labour Government, faced with sterling crises in April 1975, July 1975 and September 1976, responded on each occasion by announcing reductions in public expenditure, tightening control over the money supply and increasing the rate of interest. These crises allowed the financial markets, in an indirect way, to put leverage on the Government and to enforce a particular form of response.

Both Joel Barnett (1982), who was Chief Secretary to the Treasury, and Sir Leo Pliatzky (1982), in the role of Permanent Secretary to the Treasury, are agreed in their memoirs that a sort of panic gripped the Labour Government: 'There was a conflict between what was required from the point of view of restoring financial confidence and what was considered feasible and negotiable in Cabinet' (Pliatzky 1982: 149).

The story told is of Cabinet meetings being presented with papers recommending reductions in public expenditure as the only solution and of ministers feeling incompetent to counter Treasury arguments. This is certainly Barbara Castle's view:

> none of us are equipped with the sort of economic advice that enables us to stand up to the dubious expertise of the Treasury . . . A sense of hopelessness engulfs me. The only strategy that will be left to us will be one which commits us to unemployment continually

rising. The Labour Government will preside over the biggest cuts in public services since 1931.

(Castle 1980: 454–7)

However, the issue at stake was not whether an alternative strategy to that of the Treasury was available. Indeed, this had been articulated by some Cabinet ministers. Crosland seems to argue that he eventually supported the Treasury strategy, not because of a lack of an alternative strategy – he had already presented one to the Cabinet – but rather to avoid what would have appeared within the financial markets as the defeat of the Prime Minister and the Chancellor. Susan Crosland has recorded Tony Crosland's decision as follows:

> it's true that if the Prime Minister joins with the Chancellor, they probably are unbeatable and indeed shouldn't be beaten. If it became known that Jim had been defeated by Cabinet it would be murder. He is our strongest card. I may well switch my argument halfway tomorrow and say this: that we cannot afford not to support the Prime Minister. He's crucial! Tony then went down the corridor to the Prime Minister's room. 'In cabinet tomorrow I shall say I think you're wrong but I also think that the Cabinet must support you.'

(Crosland 1982: 381)

What this evidence tells us is that a short-term crisis could appear to have been beyond the control of the Government and that this eventually forced the Government to seek help from the IMF. The question is whether the Government had no alternative but to respond in a particular way. Although some ministers claimed that they were opposed to the reductions in expenditure, equally they argued that they felt they had no alternative but to vote in favour of the Treasury advice.

The oil price shock of 1973

A different sort of shock, which could be described as pushing the Government off course and which had not been taken into account by the Labour Party, was the consequence of the increase in the price of oil in 1973. Although there are disagreements about the impact of oil prices, the price increase has been described as having both deflationary and inflationary effects on the British economy. First, the oil price increase led to an income transfer from the non-oil producers to the oil producers, which meant a fall in real income in the UK. Second, the increase was inflationary in that it led to higher prices of oil-based products.

During 1974 and 1975, the Labour Government sought to minimise the effect of falling income by generating demand through public expenditure. However, it soon found that it was out of step with the other non-oil producers, who were searching for their own national solutions. Eventually the Labour Government could not sustain the effort, as sterling came under pressure accompanied by signals from financial markets for the Government to control its spending. Barnett (1982) argues:

> Instead of cutting public expenditure to take account of the massive oil price increase of 1973 which in our case cut living standards by some 5 per cent, the Chancellor decided to maintain our expenditure plans and borrow to meet the deficit; this had dramatic consequences for me personally and the country in general.
>
> (Barnett 1982: 23)

Long-term adjustment explanations

The influence of monetarism

In this section the aim is to explore the thesis that the Labour Government presided over the break with the post-war economic consensus and orchestrated the emergence of a new consensus around the economics and politics of monetarism, which S. Holland (1980) originally described as Howleyism, in contrast to Butskellism. Holland sought to introduce the argument that the economic strategy adopted by Denis Healey, as Labour Chancellor, in 1975 was adopted by the Conservative Chancellor, Sir Geoffrey Howe, after 1979. He argues that

> in practice it was not the Conservatives in government who first denounced Keynes and embraced Friedman. It was not Mrs Thatcher but Jim Callaghan as Prime Minister who declared that we could no longer spend our way out of a slump.
>
> (S. Holland, 'The meaning of Howleyism', *Guardian*, 16 June 1980)

Despite the numerous interpretations that can be classified as monetarist, there are some specific characteristics that, when brought together, constitute a coherent monetarist view (Laidler 1981). These are:

(a) an acceptance of the classical quantity theory of money, which says that the demand for money is stable and that inflation is caused by an increase in the money supply brought about by the Government;

(b) that a relationship between unemployment and inflation is ruled out;

(c) an antipathy to state intervention through fiscal/monetary or incomes policy, but support for the publishing of rules for monetary targets.

Under propositions (a), (b) and (c), the Government is perceived as being one important source of monetary creation and the cause of inflation. The Government does not influence the level of economic activity and employment and should, therefore, not seek to intervene in the economy in the misguided belief that it could exert some direct control over these aggregates. The role of government is confined to that of providing sound money.

According to this thesis, therefore, the reduction in expenditure, the adoption of monetary targets and the downgrading of fiscal policy confirmed the acceptance of these monetarist tenets by the Labour Government. First, the Labour Government certainly began the practice of announcing monetary targets after 1976. These targets indicated that the Government was planning to reduce the rate of monetary growth and government borrowing during subsequent years (Mosley 1984). The policy of published monetary targets rests on the monetarist axiom that bargaining agents such as trade unions and employers are rational agents who need firm statements of the Government's intentions for inflation. Negotiators can, within this framework, anticipate accurately the movement of prices. The concept of monetary targets, therefore, would indicate that the Government had accepted the monetarist postulate that governments do cause inflation. *The Times* took note of this shift in government policy:

> The Chancellor and the Prime Minister have become acutely concerned with the monthly figures for the series M1 and M3 when 10 years ago the government could serve from one year to the next without even being told that the money supply existed.
>
> (*The Times*, 20 December 1976)

Second, a statement by the Prime Minister, James Callaghan, seemed to indicate that the Labour Government had also accepted the second monetarist tenet, namely, that the Government could not influence the level of economic activity:

What is the cause of high unemployment? Quite simply and unequivocally it is caused by paying ourselves more than the value of what we produce . . . It is an absolute fact of life which no Government, be it left or right can alter . . . We used to think that you could spend your way out of a recession and increase employment by cutting taxes and boosting Government spending. I tell you in all candour that this option no longer exists and insofar as it ever did exist, it only worked on each occasion since the war by injecting a bigger dose of inflation into the economy, followed by a higher level of unemployment as the next step. Higher inflation followed by higher unemployment.

(Callaghan 1987: 426)

This often quoted speech by Mr Callaghan has in itself become an area of academic debate. Callaghan has been accused of having this part of his speech written for him by his son-in-law, Peter Jay, then a prominent convert to monetarism in the 1970s (Blackaby 1980; Keegan 1984):

I have left until last the point most often made about this speech; namely that at the time Callaghan was under the monetarist influence of his son-in-law Peter Jay. Indeed I understand that Jay drafted the passage himself. It is not difficult to assess who was using whom most; the message was certainly immediately useful to Callaghan, but it served the monetarist cause for years to come.

(Keegan 1984: 91)

Lord Callaghan (1987) did accept in his memoirs that he had consulted with Peter Jay in the drafting of his conference speech and that 'Jay had produced one paragraph that made the fur fly' (Callaghan 1987: 425). However, Callaghan does go on to argue that his speech did not indicate that his Government had adopted a monetarist doctrine but, rather

I see no reason to retract a single word of what I then said. The passage I have quoted does not say that governments should never increase public expenditure or reduce taxation as methods of boosting employment. My argument was that in the circumstances of 1976 these measures were not appropriate . . . I am no theologian in monetary doctrine.

(Callaghan 1987: 427)

Whilst Lord Callaghan might argue that his major concern was to provide an immediate response to the problems of the Government seeking to finance a PSBR of £9 billion, which in turn was leading to a loss of confidence in the financial markets, nevertheless his speech still tended to take a long-term view of economic policy-making. As the extract makes very clear, Callaghan had pointed to what he perceived as the failures of public expenditure to reduce unemployment in the long term.

The likely impact of monetarist influences was, therefore, to be long term. The Labour Government had provided the foundations for the Thatcher Government's argument that there was 'no alternative'. The Labour Government was abandoning the commitment to full employment, absolving future governments from a tenet that had been accepted by all administrations since 1945. Unemployment was now to be blamed on workers pricing themselves out of the market, whilst public expenditure was to be associated with inflation. The argument that the period of the 1974–9 Labour Government represented a watershed was a view to be shared by various economic commentators. H. Stephenson of *The Times* argued:

> The government is letting a steadily deepening recession to squeeze out price inflation whilst all the time asserting that it will be unthinkable for a Labour government to use high unemployment as a deliberate weapon of economic policy.
>
> (H. Stephenson, *The Times*, 5 January 1976)

By 1979, Peter Riddell, the political editor of the *Financial Times*, was writing a requiem for the commitment to full employment: 'One of the most curious of casualties of five years of a Labour government has been the abandonment of any specific economic growth or unemployment targets' (P. Riddell, *Financial Times*, 7 February 1979). This view also was endorsed by Terry Ward, Adviser to the Select Committee on Public Expenditure: 'the impression conveyed is that the expansion of the economy is largely outside the government's control, that budgetary policy, of which public expenditure is one, is accorded the role of overcoming inflation' (House of Commons 1979: 6).

So had the Labour Government accepted the economics of monetarism and had the decision implied a process of policy choice? Was a Keynesian alternative therefore still a viable option and did the retreat from Keynes reflect a new politics? In attempting to provide some of the answers to these questions the author (Mullard 1987) relied on research conducted at the Labour Party where confidential minutes of the two Key Committees had been made available. The

Home Policy Committee included representatives from the trade unions and the Labour Party, both of whom had direct access to Cabinet ministers. These included the TUC/Labour Party Liaison Committee, whose members included the Prime Minister, James Callaghan, and the Chancellor, Denis Healey, and trade union leaders including Hugh Scanlon of the AUEW and Jack Jones of the TGWU. All these people were members of the Home Policy Committee, which also included leading members of Labour's NEC, such as Tony Benn. The study of these minutes suggested that the Labour Party, as represented by the NEC, the trade unions and the Government, was for most of the time in agreement with the strategy adopted by the Cabinet.

In this context some specific remarks extracted from confidential documents for the period 19 July to November 1976 that were made available would confirm the degree to which the Labour Party had come to accept some of the major aspects of monetarist thinking. The timing of these documents was significant because the meetings were taking place concurrently with discussions in the Cabinet at which ministers were trying to find an acceptable package of public expenditure reductions. The meetings of the Home Policy Committee were, therefore, opportune times for members of the NEC and the trade unions to present their views. The resolutions passed by the Committee and quoted below and on pp. 142–3 tend to confirm, however, that there was no disagreement between members of the Cabinet and members of the NEC, as guardians of conference policy, and the trade unions. The Resolution of November 1976 states:

> the public sector can finance its deficit only in one of two ways – by borrowing from other economic sectors through the sale of public sector debt outside the banks or by borrowing from the banking sector which in effect amounts to printing money. The choice is between high interest rates which will hinder private investment or increasing the money supply and the rate of inflation.
>
> (Home Policy Committee, November 1976,
> RE/514/ CONFIDENTIAL)

This is a very sound endorsement of the monetarist exposition of the cause of inflation and, by implication, the policy that was adopted to reduce government borrowing to correspond with that diagnosis. The Committee had accepted that the Government could not seek a policy that increased the deficit because this was likely to lead to further inflation or higher interest rates. So, despite the increase in the level of unemployment, members of the NEC and the trade unions had come to the same conclusion reached by James Callaghan, namely, that demand management was no longer appropriate. The only difference was that Callaghan had made his views public, in his speech to the Labour Party conference, whilst others agreed, but within the confines of confidential meetings.

The no-growth state

In explaining the uninterrupted growth in public expenditure from the 1950s to the early 1970s, Klein (1975) concluded that this had been made possible by the equally uninterrupted growth in the British economy. Economic growth had allowed for the expansion of both individual and public consumption:

> For the past 30 years social policy has been the residual beneficiary of economic progress. The Welfare State flourished because the Growth State prospered . . . Perhaps for the first time in the history of mankind it was possible to combine public compassion with private self indulgence.
>
> (Klein 1975: 2)

Klein argues that during the 1970s the combination of higher inflation with a fall in economic growth provided an environment where the Government had to make a choice between higher taxation or lower public consumption. This dilemma was recognised by the Labour Government when it announced:

> popular expectations for improved public services and welfare programmes have not been matched by the growth in output, or by the willingness to forgo improvement in living standards . . . The tax burden for those on average earnings has risen to a level of 25 per cent in 1976, in contrast to 10 per cent in 1961, and those on two thirds average earnings to a level of 20 per cent in 1976, compared to 8 per cent in 1961.
>
> (HMSO 1976b: 3, 4)

Whilst in 1973 the Labour Party had declared that in expanding the public sector it recognised that it might be necessary to increase taxation, by 1976 this policy was being abandoned:

> perhaps and not unconnected with our low level of output is that people at work are already highly taxed on their income. I do not

believe that it would be right to burden them with the lion's share of taxation. Furthermore, taxation adds to the problem of inadequate financial incentives to work and to invest and this could put our economic recovery at risk.

(J. Barnett, cited in *Hansard*, 25 December 1976, Vol. 922, col. 1525)

However, this view was not confined to Treasury ministers: it was reinforced in a joint TUC/Labour Government document in February 1979:

An adequate rate of economic growth is vital if we are to make progress on our social programmes. It is doubtful whether the British people would be prepared to pay the tax rate which would be necessary to finance such programmes if our economy was growing only very slowly.

(Labour Party/TUC 1979)

The statement agreed by the TUC and the Government reflects the uneasy coalition of interests within the TUC. Trade unions with memberships concentrated in the private sector had made their priority the reduction of taxation in contrast to public sector unions, who had urged higher public expenditure even if this meant higher levels of taxation. The argument by private sector unions was that their members were paying too much tax, and that reduced taxation would increase economic demand, which was the best way to expand employment. Public sector unions, on the other hand, argued that reductions in public expenditure would inevitably mean losses of jobs and services.

The crowding-out debate

A further argument deployed by certain members of the Cabinet, and also endorsed by the Home Policy Committee, was that the continued expansion of the public sector would hinder the recovery of the economy because it was taking away resources that would be used for private sector investment. This became known as the resource crowding-out debate, introduced in the columns of the *Sunday Times* during November 1974. The relevance of the debate to this chapter is the language that was used by the two Oxford economists, R. Bacon and W. Eltis in initiating the debate, and the readiness of the Labour Government to endorse that language and deploy it to justify the reductions in public expenditure.

Bacon and Eltis suggested that the British economy was divided into two sectors: the marketed sector, which contributed to the growth in the economy, and the non-marketed sector, which included most of the public sector. In pursuing their argument Bacon and Eltis went on to point out that the non-marketed areas of the public sector were financed by workers in the marketed sector and that, by implication, any increase in public expenditure had to be financed by growth in the economy or an increase in the tax burden of marketed-sector workers. In response to such increases workers bargained for higher wages, which eventually led to a squeeze on profits, a fall in investment and unemployment:

> The increase in non-market expenditure has produced two kinds of adverse effects – higher taxes, which have accelerated wage inflation and allowed investment to suffer. A fall in investment had led to a decline in the growth rate of the economy which has led to higher redundancies.
>
> (Bacon and Eltis 1978: 110)

In the statement on the cuts package in April 1975, the Government justified the cuts as being related to 'the paramount need to move resources into exports and investment makes it essential to contain the demand on resources made by public expenditure. The government therefore aims to continue to reduce the public sector borrowing requirement' (HMSO 1975: 3).

Bosanquet and Townsend (1980) and Keegan (1984) have argued that the Labour Government was heavily influenced by these views: 'the thesis put forward by Bacon and Eltis found converts among Labour cabinet members . . . the Labour government fell heavily for this thesis when first announced' (Bosanquet and Townsend, 1980: 29–30). Once again, these views were not confined to Labour ministers but were also supported by trade union leaders and members of the Labour Party NEC, suggesting that here too there was synchronisation in the thinking of government ministers, of members of the NEC and the trade unions. This agreement was reflected in the resolution passed by the Home Policy Committee in July 1976:

> We cannot continue in serious deficit for very long nor can we afford to follow policies which threaten to make the present deficit worse. We can only remain in deficit as long as the rest of the world allows us to do so, by accumulating holdings of sterling. Furthermore, industrial recovery will be accompanied by the industrial sector

seeking funds which will lead to the public sector pre-empting resources or even worse bring a spiral of interest rates which would chasten that recovery.

(NEC/Cabinet Working Paper, RE 1793/July 1976, Page 8
CONFIDENTIAL)

CONCLUSIONS

The Labour Government reversed the trend in the growth of public expenditure. To achieve this it reduced capital expenditure whilst holding down the growth in current expenditure. All programmes except for social security, health and PSS were reduced. The record on public expenditure leads to two forms of explanation. First, that the reductions in public expenditure represented a watershed – the Labour Government had broken with the post-war trend of continuous expansion – and second, that the record seemed to be a paradox in the sense that the Government had made the expansion of the public sector the foundation of its policies on inflation, regeneration of the economy and redistribution of income.

The major concern of this chapter has been to outline an argument which suggests that any explanation of the Government's shift from its plans to expand the public sector has to take into account what can be identified as a process of events and autonomy. Government policy was very often influenced by external factors, but the responses of the Government involved political choice. The concept of events implied that certain factors, which were both of a short-term and long-term nature, seemed to require an immediate and a particular form of response from the Government. These included the response to the oil price shock of 1973, the sterling crisis and the conditions set by the IMF, where, on each occasion, the Government had to pursue policies that would gain the confidence of financial markets.

In addition to short-term factors were the arguments that suggested that the period had witnessed a series of influences that had long-term implications. These included the perception that public expenditure was the cause of inflation, that the problem of growth in the economy could no longer be taken for granted and, in conjunction with that, the argument that the public sector was crowding out the private sector in competing for financial and human resources.

The significance of this array of explanations is that it points to the emergence of an alternative language to be associated with public expenditure. Whereas in 1974 public expenditure had been described by the Labour Government as being the healer of the nation, it had by 1979 become associated with inflation, and with being the cause of higher taxation, lower rates of growth in the economy and unemployment. The period of the Labour Government points therefore to the beginnings of alternative perceptions, when new parameters and limits on the role of government were being influenced by monetarist interpretations, which in turn provided the intellectual and practical means for containing growth and reducing the levels of public expenditure. This task was made easier by the trade unions, who agreed to three years of voluntary incomes policy and to withholding opposition to the reductions in public expenditure. The incomes policy contributed to the reductions in public expenditure directly because it minimised the impact of the relative price effect on current expenditure.

The Labour Government managed to achieve a combination of a wage policy and reductions in public expenditure. In contrast, the Heath Government had worked on the assumption that an incomes policy could only be achieved through the willingness of the Government to increase expenditures. In this sense the Labour Government had crossed a watershed. The question of why the trade unions accepted a combination of pay policy and reductions in public expenditure during the years of the Labour Government, a strategy they had opposed during the years of the Heath Government, can be answered by pointing to an article in *The Times* by David Basnett in September 1975, where he argued:

> The TUC endorsed the #6 policy not because the direct effects of wage restraint will solve our economic problems but because acceptance was the only alternative to massive cuts in public expenditure and the almost certain fall within a short time of the Labour government. It would appear that its replacement by a Conservative government or Tory dominated coalition would have been prepared to take even more draconian measures on public expenditure.

(D. Basnett, The Times, 26 September 1975)

It would seem that the trade unions' support for the Labour Government's policies was based on the strategy of reluctant acquiescence – a fear that if the Labour Government fell a Conservative Government alternative would implement even larger cuts. However, it would be misleading to imply that trade union support for the Labour Government was universally harmonious. Trade unions were fragmented in their response to incomes policy and in articulating their priorities to the Government. Some trade unions, especially public sector unions such as NUPE, SCPS, NALGO and CPSA, supported incomes policy and an expanded public sector. In contrast, other trade unions, including the TGWU and AUEW, were arguing for policies which favoured a return to free collective bargaining and reductions in personal taxation as a way of regenerating the private sector – even if this was at the cost of reducing the size of the public sector. This fragmentation is most evident in the analysis of various positions taken by the TUC. These appeared in the Annual TUC Economic Reviews, where demands for combined packages of increased public expenditure and reduced taxation came to reflect the uneasy alliance within the trade union movement. The extent of that fragmentation was eventually enshrined in the 'Winter of Discontent' of 1979.

In explaining why the Labour Government abandoned its original intentions, the major concern of this chapter has been to outline an argument that suggests that it would be misleading to construct an explanation around the theme of Labour leaders who, because of lack of commitment, abandoned Labour's programme. Indeed, the change of policy was constantly endorsed by members of the Cabinet, leaders of trade unions and members of the NEC. It was this process that enabled members of the Cabinet to make reductions in public expenditure with little opposition from within the labour movement.

Chapter 7

The Thatcher Government 1979–83

INTRODUCTION

This chapter attempts to explain the nature of the politics of public expenditure during the years of the first Thatcher Government. During previous studies of the Thatcher Governments (Mullard 1987, 1990) the author was concerned with explaining the nature of Thatcherism and with what seemed to be a paradox concerning the central issue of public expenditure. During the period 1979 to 1983, despite the various commitments by Mrs Thatcher to reduce public expenditure, either in real terms or as a ratio of national income, public expenditure resumed an expansionary path, so that by 1983 the ratio of public expenditure to GDP was higher than in 1979 and control of the rate of growth was achieved only after 1985.

The nature of 'Thatcherism' and the impact of the Thatcher Governments on public expenditure has been evaluated at two levels. At one level is what can be described as a 'fundamentalist' interpretation, which suggests that the Thatcher Governments were seeking a radical departure from the politics of the post-war settlement. In contrast are the sceptics who have pointed out that the Governments of Mrs Thatcher did not seek to challenge vested interests, and have suggested that these Governments, like all previous governments, were working within the context of political judgement, expediency and political arithmetic.

Despite the language of changed expectations contained in major policy statements, the study of public expenditure confirms that, even taking into consideration the recent election victory of John Major, the fourth Conservative Government is still committed to planned public expenditure of 43 per cent of national income, which is still higher than when the Conservatives first took office in 1979. There is, however, a need to recognise that there have been elements of radical change as well as commitments to continuity within the experiences of the last fourteen years. The Conservative Governments have been radical in the context of public expenditure and macro economic policy. Fiscal policy has been downgraded as the major instrument available to government to influence the economy through public expenditure, despite the high levels of unemployment throughout the 1980s and early 1990s. During the last decade Keynesian economics have been in retreat. During the last fourteen years the UK experienced two major recessions when the levels of unemployment were higher than at any time in the post-war period. However, the Governments of Mrs Thatcher were also associated with continuity in that they did not seek to challenge certain vested interests, including the subsidies to home owners, pensioners, transport, agriculture and grants to students. Equally, the Government has continued to finance the National Health Service and public sector education through taxation, despite the commitments to push back the frontiers of the State.

The first Thatcher Government can best be viewed as a group of apprentices learning 'on the job', that is, learning what was both feasible and politically possible. It is an approach that confirms that the Government was both radical and pragmatic, and suggests that the Thatcher Government was willing to experiment, challenging certain taken-for-granted views and then seeing to what extent these could be remoulded or left alone. The record on public expenditure shows that some areas of public expenditure could be challenged whilst others had to be left well alone.

INTERPRETATIONS OF THATCHERISM

The Fundamentalist approach

The election of Mrs Thatcher as leader of the Conservative Party in February 1975 has been described as confirming the ascendance of market liberalism. Mrs Thatcher, it is argued, brought into prominence a Conservative philosophy that encouraged the freedom of the individual, and which placed emphasis on self-help, thrift, the importance of the family and the need to push back the frontiers of government.

On the other hand, some have refuted this view and have suggested instead that the election was more of a 'peasants' revolt' (Keegan 1984), a situation mishandled by the Party managers and politically misjudged by Mr Heath (Pym 1985):

> I think he [Mr Heath] lost the leadership for reasons that were
> entirely of his own making and that it is truer to say that he forfeited
> his claim to the loyalty of the Parliamentary Party than that he was
> betrayed . . . Not only did Ted Heath's attitude ensure he would lose
> the leadership but it also made it likely that his successor would be
> someone very different. All the front runners, Willie Whitelaw
> especially, were loyal to Ted Heath and found it impossible to stand
> against him in the first ballot.
>
> (Pym 1985: 21)

The concept of Thatcherism as representing a politics that sought to
break with the postwar settlement is described as a Fundamentalist
perspective because it implies that the Conservative Party had broken
with the past, both in terms of the Party's politics and the politics of
government. This approach suggests that the Conservative Party
broke with the politics of pragmatism and expediency to become a
Party dominated by ideology. The Conservative Party, it is argued,
had under Mrs Thatcher become evangelical in its commitment to
monetarism. As Cosgrave (1978) has argued, 'it is clear that the
struggle between Edward Heath and Margaret Thatcher was not
merely a struggle between proved defeat and possible success but
between two different visions of the future' (Cosgrave 1978: 36).

Bruce-Gardyne (1984) has suggested that Mrs Thatcher represented a reaffirmation by the Party of its confidence in private
enterprise and less government, which implied breaking with the
politics of post-war Conservative Governments. Whilst previous
governments saw the market economy as a means to an end, the end
being industrial modernisation and economic growth, Mrs Thatcher,
in contrast, saw the market as an end in itself: 'I do not know of any
other way than the one I am using at the moment nor of any that will
work in the long run' (M. Thatcher, cited in *Financial Times*, 1
September 1984).

In addition, according to the Fundamentalists, the suggestion is that
the record of the Government has to be evaluated in the longer term.
This is how Mrs Thatcher wanted her Government to be judged:

> For this government it is not the first 100 days that count – it is the
> first five years – and next five after that. We have to think in terms of
> several Parliaments. We have to move this country in a new
> direction to change the way we look at things, to create a wholly
> new attitude of mind.
>
> (M. Thatcher, Conservative Party Conference, October 1979,
> cited in *Politics Today*, October 1979: 322)

The commitments on public expenditure, therefore, were not a short-term crisis response, but a laying to rest of the ghost of Keynes. Bruce-Gardyne (1984) describes the commitment on public expenditure as having 'formally abandoned the pretence that full employment and economic growth were in the gift of the government, accepting by implication that the achievement of these desirable objectives depended on the ability of British commerce' (Bruce-Gardyne 1984: 59). Gamble (1979b) has also argued that the Government of Mrs Thatcher has to be understood as being an attempt to break with the past and of seeking to change the conventional wisdom concerning the claims which legitimately could be made on government:

> Thatcherism represents a clear-cut repudiation of social democracy . . . the Thatcher government has marked the moment when the break with social democratic politics is explicitly acknowledged. The strategy which can only lead to a shrinking industrial base is now justified no longer as an expedient and temporary tactic, but the only possible course of action.
>
> (Gamble 1979a: 14, 19)

According to Gamble, the politics of social democracy represented a process whereby governments recognised the twin responsibilities of maintaining full employment and of continued commitment to welfare expenditure. However, the commitments to markets and collectivist politics have proved to be incompatible. If one therefore accepts the premise that governments in Britain during the post-war period sought to meet such claims, then understanding the impact of the Thatcher Governments requires an assessment of the extent to which they have been successful in renegotiating those claims. Has the Conservative Government radically changed expectations so that governments will, in the future, no longer be held to account for the levels of unemployment, the numbers of people in poverty and the quality of public welfare services?

In addition, Gough (1983) argues that the attempt to make this shift was expressed in the Government's plans for public expenditure. A comparison of the outgoing Labour Government's White Paper with the plans of the Conservative Government of 1980 leads Gough to the conclusion that the change amounted to a restructuring of the welfare state. Restructuring was taking place at two levels: quantitatively, in terms of reduced expenditure; and qualitatively, in that the plans tended to embody a shift from universal to selective welfare and to privatisation of certain services. According to Gough, changes in public expenditure reflected changes in class relations:

Drawing together the threads of these policies we see a major attempt to reprivatise parts of the welfare state; higher charges on consumers, explicit decisions to weaken the organised working class, to widen the gap between deserving and undeserving claimants. It is difficult to avoid the conclusion that the welfare state is being attacked by the new conservatism at least as much for ideological as for economic reasons.

(Gough 1983: 153)

The theme of public expenditure is, therefore, central to a Fundamentalist framework. Reductions in public expenditure would confirm whether or not the Government had succeeded in constructing a new political agenda, and possibly a new consensus that included a number of tenets.

The end of demand management

Monetarism rules out the possibility that government can influence the level of employment. If public expenditure does influence the level of demand, it only does so in the short term and at the cost of higher inflation. The role of government is to curb inflation through the control of its own borrowing requirements.

Reducing government spending and reducing taxation

The Government has to give meaning to the principle of getting the State off people's backs and of creating an environment that encourages individual responsibility. To do this, it has to construct a policy framework in which there is a path for the reduction in taxation and also for reductions in public expenditure. A reduction in personal taxation allows individuals to keep more of what they earn, whilst reduced public expenditure means less state direction. The State crowds out the private sector because of high interest rates associated with government borrowing and also crowds out out the private sector in the reallocation of resources to government projects.

Less intervention in industry

The Government has to put what it considers to be a quietus on socialist intervention in industry through such measures as the phasing out of the National Enterprise Board, setting in motion the process of de-nationalisation of industries and the curtailment of subsidies on regional support and employment. The Government has to abandon the concept of picking industrial winners, of seeking to construct corporatist politics and extending benefits to specific privileged groups, whether they be manufacturing industry or public sector professionals and the bureaucracy.

All these propositions involved changes in expectations and in commitments to public expenditure. Reductions in public expenditure in real terms were essential if the Government was going to achieve a lasting change in the political climate. As the Government declared in its 1979 expenditure White Paper: 'Public expenditure is at the heart of Britain's economic difficulties. Higher output can only come from lower taxes, lower interest rates and lower government borrowing' (HMSO 1979b: 1).

The study of public expenditure within a Fundamentalist framework is, therefore, founded on the premise that the Government in 1979 had a coherent strategy. Fundamentalists would argue that the break with the past was expressed in the Medium Term Financial Strategy (MTFS), published in March 1980. This provided targets for the money supply and the PSBR, indicating that a money supply policy had to have congruent targets for the PSBR. Whiteley (1983) has argued that the MTFS represented a fundamental departure:

> now that the Thatcher administration in Britain is in its sixth year of office it has become possible to clearly assess the impact of the monetarist experiment on the British economy. Experiments are comparatively rare phenomena in social science and there is a sense in which the academic community should be grateful to the Thatcher government for testing monetarism on the British economy.
>
> (Whiteley 1983: 1)

The implications of the MTFS for public expenditure decisions were important since a declining PSBR figure implied that if the Government was to reduce its borrowing it had to achieve this either by reducing expenditure or by increasing its revenue. Presumably, since the Government had been elected on the pledge to reduce taxation and had by June 1979 already reduced surtax and the ordinary tax rate at a cost of £4 billion, this only left the option of reducing the PSBR through reduced expenditure.

However, despite the MTFS intentions, by 1983 the Government had not been able to reverse the trend in the growth of public expenditure. Expenditure had expanded from 39.4 per cent of GDP (market prices) in 1979 to 43.8 per cent in 1983, an overall increase of 11 per cent since 1979. Fundamentalists argue the Government never abandoned its central objective to reduce public expenditure and tend to offer two forms of explanation for this apparent 'failure'.

First, they point to factors which the Government could not control in the short term. Bruce-Gardyne (1984) has included among these the growth of demand-related expenditures, created by the recession, and the increase in the number of pensioners. In addition, Mrs Thatcher has blamed the increase on the costs incurred by the Clegg Commission:

> It has been particularly difficult to reduce public spending when we have had to meet the cost of the Clegg awards and other comparability awards. That catching-up process – which follows the inevitable collapse of incomes policy – is now nearly over.
>
> (M. Thatcher, cited in *Hansard*, 29 July 1980: Col. 1303)

Second, Fundamentalists argue that the Government made pledges to restore the morale of the police and to commit more resources to NATO. Both these pledges involved new expenditures, which in the end proved to be incompatible with the policy of reduced expenditure. This is a rather limited type of explanation, in that it can be countered by an argument that says the failure to reverse this trend cannot be explained in terms of the new pledges since these should have already been discounted. This failure, by implication, needs to be explained in terms of the lack of agreement within the Government as to what other expenditure budgets had to be reduced to make room for these new commitments.

The sceptical approach

The sceptical perspective questions the assumption that the Thatcher Government aimed to break with the past. Market liberal sceptics tend to dispute, first, the extent to which the Thatcher Government had really tried to import thoroughgoing market liberal concepts into the British economy. Among these commentators are included Brittan (1977, 1983) and Minford (1980, 1984). Second, there are those whose scepticism arises because they do not see the Thatcher Government as either fundamentalist or employing continuity, as implied by market liberals, but rather that it was a government that was involved in politics as the art of what was both feasible and possible.

The market liberals

According to this perspective the 1979–83 Conservative Government failed to reduce public expenditure because it did not seek to break public sector monopolies involved in the delivery of health care and education, which are seen by Minford (1984) as the cause of the ever-increasing cost in the delivery of services. According to Minford the reduction of public expenditure inevitably involves the wholesale privatisation of major areas of the welfare state:

> Long experience of political pressures shows that if something is produced by central or local government it is very hard to avoid the addition to it of substantial monopoly power or protection. It is utopian to think that production could remain public and yet be disciplined by the market. The only remedy is for production to be private and simultaneously for monopoly power to be broken up.
>
> (Minford 1984: iii)

Brittan (1984) tends to agree in part with the Minford thesis, in that he also sees the public sector as a coalition of vested interests. However, he also disagrees with Minford's view that if the Government wanted to succeed it had to put the privatisation of major parts of health or education on to the political agenda. He argues that:

> When it comes to health and education my reaction is not so much to throw up my hands in horror . . . but to ask the basic question whether the ordinary taxpayer who will pay much less tax but have to dip in his pocket for health insurance . . . is going to feel better off or possess much more freedom of choice . . . My main fear is that to concentrate on privatising welfare would be an unfortunate diversion.
>
> (Brittan, *Financial Times*, 19 April 1984)

Brittan starts from the premise that the increase in government spending has been the product of politicians seeking to outbid each other in making promises, whilst raising the expectations of the electorate. Brittan (1982) describes this as the 'Wenceslas syndrome' and asks whether the Thatcher Government did seek to break this myth. He concludes:

> On earlier occasions I have defended the government from opponents who wanted it to act like a Good King Wenceslas who had the power to increase the supply of satisfaction enjoyed by the people if only he chooses to do so. Now, however, it is the

government itself which is claiming the mantle of the Good Old King, it is the job of non-partisan analysts to point out that monarchs with the resources to act that way disappeared with the waning of the Middle Ages.

(Brittan, *Financial Times*, 22 March 1982)

Brittan's conclusion is that the Government continued to maintain the privileged positions of specialist interest groups. He argues that the Government's failure was due to its unwillingess to challenge those in receipt of various forms of subsidy, in agriculture and industry, and to mortgagers and council tenants, at a cost of £11 billion per annum in lost revenue and public expenditure.

The politics of statecraft

There are similarities in the arguments of Fundamentalists and market liberal sceptics, in that both fail to consider the political dimension of public expenditure. Public expenditure and tax reliefs on mortgages and pensions represent potential voters. The aim of a political party is to win elections and, therefore, it needs to nurture and seduce its social base. To achieve the twin objectives of reducing public expenditure and at the same time not threaten its electoral base the 1979–83 Conservative Government had to make reductions that were politically viable rather than reductions that would have formed a coherent market liberal strategy. The failure to halt the trend has to be explained in terms of a government working within the politics of statecraft. Riddell (1983) defines the nature of Thatcherism as follows:

> Thatcherism has won the political initiative in Britain but after four years the Thatcher government has still achieved relatively little. The balance sheet of the first Thatcher term shows a Britain divided between haves and have nots, between north and south, between 'new' industries and traditional manufacturing and between owner occupiers and council tenants.

(Riddell 1983: 230)

According to Riddell, therefore, the story of the Thatcher Government was one of continuity, of a Conservative Government which, like the Heath Government before it, ensured during its early months tax cuts to the better off whilst for the rest of the period it looked for public expenditure savings to finance the tax reductions. The Government was obeying the basic rules of the electoral business cycle, of meeting its manifesto commitments during the early period of office.

THE GOVERNMENT'S RECORD ON PUBLIC EXPENDITURE

The index of expenditure White Papers

The study of the first full White Paper, published in January 1980, when contrasted to the White Papers of 1981 and subsequent years, confirms the changes in policy objectives. In the first full review in 1980 the expenditure White Paper, outlining the reductions, argued that:

> The government intend to reduce public expenditure progressively in volume terms over the next few years. This is a substantial change from the plans published by the previous government White Paper of January 1979.
>
> (HMSO 1980a: 3)

In contrast, the 1981 expenditure White Paper confirmed that expenditures were higher than the Government had planned:

> The outturns now estimated for 1980–81 and the planning totals for future years are higher than in Cmnd 7841, and higher than the government would wish in the light of their financial and economic objectives. The government regard this development as one which requires the most serious attention.
>
> (HMSO 1981a: 3)

By 1981 therefore, the Government seemed to be admitting that it did not have control over the growth in expenditure and that this would require 'attention' – an unexpectedly feeble word considering the centrality of public expenditure to the Government's objectives. The implication was that if the problem was to be resolved then there had to be whole-hearted commitment in the Cabinet to the severe restraint needed.

The study of the intentions contained in the White Papers indicates the extent to which the Government had departed from its original plans on assuming office. In 1980 the Government possessed a strategy for a continuous reduction in public expenditure during the period to 1983–4. The changes in subsequent plans represent the magnitude of the shift away from that strategy.

The record on expenditure by programme

A detailed analysis of public expenditure by programme for the period 1979 to 1983 follows.

Housing

Within this programme the Government continued where the previous Labour Government had left off; in other words, it carried on with the policy of major reductions. Expenditure fell in monetary value from £6,274 million in 1979 to £6,115 million in 1983. As a ratio of GDP (market prices) expenditure was reduced from 3.3 per cent in 1979 to 1.9 in 1982 – an overall reduction of 33 per cent of the 1979 level. These changes reflected the increase in finance to the Housing Revenue Account from council house sales and also reductions of expenditure in house building. The reductions in house building also confirmed the Government's approach to capital expenditure projects in the public sector.

Trade and industry

The Government reduced its commitments within this programme through redefining areas of Britain eligible for development area status and through the phasing out of some of the industrial training boards. Expenditure fell from 2.5 per cent of GDP to 1.9 per cent of GDP and also as a percentage of total expenditure.

Education

The third area to experience a reduction was education, which fell as a ratio of GDP from 5.3 per cent to 5 per cent in 1983 – a reduction of 3 per cent of the 1979 level. Despite this slow-down, the Government claimed that it had maintained educational standards. Whilst the number of state school pupils fell from 8.5 million in 1979 to 7.8 million in 1983, pupil–teacher ratios improved from 22.4 in 1970 to 19.2 in 1983. However, the Government also pointed out that the education budget had to reflect what the economy could afford, which implied that the education budget must take its share of the misery. Furthermore, the Government's imposition of cash limits seemed to put the onus on the teachers, since now they had to decide between bargaining for higher wages for themselves and acquiescing to lower expenditures for pupils in the form of reductions in capitation allowances.

Health

In contrast, expenditure on health continued to expand during the period. The health budget grew faster than the rate of GDP, from 4.6

per cent in 1979 to 5.3 per cent in 1983 – an increase of 14 per cent of the 1979 level. The Government pointed out that some 56,000 more people were employed by 1983 in the delivery of health care within the NHS. At the same time, however, it urged health authorities to put out to tender contracts for hospital cleaning, catering and laundry. The Government argued that competition, whether it led to the privat-isation of such services or to the awarding of contracts in-house, would lead to lower costs, thus leaving more resources for patient care.

Personal social services

The framework adopted for the Health Service was also argued to justify increases in expenditure on social services. The budget was expanded from 0.93 per cent of GDP in 1979 to 1.00 per cent in 1983. The Government claimed that this increase would meet the needs of the growing number of elderly people and new commitments imposed on social services departments. Yet this represented a reversal of policy. The Government had originally aimed to reduce the social services budget in line with other local authority expenditures: 'The figures in future years reflect the Government's call for additional savings in overall local authority spending. It is however for local authorities themselves to determine the actual level of expenditure on individual services' (HMSO 1981a: 118).

Expenditure on social services, therefore, reflected more the tension between central government attempts to control public expenditure and local authority autonomy. This will be explored further in the following section.

Social security

The fastest area of growth was the social security programme. This partly reflected the increase in the number of unemployed during the period. Unemployment had increased from 1.6 million in 1979 to over 3 million by 1983. In the meantime expenditure on social security had increased from 9.75 per cent of GDP in 1979 to 11.20 per cent in 1983 – an overall increase of 15 per cent of the 1979 level. Social security expenditure also increased as a percentage of total expenditure from 24.7 per cent to 27.77 per cent.

The expansion of this programme contributed to the undermining of the Government's plans of 1980 to reduce public expenditure. The problem here is whether the increase in unemployment was unexpected, thereby subverting the Government's plans for public expenditure, or had the resulting levels of unemployment been envisaged all along? Although the policy of the Government had been to refrain from providing forecasts for unemployment, some economists, including Tobin (1981), Kaldor (1982b) and Galbraith (1981), would argue that the Government had been made aware that its policy of tight monetary control and high interest would lead to higher levels of unemployment. The Government, in limiting itself to the control of the money supply, had launched a monetarist experiment on the British economy:

> The question I have is that the UK has embarked upon a very interesting and, if I may say so, risky experiment in macroeconomic policy and monetary policy . . . The hope of the protagonists is that it will so melt the existing core of inflation in the economy that the response to it will be much quicker . . . From that point of view I must say that the UK is a very interesting laboratory experiment for economics.
>
> (Tobin 1981: 208–9)

According to these economists, ministers were aware of the consequences of their policies but were prepared to finance a high level of unemployment. The rise in the social security budget, therefore, reflected more of a policy choice by the Government.

The study of expenditure programmes also confirms that the Government did provide for expansion in those areas it had defined as political priorities. These commitments included the Government's aim to increase defence expenditure by 3 per cent per annum. However, after 1982 there were further added expenditures due to the cost of replacing equipment lost during the Falklands War, the expense of maintaining a garrison in the Islands, and the reprieve of some Royal Navy shipyards. Between 1979 and 1983 defence expenditure increased from 4.73 per cent to 5.23 per cent of GDP – an increase of 11 per cent since 1979 and, as a percentage of public expenditure, from 12 per cent to 13 per cent.

Furthermore, the Government announced in 1983 that there had been an overspend in the defence budget, as a result of defence contractors completing contracts more promptly than expected. This again seems to confirm that defence was a government priority when compared with the treatment of local authorities and their overspend on the housing programme. In the latter case, the Government responded with a moratorium, whilst on defence it accepted the overspend.

The law and order programme also enjoyed a continuous increase in resources. Expenditure increased from £2.9 billion in 1979 to £5.5 billion in 1983. This represented an increase in the rate of growth from 1.53 per cent of GDP to 1.84 per cent in 1983 – an increase of 20 per cent.

The breakdown of expenditure programmes by economic component

Capital expenditure

Between 1979 and 1983 total capital expenditure continued to decline from 2.6 per cent of GDP (market prices) in 1979 to 1.8 per cent in 1983. The main reductions were achieved in the housing capital programme. The implication of this reduction was that whilst in 1975 there were 144,700 new dwellings started, in 1979 this had fallen to 48,000 and by 1980 had declined further to 44,000.

This pattern of continuity with the experience of the previous Labour Government was repeated in education, where successive administrations justified their policies by pointing to falling school rolls within the primary and secondary school sectors. Between 1979 and 1983 capital expenditure on school buildings fell by 32 per cent of the 1979 level.

In health, it would seem that the Conservative Government reversed the previous government's policy of delaying hospital building. During the period 1979 to 1983 expenditure on health capital increased by 0.05 per cent of GDP, compared with a reduction of 0.08 per cent between 1974 and 1979. Indeed, the Conservative Government was able to claim that 26 new hospitals had been completed, whilst another 49 were under construction (HMSO 1983a).

In its plans to reduce public expenditure, the Conservative Government seemed to follow the well-trodden path of securing reductions through the capital component of some expenditure programmes. However, the Government was unable to achieve the same magnitude of reductions as the previous Labour Government, which had the advantage of getting to these programmes first. Between 1974 and 1979 capital expenditure overall was reduced by 49 per cent, compared to a reduction of 30 per cent between 1979 and 1983.

Both the roads and environment programmes experienced decreases. The roads programme fell from 1.83 per cent of GDP (market prices) in 1979 to 1.72 per cent in 1983, whilst environment expenditure fell from 1.67 per cent to 1.63 per cent in 1983. However, these reductions were small when compared to the housing capital programme, which again indicates that the Government was willing to protect some programmes more than others.

Current expenditure

Between 1979 and 1983 current expenditure grew from 20 per cent of GDP to 21 per cent. In contrast, during the period of the previous Labour Government current expenditure had only increased by 0.1 per cent. The analysis by programme indicates that the fastest area of growth was the health programme. Expenditure on health increased from 4.0 per cent to 4.8 per cent of GDP in 1983. The record on current expenditure raises the question of why the Government apparently failed to control this area of expenditure. One explanation suggested that the Conservative Government had inherited from Labour the awards made by the Clegg Commission. The Government argued that these settlements had added some £500 million to the cost of the public sector.

The detailed study of the relative price effect on public expenditure (Price 1979; Mullard 1987) confirms that the additional increases in current expenditure of 2.14 per cent of GDP were to both output and relative price effects (RPE), where the RPE and output effects were of equal influence. However, the study also showed that the analysis by programme indicated that in some programmes the output effect was the major component. This included law and order, defence and health, whilst in contrast the increase in education expenditure had been mainly attributed to higher wage costs. As the author concluded at the time:

> This suggests that the growth in current expenditure cannot be explained just in terms of the government having had to meet the pay increases awarded by Clegg (Price 1979). Whilst Price suggested that the government plans to reduce public expenditure were their response to the expansion of the RPE, this suggests the expansion in current expenditure was not a problem of control but the product of the government's policy to provide for a genuine growth in the volume of goods and services available.
>
> (Mullard 1987: 175)

EXPLAINING THE GOVERNMENT'S RECORD

The previous section pointed to how public expenditure was expanded between 1979 and 1983 and how this reflected changes between and within expenditure programmes. These changes represented both political choices and political constraints. This section attempts to explain the extent to which the expansion of public expenditure was deliberate policy and the extent to which this expansion involved expenditures that were not within the control of the Government.

The concept of political choice

The impact of pledges made before the election

The Conservative Party in 1979 pledged that it would increase expenditure on military defence and law and order. Furthermore, the Party made commitments to protect pensions and to meet the previous Labour Government's plans on health expenditure. However, the Conservative Party also pointed out that these commitments were to be fulfilled within the context of restraint on public expenditure. In 1977, the Party declared: 'the state takes too much of the nation's income, its share must be steadily reduced' (Conservative Central Office 1977: 2).

How then was the Government to make compatible the reduction of taxation and the reduction of public expenditure overall and yet provide new resources? The short answer to this question is that the Conservative Party presented a series of images in an attempt to attract a variety of audiences. This was reflected in the document *The Right Approach to the Economy* (Conservative Central Office 1977). Described as the strategy document to be completed by the Conservative Party under Mrs Thatcher's leadership (Patten 1980), it expressed a treaty between factions within the Party. It provided common ground on which all could agree – the need to reduce public expenditure. The document emphasised that the Government would achieve reductions by cutting back on activities that could be plausibly tagged as 'extravagant', particularly those which could be presented as the pet projects of the Labour Government:

> We shall look for major savings in the cancellation of Socialist programmes (such as the pointless community acquisition of building land); an end to nationalisation; the reduction of indis-

criminate subsidies . . . We shall also press for a major increase in the
efficiency of local government including much less duplication with
Whitehall, we shall be looking for very substantial savings here over
a five year period.

(Conservative Central Office 1977: 11)

In addition, the Party wanted to construct an image that also
emphasised continuing commitment to welfare expenditures including
health and pensions:

not being a prescription for poorer social provision, it is a recipe for
better housekeeping in all the public services. If we are to maintain
standards of services we must root out waste and unnecessary
bureaucracy.

(Conservative Central Office 1977: 11)

However, the document also reflected the influence of those who
wanted to associate public expenditure with the individual's right to
choose, inflation and the money supply:

the share of public expenditure to national income was allowed to
rise by a staggering 11.5 per cent in real terms. The government
borrowing needs soared to the highest level in our peacetime history
. . . The consequences are now before us in the shape of an inflation
rate still twice as high as that of our competitors.

(Conservative Central Office 1977: 10)

Although both the objectives of reducing inefficiency and of controlling
inflation led to the conclusion that there was a need to reduce public
expenditure, the issues of how and to what extent led to different
interpretations. Whilst Sir Keith Joseph and Sir Geoffrey Howe
argued that the reductions in public expenditure were a radical
departure from Keynesian practices, James Prior accepted the
reductions of public expenditure only as a short-term necessary
response in the context of high inflation (Riddell 1983; Keegan 1984).

The Conservative Party entered the 1979 election, therefore, as an
uneasy coalition around a policy document that was a treaty between
signatories rather than the product of a group of leading politicians
who thought as one. This alliance proved difficult to hold together
when the Conservative Government took office and in the years that
followed. Tensions arose because there was no agreement within the
Party about the exact nature of the pledges that had been made, about
the methods for reducing public expenditure that should be adopted,

and about whether the Party had set out with a new and coherent strategy. Over-optimism about the savings that could be achieved through improving efficiency and the other objectives it had articulated proved to be incompatible in the event.

Resistance within the Cabinet

This section examines the view that the commitments made during the election closed down some options for the Government when it came to decide which expenditure budgets could be reduced. As was suggested in the previous two chapters, both the Conservative and the Labour Governments of 1970 and 1974 broke with their original intentions. The question is, why did the original intentions act as a constraint on the Thatcher Government?

Heclo and Wildavsky (1982) have suggested that the ability to win reductions in public expenditure depends on whether the Prime Minister supports the Chancellor against spending ministers during the cycle of the public expenditure survey. The implications of the Heclo and Wildavsky approach are, first, that during the period 1979–83, the Treasury and the Prime Minister were not always on the same side, and second, that they were defeated during the annual negotiations with spending ministers, which would suggest that the Heclo/Wildavsky thesis did not hold for the period.

When Mrs Thatcher became the leader of the Conservative Party, she inherited a Shadow Cabinet, in which she did not have a majority of colleagues who were in agreement with her approach (Bruce-Gardyne 1984; Holmes 1985a). The significance of this was that the Shadow Cabinet became the Cabinet after the election. Burch (1983) has argued that after the post-election budget of 1979, spending Ministers were successful in thwarting demands by Treasury ministers for lower spending targets. During the 1980 negotiations Treasury ministers had asked spending ministers to reduce their bids for the year 1981–2 by £4 billion, but only achieved £2 billion. This was repeated during the 1982–3 settlement, when the Treasury was again defeated in its plans to hold expenditure to a total of £110 billion. The negotiations ended up with an increase in estimates of another £5 billion. Thus, from this standpoint, the revision of plans in an upward direction was the consequence of spending ministers defeating the Treasury and Mrs Thatcher. The Cabinet changes announced in January 1981 and in September 1981 reflected the extent of dissent in the Cabinet and were, therefore, a response by Mrs Thatcher aimed at creating a Cabinet more to her own liking.

Furthermore, the frustration of these defeats seemed also to force Mrs Thatcher to express the antagonisms within the Cabinet out into the public sphere, indicating her weak position inside the Cabinet:

> What really gets me furious is that those vociferous in demanding more tax cuts and more expenditure are not prepared to accept the consequences of their actions. I wish some of them had some guts and gumption . . . these people want us to print more money with all the consequences this would have for future inflation.
>
> (M. Thatcher, cited in the *Guardian*, 12 March 1981)

How then are we to assess the impact of disagreement within the Cabinet? What weight ought to be put on ministerial speeches? Were they forms of coded messages that the Prime Minister could not afford to ignore if she was to hold the Party and the Government together? Certainly, the evidence of such messages is plentiful. A series of speeches had been made between June 1981 and October 1981 that indicated the pressure that the Treasury was under. For example, on the television programme *Weekend World* on 24 October 1981, Sir Ian Gilmour, who had just lost his job inside the Cabinet, gave explicit recognition to the presence of dissent within the Cabinet:

> it is quite impossible for Mrs Thatcher – and I give her credit for that – I do not think that she would want to ignore the very heavy weight of opinion. It is there. She cannot wish it away. She has to pay attention to what I call the emerging consensus.
>
> (Gilmour, *Weekend World*, ITV, 24 October 1981)

This 'emerging consensus' had been articulated also by Michael Heseltine, who was Minister at the Department of the Environment, at the Party Conference in October 1981. Heseltine found it necessary to ask whether the Conservative Party was drifting away from the One Nation tradition in pursuing dogmatic policies. He went on to say:

> Those traditions are not ours to squander or abuse. For a brief time they are entrusted to us to make relevant in today's world. They are the traditions that have kept our party in the forefront of British politics.
>
> (M. Heseltine, cited in Conservative Party 1981: 127)

Michael Heseltine was signalling his agreement with some of the views developed by Sir Ian Gilmour (1977), namely, that the Conservative Party had electorally been the most successful right-wing party in

Europe because it had eschewed ideology and had responded to circumstances. The Conservative Party had always accepted that the State would recognise the legitimate claims and expectations of the electorate. Any attempt, therefore, by the Party to embrace a whole-hearted doctrine of following market forces was against what Conservatism had stood for. The coded message was that a Conservative Government had to be interventionist:

> People expect and demand action and if they do not get it they are likely to look elsewhere or take action themselves. If the State is not interested in them, why should they be interested in the State? Complete economic freedom is not, therefore, an insurance of political freedom. Indeed it can undermine it.
>
> (Gilmour 1977: 118)

The impact that these messages had on the Treasury and Mrs Thatcher can be gauged by looking at speeches made by Mrs Thatcher in April 1981, during the Cabinet discussions in October and also in separate speeches by Leon Brittan, the Financial Secretary to the Treasury. Mrs Thatcher, in a speech on 5 February 1981, reasserted the aims of the Government: 'The second aspect of the government's strategy is the sustained effort that we are making to reduce the pressure on the economy created by excessive government spending' (M. Thatcher, cited in the *Guardian*, 6 February 1981). However, in her address to the House of Commons on 28 October 1981, Mrs Thatcher seemed to emphasise that the Government needed to be flexible on public expenditure, whilst she also wanted to take credit for that flexibility:

> We must exercise restraint but we are not considering a lower total for next year than that published in the last White Paper – indeed the total will be higher. We are resolute in the pursuit of the strategy but accusations that we are inflexible in our tactics in the face of recession are wholly refuted.
>
> (M. Thatcher, cited in *Hansard*, 28 October 1981, Col. 883)

Mrs Thatcher then carried on with a list of the areas of new expenditures in which the Government had become involved. Increased expenditures seemed to have become a virtue and no longer a burden:

> Well before last July we had increased expenditure on special employment measures . . . We increased the financial limits for the

nationalised industries for coal, steel and the railways. We raised the spending limits for British Telecommunications . . . We have given help to Harland and Wolff . . . To accuse me of being inflexible is absolute poppycock.

(M. Thatcher, cited in *Hansard*, 28 October 1981, Col. 884)

The message of the new flexibility also entered the speeches made by Treasury ministers. A comparison of two speeches made by Leon Brittan again shows the shift in emphasis. In an interview with the *Financial Times* on 12 October 1981, Mr Brittan declared that he 'would not favour a position where the total level of spending is going up deliberately as a result of conscious government policy decision' (L. Brittan, cited in the *Financial Times*, 12 October 1981). However, when the White Paper on public expenditure was published in December 1981, Mr Brittan went on to justify the Government's deliberate policy choice to increase public expenditure:

The White Paper has disposed effectively of the notion that the government refuses to adjust its plans to circumstances. The decision to increase spending is a conscious and deliberate collective policy response by the government to the realities of the present.

(L. Brittan, speech to the Manchester Chamber of Commerce, 4 December 1981)

So did the changes in expenditure described here confirm a change in policy away from the radical to the pragmatic approach? This study of the political record indicates that certain members of the Cabinet were willing to put in bids for new expenditures, in the full knowledge that this would not be consistent with the Government's economic policy, and seemed to be getting their way during the expenditure cycle. Mrs Thatcher and the Treasury bowed to the pressure. However, it remains arguable that there was no basic change in the Government's economic policy. The need is to differentiate between 'economic' and 'political' monetarism. Mrs Thatcher and her supporters might have surrendered some of their economic monetarism by allowing ministers to expand their budgets, but they had sustained their political monetarism. As Holmes (1985a) argues: 'To claim as critics of the Thatcher policy have done that monetarism was abandoned . . . is to misunderstand Mrs Thatcher's approach. Essentially the policy was to resist reflation and any shift towards Keynesian demand management' (Holmes 1985a: 50).

Since spending ministers were not involved in the construction of the budget, their successes in increasing public expenditure were offset by

Treasury decisions to raise further taxation and interest rates. Holmes (1985a), in an interview with a Treasury minister, shows how this was resolved: 'According to one Treasury minister, "the Treasury having been defeated on public expenditure in Autumn 1980 convinced Geoffrey (Howe) that what had been foregone must be recouped" ' (Holmes 1985a: 63).

However, dissent within the Cabinet was limited to the expenditure cycle. The dissent did not lead to a change in policy; new expenditures did not change the Government's fiscal stance. Furthermore, the dissent was confined to the period 1980–1, so that the Cabinet reshuffles, together with the aftermath of the Falklands conflict, were sufficient to consolidate Mrs Thatcher's leadership within the Party and inside the Cabinet. The direct consequence of this was that the public expenditure exercises after November 1982 were carried out relatively smoothly. This is confirmed by a study of the expenditure out-turns, which tend to show that the rate of growth in expenditure did level off after 1981.

Constraints on the Government

This section deals with those events which could be described as being outside the direct control of the Government. This approach encompasses those arguments that point to the impact of demand-related expenditures, such as social security and health, and how these programmes imposed a limit on the autonomy of the Government.

The problem with this approach is in separating what can be explained as the demand-related aspect of an expenditure and the degree of autonomy the Government has to alter that expenditure in the short term. For example, it was argued earlier that it would be insufficient to seek an explanation of public expenditure changes in the rise of unemployment, based on the assumption that this was unforeseen. Certainly, it can be argued that once eligibility to unemployment benefit had been defined, then the numbers of unemployed decide the cost of the programme, but this is different from the argument that suggests that the increase in unemployment was not predicted or that it was beyond the control of the Government. Indeed, the Cambridge Economic Policy Group had warned the Government in 1980 that unless it changed policies unemployment would rise to 4.5 million by 1984, to which Nigel Lawson replied, 'perhaps the ultimate lunacy in economic forecasting is the annual report from the Cambridge Economic Policy Group . . . If this is really

the choice we face, then the only rational answer would be emigration'
(N. Lawson, cited in the *Evening Standard*, 29 April 1980).

The autonomy of the Government is certainly constrained in terms
of whether or not it has complete control over an expenditure
programme. The education budget illustrates the problem that
confronted the Conservative Government in seeking to control the
expenditure of local authorities. Changes in expenditure indicate that
within the education budget there was a fall in capital component,
whilst the current side of the programme was expanded. This reflected
not only central government's control over local capital expenditure,
but also the decision taken by some local authorities to protect teacher
employment at the cost of capital projects. Local authorities
consistently overspent on their education budgets, whilst the
overspend was on the current side of their programmes. Jackman
(1984) argues that:

> so substantial has been the overspend on current expenditure each
> year that figures in subsequent Public Expenditure White Papers
> have had to be adjusted upwards, so that essentially we observe a
> process of central government adjusting its planning targets to
> conform with what local authorities actually spend rather than
> local authorities adjusting their expenditure to bring it in line with
> central government spending plans.
>
> (Jackman 1984: 95)

The Government's own perception of its lack of control over local
government was expressed in the rebuke Mrs Thatcher delivered to the
local authorities in the Queen's Speech in November 1982:

> it is a sorry catalogue; housing underspend £500m; local authority
> capital other than housing £200m; water £70m. What a difference
> it would have made if those capital expenditure plans had been
> fulfilled. Most of the authorities certainly spent the money, but not
> on the purposes for which it was intended. Some of them sacrificed
> investment and, therefore, jobs in order to finance higher pay
> awards.
>
> (M. Thatcher, cited in *Hansard*, 3 November 1982, Col. 21)

Certain conclusions can be drawn from this section. First, that central
government had problems in the control of some local government
expenditures. Despite such measures as cash limits, penalties and the
control of local authority borrowing on the capital account, local

authorities continued to overspend on their current expenditures. Second, that within some programmes, including health and education, the influence of producer groups including teachers and doctors enabled these professionals to protect the level of employment and pay of their members, although the teachers seemed to have more success in protecting employment than pay. Professionals were engaged in deploying bleeding stump and sore thumb strategies to stoke up public concern over 'reductions' in their programmes (Holmes 1985a), whilst Le Grand (1985) contends that the Government's failure stems from the 'middle class' influence on certain expenditure programmes:

> The key, it seems to me, lies in the role of the professionals and managerial classes: the middle class . . . they are a powerful political force; no politician or civil servant can afford to neglect their views. Now the middle class has three sets of interests in the welfare state; as taxpayers, as suppliers and as consumers . . . The middle class elements of the welfare state have thus managed to weather the storm and I venture to predict will continue to do so.
>
> (Le Grand 1985: 109–10)

CONCLUSIONS

Studies of the 1979 Conservative Government have tended to suggest that the election of 1979 represented a break with the politics of Keynesianism and collectivism. These approaches have sought to confirm the existence of the 'Politics of Thatcherism', embodying a coherent strategy to reorder the priorities of government. Thatcherism represented the attempt to redefine what claims could be made of government, a change in which the individual was to take more responsibility, such as making private provision for health care, education and pensions.

The expansion of public expenditure during the period 1979–83 seems to lead to two types of conclusion. First, it could be said that the changes in public expenditure point to a negation of the existence of Thatcherism, if Thatcherism is defined as being an attempt to reduce the activities of the government. In 1983 most children continued to be educated in the public sector, the sick continued to look to the NHS for treatment. Tax relief to mortgagers and subsidies to agriculture had not been challenged. However, as this study points out, whilst the Government had not managed to reduce public expenditure as planned, it had nevertheless halted the rate of growth.

However, despite the expansion in public expenditure there is the added argument that the growth in public expenditure was being financed by increases in taxation and interest rates. In this, it could be argued, there was a departure; the Government had abandoned an arm of economic policy, to use public expenditure and government borrowing to influence economic activity. Research by the Cambridge Group of Economists and Nickell and Layard (1985) has tended to suggest that the Government had abandoned public expenditure as an instrument of economic management. Indeed, Terry Ward, a Cambridge economist and advisor to the Select Committee, claimed:

> The impression given by the government is that budgetary policy does not affect economic activity, which is allegedly determined entirely by factors outside the government's control . . . This impression is wholly misleading and cannot be substantiated although it conveniently absolves the government from any responsibility for the deepening recession, which its policies would have helped to create.
>
> (T. Ward, cited in House of Commons 1980b: 22)

The argument of this chapter has been that changes in public expenditure were the product of deliberate political decisions. The pledges made in 1979 represented a political calculation both within the Conservative Party and also with the electorate. The aim was to hold the party together – an alliance of interests – whilst the message to the electorate was that the aim of the Government was to curb inflation, reduce taxation and protect welfare expenditures by eliminating waste and inefficiency in the public sector. These pledges tended to limit the autonomy of those ministers who supported the radical component of the Government, and also pointed to the weakness of the Prime Minister and the Treasury.

The suggestion that changes in public expenditure need to be explained in relation to deliberate political choice has implications for the politics of Thatcherism. The idea of a 'Politics of Thatcherism' founded on the view that the Government that took office in 1979 had a coherent strategy to restructure public expenditure and alter the perception of government cannot be sustained. However, another argument suggests that the Government of 1979 represented a politics of statecraft, of ministers equipped with the tools of the MTFS and a view that there was no return to corporatist practices. Thus, having limited itself to the control of the money supply, interest rates and government borrowing, the Government could be perceived as 'learning on the job' about the viability of such policies. Within the Thatcher Government, therefore, there was less concern with strategy and more with the tactics of winning some battles and losing others. The outcomes on public expenditure represent a process of learning rather than of strategic choice.

Chapter 8

The restructuring of public expenditure 1984–90

INTRODUCTION

In the previous chapter it was pointed out that during the period 1979–83 public expenditure increased from 43.5 per cent to 47 per cent of GDP by 1983. Despite the frequent commitments made by the Government to reduce public expenditure in real terms and as a ratio of national income, it seemed to fail in achieving either of these policy objectives.

Within the context of public expenditure the concept of a 'Thatcher Revolution' could not be sustained. The careful study of public expenditure outcomes when contrasted to policy statements confirms that there is little evidence to support the view that the Government had succeeded in pushing back the frontiers of the State or that it had succeeded in breaking with the post-war commitment to public expenditure programmes. The expenditure commitments on health, education and social services reinforced the view that there had not been a qualitative restructuring of the welfare state or a redefinition of the boundaries between the private and public sectors of the economy. The study of public expenditure suggests that the Thatcher Government was not committed to some predetermined coherent strategy called Thatcherism but, instead, sought to approach decisions on public expenditure through a process of political pragmatism combined with expediency: a process of learning what was both politically feasible and possible. Nigel Lawson (1992) in his recent diaries confirms, for example, Mrs Thatcher's suspicion of the MTFS and her constant opposition to increasing interest rates in line with the MTFS proposals because she felt that interest rates were essential to the political credibility of the Conservative Party with owner-occupiers and mortgage holders. In seeking to reduce public expenditure the policy was in continuity with policies adopted by the previous

Labour Government, and was to reduce resources on programmes that seemed to be the least politically costly to the Government. These included expenditure on the housing capital programme, roads, environment and schools.

The reasons for this incremental approach were twofold. First, a large proportion of senior members of the Government during the period 1979–83 did not share Mrs Thatcher's personal vision of politics or policy, which meant that the conviction politics of Mrs Thatcher could be slowed down. Second, ministers who did share Mrs Thatcher's vision preferred to experiment with policies, ensuring that the Government did not close down on the option of electoral politics. In this sense Mrs Thatcher was as willing as her ministers in trading off her principles for political success. The theme outlined in the previous chapter aimed to show, therefore, that a project called Thatcherism as a coherent strategy did not exist during the period of the first Thatcher Government. However, the ability to win a second and a third election did increase the dominance and autonomy of Mrs Thatcher; and it was the ability to build on initial successes together with Mrs Thatcher's leadership style to which the concept of Thatcherism seems to be more applicable between 1984 and 1990.

The elections of May 1983 and June 1987 both resulted in major Conservative victories, giving Mrs Thatcher respectively a 102-seat and 144-seat majority in the House of Commons. Mrs Thatcher's ability to lead her Party to a second and a third election victory immensely increased her credibility within the Party and amongst Conservative MPs. Electoral success had now made it that much easier for Mrs Thatcher to create Cabinets that were closer to her vision, although some balance had to be maintained between different tensions and traditions within the Party. Mrs Thatcher felt confident enough in 1986, for example, to invite Kenneth Baker, a former supporter of Edward Heath, to become Secretary of State for Education in the full knowledge that Baker favoured increases in the education budget. However, to ensure that the balance between factions was maintained two supporters of Mrs Thatcher's 'Revolution' joined the Government: Nicholas Ridley, who went to the Department of the Environment, and John Moore, who took over at Transport. Peter Walker, who had been a minister during the Heath Government, continued to be in Mrs Thatcher's Cabinet until 1989, even though he had been moved to the margins of policy as Secretary of State for Wales.

In contrast to the first term, between 1983 and 1990 the Government did succeed in reducing public expenditure, both in real terms and as a percentage of national income. The year 1982–3 had been a 'peak' year in terms of growth and expansion. After the election of 1983 the Government again made a commitment to reduce public expenditure, and during this second term it succeeded.

The central message of the Conservative manifesto in 1983 emphasised continuity of policy, which meant the continued commitments to reduce inflation, to control public expenditure and to continue with trade union reform, and reform of the structures of local government and local government finance. In terms of new policies these were mainly directed towards privatisation of nationalised industries, deregulation and competitive tendering for local government services:

> The prospectus in a word was anodyne. It took no risks, canvassed no excitement. And this was a conscious choice. According to one involved in drafting, ministers viewed with distaste the habits of previous governments to make lavish promises and raise false expectations . . . Equally to be avoided were ideas themselves. This was not a period, it seemed, when bold thinking was to be encouraged.
>
> (Young 1990: 330)

This lack of direction to policy provided the Government with a double-edged sword. The absence of pledges in the manifesto meant that the Government had created more autonomy in giving direction to policy. Spending ministers could no longer hold the Chancellor or the Treasury to ransom over explicit commitments made in the manifesto. The Chancellor and the Treasury could impose their priorities over spending ministers. However, the uncertainty over priorities and commitments, rather than reducing conflicts within the Cabinet over expenditure programmes, was likely to increase tensions since there were now no specified priorities between spending programmes, which meant that all expenditure bids had to be treated with equal status. This lack of vision would therefore suggest that the Government tended to drift between 1983 and 1987, very often responding to external events rather than providing a coherent strategy and momentum. The implications for public expenditure during this period were twofold. During the early period the Chancellor and the Treasury were able to take the initiative in bringing public expenditure under control after the apparent failures of the Government between 1979 and 1983. However, the

Government also abandoned its major policy objective, which had been to reduce public expenditure in real terms. The implicit rather than explicit policy objective had changed to one of holding the line on public expenditure, of hoping that the economy would grow faster than the growth rate in public expenditure. Within this context, therefore, the strategy on public expenditure between 1983 and 1987 was mainly related to electoral politics:

> as financial and policy analysts know well, it is the radical reputation which is a mask. The record on public spending speaks for itself, its growth actually accelerated for the first five years of Mrs Thatcher's premiership and even the apparent check over the last twelve months has as much to do with the end of the miners' strike as with any success for cash limits.
>
> (*Financial Times*, 28 December 1985)

Whilst the concepts of Thatcherism and a Thatcher Revolution were associated with commitments to market liberal principles and the rolling back of the State, the reality of policy confirmed the view that the Government was, like previous governments, committed to the continuity of grants and subsidies to specific vested interest groups. The politics of the pig trough and the syndrome of 'what is in it for me' had not changed during the years of the first Thatcher Government. Pressure groups and other vested interests continued to queue for their share of public sector resources. The National Farmers Union (NFU), representing the 100,000 farmers, continued to ensure that its members received subsidies despite Mrs Thatcher's commitments to market principles. Overproduction of food and subsidies to farmers continued despite protestations to the EC over the Common Agricultural Policy (CAP).

Within the context of electoral politics the major concern of the Government was to ensure that the electoral calculus produced a majority vote for the Government, and that involved having to substitute policy principles to the politics and pressures of vested interest groups. In this context Mrs Thatcher was unwilling to support her Chancellor, Nigel Lawson, in phasing out mortgage tax relief, because mortgage payers constituted an influential part of the electorate. Within the principles of a government committed to removing distortions from the market, mortgage tax relief did distort the housing market by reducing the cost of housing, thus leading to overconsumption in housing and inflation. Nigel Lawson preferred to use the tax system to provide incentives. The phasing out of mortgage tax relief would have provided the Chancellor with an extra £7 billion in tax revenues. The only commitment that the Chancellor was able to achieve was that a ceiling of £30,000 would be imposed on mortgage relief.

Equally, Mrs Thatcher very quickly disassociated herself from the proposals of Sir Keith Joseph to replace student grants with loans. Joseph argued that lower income groups were providing a subsidy for the education of the children from higher income groups. However, the pressure from middle-class parents seemed to force Mrs Thatcher to abandon another radical policy and relent to the pressures of another group dependent on a government subsidy. The major pressure groups that did not benefit during the Thatcher years were certain public sector employees, including nurses, doctors and teachers, although others who seemed to be more favoured by the Government, including the armed forces and the police, did receive much better pay settlements.

POLITICS AND PUBLIC EXPENDITURE 1983–7

The politics of the electoral business cycle

The politics of the electoral business cycle points to the following proposals:

(a) that within the electoral cycle governments will seek to do what is unpleasant and unpopular during the early part of the electoral cycle – that is, within the first 18 months after the election. According to this proposal, electors do not judge the performance of the Government over the whole cycle but on events that are closer to the election. The early period therefore is seen as offering the Government a window of opportunity to realise its policy objectives and to adhere to its manifesto commitments. During the first phase, therefore, there seems to be more room for governments to be ideological in their approach to policy.

(b) that during the second half of the cycle the government will seek to produce a congruence of objectives between the political and the economic cycle, which means that trends within the economy have to start pointing in a favourable direction, with unemployment falling, inflation pointing downwards, and living standards and prosperity increasing. During this cycle the Government has some levers to ensure that the cycle becomes favourable; these include public expenditure, taxation and interest rates. During this cycle the Government appears to be less ideological and more consensus seeking, in order to please the majority of the electors, since the aim is to win the forthcoming election.

(c) that within an electoral cycle model the implications for public expenditure are twofold. First, that governments will increase public expenditure prior to an election, and second, that after the election will seek to curb the increases announced in expenditure programmes because of problems of inflation, of overheating the economy and of increasing the Government's borrowing requirement. This means that negotiations on public expenditure would tend to emphasise issues of constraint and reductions during the first two years. However, spending departments will have lost out during the early period and will increase their bids to make up these losses during the second part of the electoral cycle, so that, as the election approaches, programmes that would have been constrained will appear as winners.

The strategy pursued by the Government between 1983 and 1987 has to be considered in the context of the decisions it made between November 1982 and the budget of March 1983, which set the context for the election of June 1983. Within the framework of the electoral business cycle the expectation would be that the Government would have relaxed its macro-economic policy objectives, to allow for reductions in taxation and for increases in public expenditure in an attempt to produce a 'feel good' factor in time for the election. The problem for the Government when re-elected was whether the increases in public expenditure and reductions in taxation would be sustainable over the period of a Parliament.

The politics of the March 1983 Budget

This was the last Budget before the election of June 1983. The proposals outlined in the Budget were all politically highly visible and had immediate effects on the electors. The Government increased personal tax allowances by 14 per cent – much higher than the predicted inflation rate of 6 per cent. Furthermore, there were increases in child benefit to £6.50 per week (an increase of 11 per cent) and a reduction of the national insurance surcharge. The Budget helped to please those Conservative critics who wanted their Government to be more caring. The uprating of child benefit and restoration of cuts in unemployment benefits aimed to show that ministers were listening to all views within the Party and that the Party was therefore not being dogmatic or following any coherent ideology. The Budget was judged also as being reflationary. Although the Government did not announce increases either to the public expenditure total or changes to the PSBR, it had reduced the contingency reserves and allocated these funds to expenditure programmes.

However, the stimulus to the economy had already been provided during the November 1982 Autumn Statement when the Government agreed to increases in public expenditure and allowed sterling to devalue. There had also been a relaxation of monetary policy since 1982, which meant that, together, the measures announced between November 1982 and March 1983 did produce a strategy of reflation. The fall in oil prices in 1982 was seen as likely to lead to increases in world trade as countries had to pay less for primary commodities. Furthermore, the Government of the USA had, despite its large deficit, announced a lowering of interest rates, which resulted in an easing of pressures on sterling. The value of sterling fell by 10 per cent between November 1982 and April 1983. Wage settlements had also fallen by 11 per cent in 1982 and 8 per cent in 1983, thus leading to increased UK competitiveness. Despite the fall in wages there was also an increase in real living standards for those in employment as inflation had fallen faster than the rate of wage settlements.

The forecast after the March 1983 Budget was that in future the Government would have to adopt a deflationary policy. The stimulus given to the economy was seen as exceeding the capacity utilisation of the UK economy. Despite the high levels of unemployment the recession of 1981 and 1982 had led to de-stocking and the closure of capacity in the manufacturing sector, which meant that any stimulus to demand was likely to be met through increased imports and future pressures on the balance of payments and sterling. In this context the March 1983 Budget strategy could be described as being short-term, directed mainly at the election since it was likely that the Government would seek to reduce demand after the election. The fiscal and monetary stimuli were likely to lead to increases in imports and inflationary pressures.

In addition to the economic uncertainties created by the Budget the absence of coherence in the manifesto was also likely to create political uncertainty for the Government. Since the manifesto had not contained any specific commitments, there were tensions between those who wanted to consolidate the achievements of the first term in office and those who argued that the Government had already missed opportunities in its first term. The second electoral victory had opened a new window of opportunity for the Government to embrace more firmly the radical agenda associated with Mrs Thatcher, which was to continue with pushing back the frontiers of the State.

Mrs Thatcher had in September 1982 allowed for the Central Policy Review Staff (CPRS) to present a paper on the future of public expenditure. Based on the assumption that the economy was likely to grow by 1 per cent per annum, the government 'think tank' had pointed out that if government expenditure plans remained unchanged public expenditure would be 6 per cent higher by 1990 than when the Government came to office. The CPRS presented the Cabinet with a series of alternatives that included the charging of fees for higher education, the use of private health insurance to finance the NHS and the non-uprating of social security benefits. These proposals seemed to provide a radical agenda that Mrs Thatcher wanted to be discussed by her Cabinet colleagues. However, some Cabinet ministers, horrified at the proposals, had strategically leaked the news to magazines and newspapers:

> it was this unauthorised act of open government that finally killed the CPRS proposal for a six month study of thinking the unthinkable. The prime minister was furious but chastened . . . Newspapers were briefed to the effect that she (Mrs Thatcher) opposed the Think Tank report and really had nothing to do with it. That was not the case.
>
> (Young 1990: 301)

In 1983, in the immediate aftermath of a second election victory, the concern for some ministers was whether the 'hidden agenda' as outlined in the CPRS report would be resubmitted to the Cabinet. The consolidators included a range of opinions within the Government from John Biffen, who had been made Leader of the House in 1983 and who had been an ardent advocate of monetarism during the years of the Heath Government, and Sir Francis Pym, who had been removed as Secretary of State for Defence in 1983 and had urged the Government to become more caring and interventionist. The concern of the consolidators was mainly the high level of unemployment, which had risen sharply to 3 million in the early 1980s and showed no signs of improving.

Rather than arguing for a change in overall strategy, some Conservatives urged the Government to relax its monetary and public expenditure policies and called instead for increases in infrastructure expenditure as a means of reducing unemployment. There was also some unease about the future of the welfare state. Although there had been widespread support for the privatisation of the nationalised industries, there was now concern whether, under the umbrella of privatisation, Mrs Thatcher would seek to privatise health care or education services. Again, there were demands for the Government to increase child benefit and to govern on behalf of the whole nation.

The 1984 Budget

During his first Budget speech in March 1984 Nigel Lawson seemed to confirm that the Government would continue with its radical strategy:

> This Budget will set the Government's course for this Parliament. There will be no letting up in our determination to defeat inflation. We shall continue the policies that we have followed since 1979. These policies provide the only way to achieve our ultimate objective of stable prices.
>
> (N. Lawson, cited in *Hansard*, 13 March 1984)

The March 1984 Budget aimed to stabilise the growth of public expenditure and to allow for the growth in revenues to be used for reducing government borrowing and reducing taxation. The Budget reinforced the Government's commitment to continue with the Medium Term Financial Strategy. In the MTFS for the period 1983–4 to 1988–9 the Government aimed to reduce the PSBR from a ratio of 3 per cent of GDP in 1983–4 to 1.25 per cent of GDP by the end of the cycle. The Budget also reinforced the Government's commitment to supply side economics; it outlined the phasing out of capital allowances on investment and abolished the national insurance surcharge. Capital allowances were seen as a subsidy to the industrial sector aimed at increasing capital investment at the cost of labour, whilst the national insurance surcharge was seen to increase labour costs. The abolition of capital allowances and the national insurance surcharge were therefore seen as removing distortions from the labour market.

With money supply growth 'exceeding' its target range, the increases in house prices and the weakness of sterling on the foreign exchanges confirmed that the UK Government had relaxed monetary policy. In the meantime, the strengthening of the dollar had put pressures on UK interest rates and sterling. The increase in interest rates in the USA to fund the public sector deficit meant that the dollar rate against the Deutsche mark increased from Dm 1.7 to Dm 2.7, in contrast to the expected rate of about Dm 2.1. The decline of sterling against the dollar meant that the Government had to increase interest rates despite the high rates of UK unemployment.

In early 1984, therefore, the message to the consolidators from the Chancellor was clear. First, he seemed to confirm that the Treasury would continue to make the control of inflation the economic priority for the Government, and that meant continued commitment to the MTFS, which was seen as the Government's major weapon against inflationary expectations. Second, Nigel Lawson aimed to show that his priority was to control the growth of public expenditure and to utilise any growth in the economy to reduce taxation. In this context, Lawson had reinforced the view that he would not use fiscal policies to stimulate the economy but that he would prefer the process of tax incentives and reducing distortions in the market-place to be the means of achieving growth and reducing unemployment. Furthermore he also seemed to suggest that the Government would prioritise reductions in taxation rather than increases in public expenditure.

Mrs Thatcher's commitment to a radical approach to government was reflected in her replies to what she perceived to be the consolidators:

> Some of our critics and fair weather friends would like us to slow down a bit; to take stock; even to let a few sleeping dogs lie. 'Consolidate', they say, 'Forget about radical reform'. No, there are still too many tasks to be done . . . we will continue to be radical . . . I am a more passionate Conservative now than on the day I stepped into No. 10 – and I was pretty passionate then.
>
> (M. Thatcher's speech to the Conservative Women's Annual Conference, February 1985)

The slide in sterling during January 1985 forced the Government to increase interest rates from 12 per cent to 14 per cent, and also reduced the Government's room to manoeuvre in the Budget. The hoped-for fiscal adjustment of £2 billion to be used for tax reductions had become more difficult with increased pressures of inflation. Having just increased interest rates, the Chancellor could not relax on fiscal policy without creating further problems for the financial markets and affecting confidence in sterling. The major concern of the Chancellor therefore was to restore the confidence of financial markets and prevent further pressure on sterling. The PSBR planning for 1984–5, which had been £7.5 billion, had resulted in an out-turn of £10 billion, which reflected the cost of the miners' strike. In his Budget speech the Chancellor argued that the increased PSBR was worthwhile paying for in the long run.

The 1985 Budget

The theme of the 1985 Budget was that this was a Budget for jobs aimed at improving the supply side of the economy. Examples of supply side economics included expanding the Youth Training Scheme for 16- to 17-year-olds from one year to two years – at an estimated cost of £250 million plus £40 million for higher education places directed at engineering and technology. The Government also expanded the community programme for 18- to 24-year-olds who had been unemployed for more than 6 months from 100,000 to 200,000 – at a cost of £400 million. The Government also announced plans for abolishing wages councils for young people and for amending the legislation on dismissal to the minimum of 2 years in employment.

The Autumn Statement of November 1985 represented a further indicator by the Chancellor that the Government was still committed to the strategy of controlling public expenditure and reducing inflation. In his statement the Chancellor confirmed that the objective of the Government was to flatten the growth of public expenditure. The projected total for public expenditure was a fall from 46 per cent of GDP in 1983–4 to 43 per cent by 1987–8. There were no announcements of any major increases in any of the expenditure programmes. However, in the context of increased expenditure, the housing capital programme received an additional £200 million but this must be located in the context of additional bids by Kenneth Baker for £600 million and a Department of the Environment report (DoE) that showed that the housing capital programme required approximately an extra £18.8 billion to meet the cost of housing repairs. The DoE internal report showed that 84 per cent of the country's 4.6 million local authority dwellings were in need of repair.

On health the Government indicated an additional £250 million in 1986–7 and £300 million in 1987–8. This meant that the planned increases outlined in the Autumn Statement of 1984 had been revised upwards from 5.5 per cent to 7 per cent of GDP. The pressures of demographic changes, however, especially the increase in the number of people aged 75 years and over meant that NHS spending had to be increasing by an average of 1 per cent above the inflation rate just to maintain the standard of service. The settlement meant therefore that growth in the NHS budget was only just sufficient to keep spending in line with inflation.

The Autumn settlement also showed that the social security budget had received the lowest increases. The uprating of benefits was limited to a 1 per cent increase as the Government changed its uprating review from November to April. Increases in pensions, for example, meant an additional 40p for a single person and 60p for a married couple per week; child benefit was increased by 7p per week.

There were no new resources announced for education despite the teachers' pay settlement, which had been above that estimated by the Government, who, furthermore, had planned to reduce the education capital programme. The Department of Education budget of £14.2 billion represented an increase of £210 million, or about 5.8 per cent over the previous expenditure White Paper. This represented a shortfall of £500 million for local authorities in meeting the teachers' pay settlements. In the meantime, the budget allocation for universities of £1.41 billion represented a 1.6 per cent decline in real terms.

The overall message for spending ministers was that increased expenditure did not necessarily improve the quality of services and that in future years ministers had to ensure value for money in improving the quality of public services. In seeking to improve efficiency the Government could claim that within the social security budget there had been major increases in productivity as the ratio of claimants to staff increased from 75 to 1 in 1979 to 119 to 1 in 1986. The plan was to extend this productivity gain to 130 to 1 by 1989.

The Autumn Statement, however, did not seem to clarify the principles for fiscal and monetary policy and the impact of the public expenditure plans on the economy. The additional revenues coming to the Government as a result of asset sales meant that, despite the rhetoric of the Autumn Statement, the Government was aiming at a fiscal stimulus of the economy. The privatisation of British Telecom had brought an additional £1.7 billion of revenue to the Treasury in 1985, whilst the planned sales of British Gas (estimated at £6 billion), British Airways and Rolls-Royce Engines were likely to bring an extra £4.75 billion to the Treasury for each year between 1986 and 1989. Since the Government had not aimed to use asset sales to reduce the PSBR, it seemed that it was planning to either increase public expenditure or reduce taxation in future years.

The public expenditure cycle July–October 1986

The June 1987 election

Despite protestations for additional resources the final settlements for public expenditure between 1983 and 1985 reflected the ascendancy of the Treasury over spending ministers. The disagreements and tensions that had characterised the years between 1980 and 1982 had been replaced by a new consensus during the Government's second term. Mrs Thatcher was able to promote Cabinet ministers who were more likely to agree with her vision of the public sector. However, as an election period started to get closer the public expenditure cycle also started to reflect dilemmas and contradictions for the Government, with some senior ministers arguing that the Government had to be more caring about the quality of life whilst others wanted the Government to give priority to tax reductions and personal choice.

In responding to this dilemma John Biffen suggested that within the Cabinet Mrs Thatcher needed to produce a 'balanced ticket' of consolidators and radicals, between supporters of less government and reduced taxation and those who favoured increased government expenditure. Francis Pym and Michael Heseltine produced strategies to increase expenditure on the infrastructure to reduce unemployment. Their priority was to increase public expenditure and to forgo reductions in taxation as the best means to reducing unemployment. Nicholas Ridley attacked the balanced ticket approach arguing that

> The Media and the Public Spending Brigade have interpreted it [the balanced ticket] to mean higher public spending. The flood gates are opened. But I must warn taxpayers that this balanced ticket includes a large surcharge which they will have to pay for.
>
> (N. Ridley, cited in *Hansard*, 20 May 1986)

Opinion polls during the early part of 1986 continued to show the Conservative Party in third place behind Labour and the Liberal/Social Democratic Alliance. The May 1986 local elections resulted in Conservative Party losses of a total of 764 seats, in contrast to Labour gains of 571 seats and Liberal/SDP gains of 386 seats. The Conservative Party also lost the safe constituency of Ryedale in North Yorkshire – a previous Conservative majority of 16,000. In the aftermath of these elections Francis Pym saw his chance to launch

Conservative Centre Forward, which aimed to produce new thinking on economic and social issues. Pym saw this initiative as an attempt to bring together the One Nation group of Conservatives and those Conservatives disenchanted with Mrs Thatcher's leadership.

These tensions were reflected in the public expenditure cycle as ministers sought to increase their additional bids by £4.7 billion above the planned targets announced in the previous Autumn Statement. The Cabinet reshuffle of May 1986 moved Kenneth Baker to take over education from Sir Keith Joseph. Baker was replaced by Nicholas Ridley at the Department of the Environment. Kenneth Baker had already submitted additional bids of £3 billion for housing and the environment. In the meantime the HMI report of May 1986 had emphasised the deterioration of school building because of reductions in capital expenditure, and had estimated a cost of £2 billion in the schools repairs programme. In 1986 education was perceived to be a major failure for Mrs Thatcher. Kenneth Baker had been appointed in the hope that he could make education a major electoral asset for the Conservative Party. The proposals to reform education, as unveiled during the 1987 election and the subsequent Education Reform Act, 1988, were seen as major achievements for both Mr Baker and Mrs Thatcher.

Inside the Conservative Party in Parliament the debate between quality of services and tax cuts became more intense as members felt that the forthcoming Autumn Statement was likely to be the last before a general election. In the end, the Autumn Statement of November 1986 represented major increases in public expenditure – and was judged as a major attempt to boost the Government's position for the forthcoming election. The areas for additional expenditure included education, social security, housing and health, a total which represented an additional £10 billion of new expenditures – £7.5 billion for the year 1987–8, the last year before election. Increases in expenditure also included £4 billion to local government to finance the teachers' pay settlement. However, in outlining his expenditure plans the Chancellor, Nigel Lawson, also warned:

> But before referring to some of the more important changes let me make one thing absolutely clear. There can be no question of allowing the projected increase in public expenditure over the next two years to undermine the prudence of the government's fiscal stance. The government's fiscal stance has been clearly set out in the

Medium Term Financial Strategy at the time of the last budget. There will be no relaxation of that stance.

(N. Lawson, cited in *Hansard*, 6 November 1986)

The aims of this statement were twofold. First, the Chancellor sought to assure the markets that the additional increases were temporary and that the Government was not slipping back into Keynesian ways. The Government was still very much committed to the MTFS and, therefore, an economic policy conducted within the context of tight monetary policy. The additional increases were planned only for a two-year period. Second, the Chancellor aimed to show Conservative MPs that the Government cared about public services and that although the Treasury was seen as giving way to pressures on the expenditure cycle it still aimed to maintain control over public expenditure.·

Samuel Brittan commented that the Autumn Statement of 1986 confirmed that 'Mrs Thatcher has abandoned her attempt not even to cut public spending but to hold it stable. She should explain her 'U' Turn to the Nation' (S. Brittan, *Financial Times*, 10 November 1986).

Mrs Thatcher seemed to respond to Samuel Brittan's challenge, although indirectly, in an interview with the same newspaper a month later:

We have got higher public expenditure than we would have wished. In so far as money has been spent, it is not available for tax relief. When we get that higher expenditure, as we have, then the only thing that I can do is what we did in 1981 – ensure that it is soundly financed.

(M. Thatcher, *Financial Times*, 12 December 1986)

Both the announced expenditures outlined in the Autumn Statement and Mrs Thatcher's interview reinforced the view that the Treasury and the Prime Minister had lost their battle during the expenditure cycle of 1986. As Mrs Thatcher seemed to admit, she had ended up with a higher level of expenditure than that she had wanted, but she now warned her Cabinet colleagues that she would repeat what she had done in the 1981 Budget. During the 1980 public expenditure settlement Mrs Thatcher had experienced a similar setback at the expense of spending ministers. However, during the Budget of March 1981 the Chancellor and the Treasury had reasserted their position by not increasing tax thresholds or reducing social security payments. In her *Financial Times* interview of December 1986 Mrs Thatcher seemed to be suggesting that the Budget of March 1987 would not be used to reduce taxes but, rather, to reduce the PSBR: 'The attitude which I have towards spending your money as the Prime Minister is the attitude I got from being in small business. I ask myself would I do this if it were my own money' (M. Thatcher, speech at Finchley, 18 February 1987).

At one level, therefore, the Autumn Statement seemed to generate a debate about the coherence of Thatcherism and whether the additional increases in public expenditure signalled a break with the commitment to push back the frontiers of government. At a second level, however, the concern was the political dimension and the extent to which the plans for public expenditure reflected the Government's political priorities in readiness for an early election in 1987. The Conservative Government had been perceived as uncaring towards issues of social concern, including health and education, and in this respect the additional resources announced seemed to be a response to its critics.

In the meantime the Labour Party had found the additional increases in public expenditure difficult to criticise, although the additional expenditures were judged as being part of the Government's electoral cycle. Neil Kinnock, leader of the Labour Party, suggested that:

> They will try to persuade everyone that the butchers have become healers and the wreckers builders . . . that they are going to spend on health and education and housing, that recovery is on its way. But after seven years of saying 'they can't afford it' this last-minute splash will be treated with contempt.
>
> (Neil Kinnock, speech at Knowsley bye-election,
> 7 November 1986)

The Autumn Statement of November 1986 pointed to the truth of the axiom that winning elections was always likely to be more important for governments than any adherence to some single set of principles. In the preparation for the March 1987 Budget, one insider to the Budget process commented that the Budget was 'as if his [Mr Lawson's] Christmases and birthdays have come at once and that the economic indicators during the preparations for the March 1987 Budget had presented Mr Lawson with the opportunity to redeem a clutch of IOUs to the Conservative Party; a series of pledges which had been outlined in the Manifesto between 1979 and 1983 but thwarted during the first period in office could now be realised' (*Financial Times*, 12 March 1987).

The strategy pursued during the previous three years had allowed the Chancellor a fiscal adjustment of £5 billion, which he could now utilise to reduce taxation or increase expenditure on certain programmes, or both. The buoyancy of revenues brought in through increases in VAT and through higher levels in consumer spending meant that the Chancellor could point to the Budget as representing the fruits of good economic management, that the supply side economics of the Government had been successful.

Despite the options available the Chancellor produced a prudent Budget – reducing taxation from 29 per cent to 27 per cent but also reducing the PSBR by £3 billion. There was also a 1 per cent reduction in interest rates. The Budget was described as being built on success and built for success. In one sense therefore, the Budget reflected Mrs Thatcher's promise after the Autumn Statement of 1986, when she had lost the battle over public expenditure. Rather than using fiscal adjustment to reduce taxation, the Chancellor had used £3 billion to reduce the PSBR.

The increases in public expenditure announced in the Autumn Statement, together with the reductions in personal taxation announced in the March 1988 Budget, meant that the Chancellor had provided a major stimulus to the economy in 1988. The question was whether the expansion could be sustained in the long term, or would the historic problems of the balance of payments and inflation again be major obstacles to economic prosperity? In addition to the fiscal stimulus, the Chancellor together with the finance ministers of the Group of Seven had agreed at the Louvre summit in November 1987 to co-ordinate monetary policy and reduce interest rates as part of a common response to the stock market crash. The received wisdom had been that the sharp fall in share prices was likely to lead to a decline in personal wealth, consumer confidence and expenditure. In agreement with the Group of Seven the Chancellor had reduced UK interest rates. However, during the early part of 1988 indicators seemed to confirm that the forecast of the November crash had been overstated and that the reduction in interest rates was likely to lead to an expansion of the money supply.

The economic landscape in June 1988 had changed when contrasted to that of November 1987. The problem was no longer of a decline in consumer confidence; now the concern of the Government was in dealing with a consumer boom that was leading to new pressures on inflation and the balance of payments. In July 1988 the forecast for the balance of payments was £12 billion, whilst inflation was rising at 6 per cent per annum. In the meantime the Chancellor had increased interest rates from 7 per cent to 12 per cent in his attempt to constrain demand. The increase in interest rates was seen as having an immediate effect on mortgage holders, since interest rates were likely to increase the cost of housing, thus leading to a fall in consumer demand. The question was whether or not the reliance on interest rates was likely to be sufficient to deal with the expansion of consumer credit, since the deregulation of financial markets in 1986 had resulted in the expansion of credit facilities.

THE RECORD ON PUBLIC EXPENDITURE 1979–90

Whilst in the previous sections the aim was to outline the events that influenced the public expenditure process, the problem remains of explaining the gap between the objectives and claims discussed in policy statements such as the Autumn Statement and the Budget and the actual out-turns for public expenditure. Whilst the Autumn Statement includes the Government's proposals for public expenditure, governments do not have complete control over the expenditure process. Despite the many attempts by the Conservative Government throughout the 1980s to bring local government expenditure under control, it found itself increasing the settlements to local authorities by at least £1 billion per annum, either because the Government had underestimated the cost of services or because local authorities had increased expenditures. Equally, the Government continued to underestimate the increases in unemployment and therefore the costs to the exchequer. Whilst politically it is always better for the Government to underestimate increases in unemployment than to admit that unemployment is increasing, in terms of planning for public expenditure this is likely to result in the Government using the contingency fund to deal with the unforeseen increases in unemployment.

Within the context of Autumn Statements and Budgets the Government continued to underline its commitment to the control of public expenditure. The process of how the Government sought to achieve its objective still needs explaining. The framework outlined in this section therefore seeks to explore the process of how the Government combined the rhetoric of policy statements with the reality of expenditure out-turns. The discussion on the actual expenditure out-turns seeks to provide a framework for analysing the

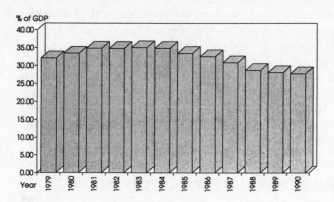

Figure 8.1 Total expenditure 1979–90

Government's record at three levels. First, an attempt is made to assess the aggregate changes in expenditure, where expenditure on programmes is assessed as a whole and then disaggregated by economic category into capital expenditure, current expenditure and transfer payments. Second, expenditure is related to actual spending programmes. Third, programmes themselves are disaggregated by economic category.

The record on aggregate expenditures

The study of the Government's expenditure in Figure 8.1 shows that between 1979 and 1983 total expenditure continued to increase from 32.5 per cent of GDP in 1979 to 35.1 per cent in 1983, when the growth in expenditure reached a peak. Since 1983 expenditure has continued to fall annually, so that between 1984 and 1990 expenditure fell from 34 per cent to 28 per cent of GDP. At one level therefore, the record on expenditure out-turns seems to confirm the view that the Government did achieve the policy objective of reducing public expenditure as a ratio of national income.

The analysis of the data in Figure 8.2 comparing year-on-year changes tends to indicate that through the period 1979–90 there were only two years, namely 1980 and 1981, when there were major additions to expenditures. For the remaining years the Government managed to hold expenditure constant, as in 1982, 1983 and 1984, and actually managed to reduce expenditure annually from 1985.

The two studies would suggest that the Government did achieve the policy objective of reducing total expenditure as a ratio of national

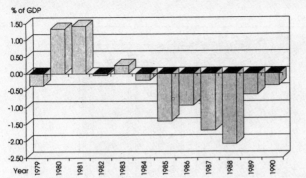

Figure 8.2 Total expenditure, year-on-year changes 1979–90

income especially between 1985 and 1988. Since 1988 the levels of reductions have been of a lower magnitude.

The disaggregation by economic category is examined on the following pages.

Total current expenditure 1979–90

The study in Figure 8.3 shows that in 1979 current expenditure consumed 17 per cent of GDP and that by 1983 this had increased to 18 per cent of GDP. The trend in the changes for current expenditure corresponds to that for total expenditure. Current expenditure fell from 18 per cent in 1984 to 14.5 per cent in 1990. The ability of the Government to control and reduce total expenditure can therefore be attributed to the Government's approach to current expenditure. Since over 80 per cent of current expenditure represents the costs of producing a service, that is, the inclusion of wage costs in the public sector and the costs of purchasing goods and services, the control of current expenditure continues to be crucial to governments.

The year-on-year changes as outlined in Figure 8.4 confirm the degree to which the Government was able to control current expenditure and the degree to which the success of the control of current expenditure contributed to the control of total expenditure. As Figure 8.4 confirms, expenditure only increased in 1980 and 1981, similar to the trend in total expenditure. Since 1981 expenditure continued to fall on an annual basis, with major reductions being achieved in 1985, 1986 and 1987.

Throughout the period of the 1980s the Government did not attempt to secure a declared incomes policy, especially after the failed

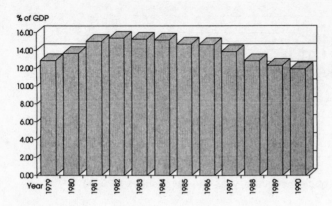

Figure 8.3 Current expenditure 1979–90

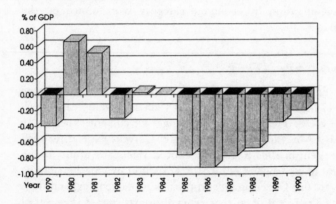

Figure 8.4 Current expenditure, year-on-year changes 1979–90

attempts of the Heath Government and Labour's Winter of Discontent. There was no official policy on incomes in the public sector. However, the discipline of cash-limited expenditure programmes and the controls imposed by central government on local government finance ensured restraint in public sector wage settlements. Throughout the period, public sector pay settlements tended to lag behind those in the private sector, whilst unlike the previous period there was no 'catching-up' factor by public sector workers. Changes in industrial relations and trade union law contributed to a shift in the landscape, resulting in a steep decline in militancy and days lost at work through strike action.

Since 1979 about 50 per cent of public enterprises have been privatised. Some 650,000 employees who were once working for the public sector were employed in private sector owned companies by 1992. Contracting out of services, including refuse collection and hospital domestic cleaning, resulted in a reduction of 20 per cent in costs as public sector employees found themselves threatened by job losses and lower wages in the context of competitive labour markets and local authorities aiming to secure efficiency and value for money (Ramanadhan 1989, Veljanovski 1987). In addition, government legislation on competitive tendering for local government services imposed constraints on local authorities; local authority employees were forced to revise their wage costs before being able to secure tenders. However, despite these major changes trade union density within the public sector remained relatively stable when compared to the 21 per cent decline in overall trade union membership between 1979 and 1992.

Government capital formation

In 1979 total capital expenditure amounted to 2 per cent of GDP (see Figure 8.5). Capital expenditure had already deteriorated during the period of the Labour Government. In 1973 capital expenditure stood at 4 per cent of GDP, but by 1978 it had fallen to 2.2 per cent, and by 1979 to 2 per cent. Between 1979 and 1988 expenditure fell from 2 per cent to 0.9 per cent in 1988, although there were some increases in 1989 and 1990. Capital expenditure in 1990 had increased to 1.4 per cent of GDP.

The study of the year-on-year changes in Figure 8.6 confirms the extent to which the Government imposed limits on capital expenditure. Over the last 12 years there have only been three years of increases to capital expenditure – 1983, 1989 and 1990.

The record on capital expenditure points to the neglect of infrastructure expenditure by UK Governments since the middle of the 1970s. Both Labour and Conservative Governments tended to use the capital expenditure programmes as the means to restrain public expenditure growth. Investment in public sector infrastructure, whether on hospital buildings, school repairs, roads or railways, was reduced over the last two decades as governments came under pressure to reduce public expenditure. There has been no attempt to analyse the different impacts of expenditure on the economy, as both capital and current expenditures have tended to be treated as aggregates by

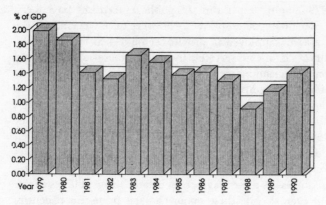

Figure 8.5 Capital expenditure 1979–90

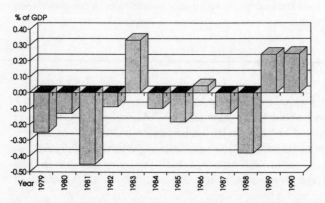

Figure 8.6 Capital expenditure, year-on-year changes 1979–90

the Treasury in its attempt to persuade spending ministers to lower their spending bids.

The golden rule on public expenditure, which is recognised within the context of the German expenditure cycle, seems to be missing in the UK public expenditure cycle. Expenditure directed towards public sector investment in Germany is treated differently to current expenditure. The German Government finances additional increases in investment expenditure through increases in government borrowing. The golden rule allows the Government to borrow in relation to the amount it spends on capital formation. By contrast, the attempts by UK Governments to reduce the PSBR from 9 per cent of GDP in 1978 to 4.5 per cent in 1981 were mainly achieved by reducing capital expenditure.

Rather than arguing that capital expenditure could be used as the automatic stabiliser during the 1981 recession, the Thatcher Government actually reduced capital expenditure further. Between 1979 and 1982 capital expenditure declined from 2 per cent to 1.3 per cent. In the meantime, unemployment during the same period increased from 1.4 million in 1979 to 3.2 million in 1983. The Thatcher Government responded to the recession by reducing the high levels of the PSBR, which they had inherited from the Labour Government, and reducing capital expenditure.

In the context of responding to the recession of the 1990s, therefore, the Conservative Government under the leadership of John Major has responded differently. Whilst Nigel Lawson in 1988 could boast a public sector surplus of £14 billion, by 1991 that surplus had been reduced to a PSBR of £7 billion, with a forecast of £28 billion in 1992, and of £37 billion in 1993. Under John Major the language of 'automatic stabilisers' has again become acceptable as the Government has sought to make its case for increasing public sector borrowing in response to the recession.

Transfer payments

This category of expenditure includes personal grants directed at individuals, including pensions, child benefits, social security and unemployment benefits. It also includes the grants and subsidies that government allocates to specific industries, including agriculture, and grants that are directed to specific regions of the UK. Most of the expenditure, however, is influenced by what is termed demand-led expenditure, since expenditures tend to change in relation to factors that are perceived to be beyond the immediate control of the Government. Changes in demography and in the number of pensioners result in changes in expenditure on pensions, whilst changes in the levels of unemployment also affect the costs of unemployment benefit and social security payments.

The record as outlined in Figure 8.7 indicates that between 1979 and 1983 expenditure increased from 13 per cent of GDP in 1979 to 15.3 per cent of GDP in 1983. As indicated above, during this period unemployment increased sharply. Since 1983 expenditure has continued to fall, reaching 14 per cent in 1987 and 12 per cent in 1990. Unemployment in 1984 peaked at 3.2 million and continued to decline up to 1990, when it had fallen to 1.6 million. The year-on-year changes (Figure 8.8) confirm that expenditure increased during the years of

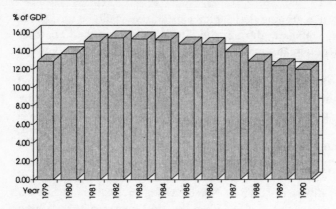

Figure 8.7 Transfer payments 1979–90

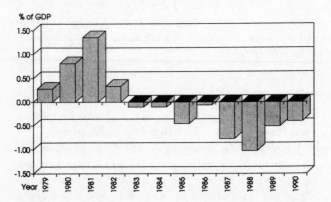

Figure 8.8 Transfer payments, year-on-year changes 1979–90

recession in 1980 and 1981 but then continued to fall every year from 1982, with major reductions being achieved in 1987 and 1988.

During the period of the Thatcher Government the commitment has been to revise changes in benefits in line with the inflation out-turns over the previous year. This represented a reversal from the previous Labour Government's policy, which had been to review social security benefits in relation to changes in earnings.

Whilst the majority of transfer payments were demand-determined, in the sense that changes in expenditure tended to reflect the economic cycle, the ability of the Government to control transfer payments also reflected its political decision to relate benefits to the rate of inflation. As the Government succeeded in curbing inflationary pressures, so it became less expensive for the Treasury and the Government to finance increases in pensions and supplementary benefits.

As earnings from employment continued to expand over the period, the income of those on fixed earnings remained tied to the level of inflation. Since the Government limited itself to protecting the purchasing power of social security benefits, this meant that those dependent on benefits tended to participate less as consumer citizens.

CONCLUSIONS

Whilst the Government could claim that it had abandoned Keynesian fine tuning of the economy, this did not mean that it had surrendered its ability to ensure a correspondence between the political and the economic cycle. Like its predecessors, the Government did attempt to manipulate the economy to improve its electoral opportunities. The difference was that instead of using fiscal policy the Government utilised interest rates. The policy of high interest rates to deal with inflation, which had been implemented during the period 1980–1 was relaxed, despite the overshoot in monetary targets after 1982. Lower interest rates reduced the costs of mortgages and helped to increase consumer and voter confidence in time for the 1983 election, even though the policy indicated by the MTFS would have suggested that interest rates should have increased in the context of an increase in monetary growth. However, the immediate threat of inflation caused by the stimulus during the 1983 election soon forced Mr Lawson, in July 1983, to announce an emergency package of £1 billion in expenditure cuts in order to claw back the Government's pre-election generosity.

In his Mansion House Speech of October 1985, the Chancellor of the Exchequer, Nigel Lawson, announced that he would suspend sterling M3 as the monetary target and that he would look at other broad monetary aggregates including M0. Sterling M3 seemed to be beyond the control of the Government, and any attempt to bring sterling back inside the path announced in the MTFS would have resulted in a steep increase in interest rates. Lawson had shifted his anti-inflation strategy from the control of the money to the control of the exchange rate by shadowing the Deutsche mark. The growth in the money supply was accompanied by a weakening of sterling on the exchange rates, so that between 1984 and 1985 the Government found itself increasing interest rates in an attempt to increase confidence in sterling and in the credibility of the Government's ability to reduce inflationary expectations.

Furthermore, it must also be noted that whilst the framework of the MTFS had produced paths for the growth of sterling the actual out-turn for the money supply had continued to outstrip the target. Between 1980 and 1986 the target for sterling M3 would have been 34 per cent. In contrast, the actual out-turn showed that sterling M3 had increased by 65 per cent and yet, despite this overshoot in the money supply, inflation had continued to fall from a peak of 20 per cent in 1980 to 6 per cent in 1985. Nigel Lawson, who has been described as a pragmatist in the conduct of economic policy, abandoned his adherence to any single monetary target. In addition, fiscal policy was less tight between 1983 and 1987, despite the steep decrease in the PSBR from 4 per cent of GDP in 1983 to 1.25 per cent in 1987. The Chancellor utilised the proceeds of privatisation as a sizeable stimulus to the economy without having to resort to the conventional Keynesian techniques of taxation and public expenditure. From 1985, in his attempt to shadow the Deutsche mark, the Chancellor also helped to engineer a major devaluation of sterling without creating a crisis of confidence in the financial markets.

In contrast to the early years of the Thatcher Government, public expenditure after 1983 was successfully brought under control. The commitment to reduce public expenditure as a ratio of GDP was a success as public expenditure fell from 45 per cent of GDP in 1983–4 to 43 per cent in 1986–7, and to 40 per cent in 1989–90. In his Autumn Statement of November 1988 Nigel Lawson pointed to the success of the Government's policy:

> public expenditure this year will be less than 40 per cent of national income – the first time this has happened for over 20 years. Not so long ago the share of national income spent by the state seemed to rise inexorably. Over the past six years that trend has been decisively reversed. Since 1982–83 public expenditure excluding privatisation proceeds expressed as a percentage of national income has fallen by 7 percentage points – the largest and the longest sustained fall since the wartime economy was unwound.
>
> (N. Lawson, cited in *Hansard*, 1 November 1988)

However, the commitment to reduce public expenditure as a ratio of GDP reflected a major shift in government policy when contrasted to the original objective outlined in the MTFS in March 1980, which had committed the Government to reducing public expenditure in real terms. After six years of this commitment it would seem that by 1986 the Government had changed its objective from reducing public expenditure in real terms to 'a best hope to hold the line', which in other words meant an objective that indicated a policy of controlling the rate of growth rather than of restructuring. The objectives in public expenditure had undergone a series of changes from that announced in conjunction with the MTFS in 1980. Whilst in 1980 the policy objective was to reduce public expenditure in real terms, which meant spending less on expenditure programmes, by 1982 the objective had changed to holding public expenditure constant, and finally to outlining the objective that expenditure should fall as a ratio of national income.

The policy objective to reduce public expenditure as a ratio of GDP did create new problems for both spending departments and the Treasury. First, there was the problem associated with the economic cycle, in that during a downturn in the cycle, as GDP fell and unemployment increased, the ratio of General Government Expenditure (GGE) to GDP was likely to increase faster, which meant that the Government was losing its battle in the control of public expenditure. During a recession, rather than the Government increasing public expenditure to counter the cycle it found itself reducing public expenditure further. Second, the comparison of GGE with GDP did not amount to measuring like with like. Areas of public expenditure including pensions and transfer payments were included in the GGE but not in GDP, which meant that the GGE was higher than estimated. Transfer payments make up some 18 per cent of total public expenditure. The policy objective also increased the problem of brutalisation by aggregation identified by Heclo and Wildavksy in 1983. Expressing public expenditure as a ratio of GDP does not allow for a rational evaluation of different expenditure programmes on the economy. There is therefore little reason to evaluate the impact of capital expenditure as compared to current expenditure on the macro economy. Furthermore, there is an assumption that holding public expenditure constant is a desirable objective because it allows for growth in private consumption since this is preferred to public consumption. According to Johnson (1991):

> The result was to starve public services and infrastructure of resources at a time when they might have been expected to share in, and contribute to, the expansion of the private sector. The curbs on public expenditure made the UK a country of private affluence and public squalor.
>
> (Johnson 1991: 105)

In the aftermath of the 1987 election victory the Conservative Party was very buoyant. Nigel Lawson had been able to achieve the triple objectives of reducing taxation, increasing public expenditure and reducing government borrowing. Decisions made in 1987 had long-term effects for the Conservative Government in its third term. Mrs Thatcher seemed to be invincible and was already guaranteed a fourth term of office. She had declared she was ready to go on, on and on. The Conservative Party was always about 10 to 15 points ahead of the Labour Party between 1987 and 1988 in opinion polls, yet in 1990 the Conservatives had dropped to 28 per cent with Labour showing a 20 point lead over the Conservative Party. There was a loss of correspondence between the political and economic cycle, as the Government seemed to be unable to provide the 'feel good' factor, as in 1983 and 1987. Decisions made by the Chancellor in the Autumn Statement of 1987 and the Budget of 1988, which included increasing public spending, and reducing interest rates and taxation when the economy was already growing too fast, had by 1989 forced the Government to increase interest rates. The economy had been growing by 4 per cent in 1987 and 5 per cent in 1988 – a rate of growth which seemed to be unsustainable in the longer term. Unemployment levels had decreased sharply from 3.3 million in 1987 to 1.6 million in 1990.

The Conservative Party in 1989 seemed to be moving towards the concept of 'a time for change', indicating that the challenges of the 1990s for the Party were not going to be similar to those of the 1980s. The debate of the 1990s was no longer going to be about defining the boundaries between the private and the public sector. The Government had already won that debate in the 1980s, and the achievements of privatisation were not likely to be eroded. Instead, Kenneth Clarke argued:

> It is probably more important for our society that British hospitals and British schools should be the best in the world than it is that British factories, British steel works and coal mines and British banks should be world leaders . . . Third term Conservatism is neither wet nor dry. The great changes of economic and industrial policy and the great battles over them are now behind us.
>
> (Kenneth Clarke, speech to the Conservative Party Conference, 5 October 1989)

Kenneth Clarke urged the Conservative Party to remain radical by generating new ideas on the effectiveness and efficiency of public services. The future challenge for a Conservative Government would be how to commit itself to the provision of high-quality public services that were responsive to the needs of the consumer. The public services had to be depoliticised by changes in the management of schools, from local authorities to governing bodies and grant maintained schools, whilst health care needed the expansion of trust hospitals and the decentralising of budgets to doctors. These changes meant shifting the provision of services to the consumer and away from the vested interests of pressure groups, professionals and bureaucrats. These themes were central to the Conservative Party manifesto in the election of 1992.

Chapter 9

Politics and public expenditure in the 1990s: the years of the new pragmatism

INTRODUCTION

The concern of this chapter is to provide a framework for analysing the processes of public expenditure decisions during the 1990s. Although any attempt to provide a forecast as to the likely outcome of such decisions would be a hazardous occupation, nevertheless there are lessons to be learned from the past that can at least be used as signposts to the future. The study of public expenditure for the 1970s and 1980s raises issues that will continue to have an influence on public expenditure. In the preceding chapters it was suggested that public expenditure outcomes were influenced by two factors: the process of continuity and the dimension of politics and choice. Changes in public expenditure reflected not only the durability of some expenditure programmes but also the day-to-day political process and the autonomy of governments to bring about change. Public expenditure was described as a process reflecting events that could be perceived as being not within the immediate sphere of government.

At one level this study has sought to suggest that, since the early 1970s, irrespective of government, there has been a common approach to public expenditure. The question is whether those factors that influenced public expenditure decisions in the 1970s and 1980s would continue to shape expenditure decisions during the next decade. During the last two decades resources for the public sector were mainly influenced by the economic context. After 1975, the view that the public sector was crowding out the private sector had become the shared paradigm for both Labour and Conservative Governments and included the argument that public expenditure and government borrowing had contributed to inflation. Within this context, therefore, public expenditure as an instrument of fiscal policy was in retreat as governments concentrated on the curbing of inflation through monetary policy and controlling public expenditure. The role of public expenditure as an instrument of fiscal policy was downgraded as was the view that governments could fine-tune the economy through marginal changes in fiscal policy.

The first part of this chapter deals with the theme of continuity in the era of John Major as both Chancellor and Prime Minister, and asks whether it would be feasible to argue that his Government represents a continuation with the past or whether it represents a break with the Thatcher years. The concerns here are twofold: first, there is a need to evaluate the impact of the Major Government on public expenditure. It shall be argued that whilst John Major, when he first became Chancellor in 1989, argued for continuity with the policy strategy of Mrs Thatcher and the outgoing Chancellor, Nigel Lawson, this policy had already been reversed in the Autumn Statement of 1990 when Mrs Thatcher was still Prime Minister and John Major had presented his second Autumn Statement. It would seem that by November 1990 'politics' had returned to public expenditure, with spending ministers showing resistance and winning additional bids for their spending departments. Second, it shall be argued that the Major Government has in a limited sense broken with the economic strategy of the Thatcher era. The move from a surplus on the PSBR to forecasts of a £40 billion deficit in 1993–4 confirms the degree to which the Major Government has been willing to use public expenditure as part of its macro economic strategy.

PUBLIC EXPENDITURE AND THE CHALLENGES OF THE 1990s

The emphasis on continuity

Mr Major, in unveiling his first Autumn Statement in 1989 as Chancellor, emphasised his commitment to the continuity of the previous Chancellor's strategy on expenditure policy, that is the reduction of public expenditure as a percentage of national income and to aim for a balanced budget. The central aim of the Government since 1987 had been to ensure that the rate of growth in public expenditure would be slower than that for the economy as a whole. The objective of reducing taxation in future years depended on the Government's ability to control public expenditure. Nigel Lawson as Chancellor had outlined a Conservative commitment to reduce personal taxation to 20 per cent. If this was to be achieved the Government had to find ways of reducing its expenditure commitments.

The Autumn Statement of 1989 reinforced the new Chancellor's commitment to the control of inflation by maintaining interest rates as high as was necessary until inflation had been brought under control. Nigel Lawson in the March 1989 Budget had maintained a tight fiscal policy despite the forecasts of a budget surplus of £14 billion. The aim was to dampen down demand inflation. In the Budget Lawson had also argued for continuity in improving the supply side of the economy and had reduced national insurance contributions, mainly targeted at low income groups, as part of the Government's commitment to improve incentives in the labour market.

John Major pointed out in his Autumn Statement that tight control of public expenditure would continue to be a central element in the Government's economic strategy. Public expenditure had fallen sharply as a ratio of national income, which had made possible the reduction in taxation and improved the Government's finances. Public expenditure as a ratio of GDP had fallen from 47 per cent in 1983 to 38.5 per cent in 1988 and was forecast to fall further in 1992 and 1993:

> Mr Speaker, tight control of public expenditure remains a central element of the Government's economic strategy. The ratio of public expenditure was nearly 47 per cent in 1982–83. In the current year it is likely to be 38.5 per cent . . . By 1992–93 the ratio is expected to fall further to its lowest levels since the mid 1960s.
>
> (J. Major, speech to the House of Commons, 16 November 1989)

The re-emergence of a politics of public expenditure and the Autumn Statement of November 1990

During the Budget of March 1990 John Major as Chancellor again emphasised that central to the Government's economic strategy was the control of inflation, and that the Government would continue to maintain high interest rates for as long as was necessary. He also planned to maintain a tight fiscal policy by outlining the Government's planning for a deficit of £2 billion. The Chancellor argued that the Government's attempt to repay some of the national debt had been a great achievement:

> For decades successive governments had spent more than they were prepared to raise honestly from taxation and made up the shortfall

by borrowing . . . Over the past 10 years we have reversed that trend; and in the last three we have repaid £25bn . . . As a result of the debt repayments we are saving over £2.5bn a year in debt interest. That is sufficient to meet the annual cost of around 150 district hospitals.

(J. Major, speech to the House of Commons, 20 March 1990)

However, the plan for a £2 billion public sector deficit could also be perceived as a form of loosening of fiscal policy when contrasted to the previous Budget, which had planned for a surplus of £7 billion. Even taking into account the decline in income generated from privatisation, John Major could still have planned for a surplus of £2 billion – instead he was planning for a deficit of £2 billion in 1990–1 and £5 billion in 1991–2. So, despite his acknowledgement of the benefits of a budget surplus, Major's first Budget was actually aiming at a budget deficit. Furthermore, rather than seeking to claw back the overspend by local authorities he seemed to be accommodating the overspend into the budget deficit. The *Financial Times*, at the time of the Budget, was able to predict that

Given the pressures on the public purse from his colleagues at the departments of the Environment, Transport, Education and Health, it seems clear that public spending rounds this Summer and Autumn will be among the toughest the Treasury has faced since the Government won power in 1979.

(*Financial Times*, 21 March 1991)

As the *Financial Times* had accurately predicted, the public expenditure round of the summer and autumn 1990 proved very difficult. The Autumn Statement of November 1990 was presented in different languages to different audiences: first, it was presented in the language of prudent government, that it was a tough settlement aimed at the financial markets; second, it also aimed to appease MPs by saying that 'billions' had been made available to offset the effects of inflation on social security, health and transport.

The annual bargain to settle the additional expenditure bids had been the most difficult since the early 1980s, when Mrs Thatcher was still working with a Cabinet that she had inherited. Now, in the 1990 'bilaterals', there seemed again to be disagreements on the relationships between the economy and public expenditure priorities. The disagreements on spending targets reflected the tensions between ministers who were concerned with the politics of public expenditure and the principled position adopted by the Treasury, which was to maintain a tight control on new expenditure bids.

Chris Patten, then Secretary of State at the Department of the Environment, had pointed to new problems over the poll tax and had argued for an extra £3 billion spending to limit the political damage of high poll tax bills. Although the Treasury did accede to these demands, it was believed that Patten had traded off the new bids for local government against those costed in the Environmental Green Paper. Patten was seen as having won on the poll tax but was not expected to win on everything. He was criticised by environmental groups for not keeping to the commitments outlined in the Green Paper *Our Common Inheritance*, where he had argued for new environmental protection agencies.

Additionally, pressures on social security caused by higher than expected inflation had increased the cost of uprating benefits by £2.3 billion. The higher than expected increase in the rate of unemployment cost £800 million. UK inflation, announced on 12 October 1990, had reached 10.9 per cent, which meant that the Government had to uprate benefits in line with the September figures for inflation. The Treasury had, however, only suggested a 6 per cent inflation, which meant that new expenditures of £2 billion had to be met in April 1991.

John McGregor, when Secretary of State for Education, had also submitted additional bids for new expenditures on education, arguing that the education reform legislation could not be carried out effectively without new resources. Additional resources were required to meet the new capitation costs of the new curriculum, and for retraining teachers and increasing their pay as a means of recovering teachers' morale. Rhodes Boyson, the Conservative MP, criticised McGregor's demands for new expenditures, arguing that it was the educational bureaucracy at Whitehall and in local government that was the major obstacle to the educational reforms. Boyson seemed to favour the break-up of national agreements on teachers' pay and suggested that the Government should encourage local governing bodies to take responsibility for teachers' pay and conditions. McGregor was seen by members of the No Turning Back Group 'as having gone native and being captured by the education establishment'.

McGregor was the last to settle with the Treasury and seemed to have received an extra £700 million in additional bids in exchange for changing his position on the assessments for seven-year-olds. He had previously accepted the National Curriculum Council advice that the tests for seven-year-olds were not appropriate. In Cabinet it would seem that McGregor came under immense pressure from Mrs Thatcher and Kenneth Baker, who saw the education reforms as being diluted. Furthermore, McGregor also seemed hesitant, in his speech to the Conservative Party Conference in October 1990, on extending the concept of vouchers from training to education, arguing instead that the legislation on education reform – the introduction of grant maintained schools and local management of schools (LMS) – was sufficient and that these reforms should be consolidated. The tensions between Mrs Thatcher and her education minister seemed to go further when, in her closing speech to the Party Conference, she went out of her way to mention the introduction of vouchers by the Training Enterprise Councils (TECs) and said she hoped that vouchers would be introduced within education.

The final area of tension during the expenditure round was related to the uprating of child benefit. The Conservative Government during the previous four years had frozen child benefit, arguing that its aim was to target benefit to those in need and that the social security reforms of 1984, which included family credit and income support, were now redirecting income to families in need. Child benefit in 1990 had re-emerged as an issue with many Conservative MPs, who argued for its uprating. The Treasury increased child benefit by £1 per week – but only for the first child – during the negotiations in Brighton. It seemed that Angela Rumbold, the Women's Affairs Minister, had managed to win an important concession. By contrast, the No Turning Back Group had argued that child benefit, as a 'universal' benefit, should be abolished.

The last-minute bargaining on public expenditure carried out during the Conservative Party Conference indicated the degree to which public expenditure was becoming more political for the Party. Disagreements within the Cabinet seemed to be returning to the intensity of the period 1981–2, when many spending ministers were in open rebellion against the Prime Minister and the Chancellor. In October 1990 the same problems seemed to be returning to Mrs Thatcher's Cabinet.

Further pressure came from the Treasury and Civil Service Committee Report of November 1990, chaired by Terence Higgins, who pointed out that the UK economy was then 'finely' poised between shallow and deep recession. The Committee recommended that in the case of deep recession the Government had to utilise fiscal policy to stimulate the economy, including public expenditure and taxation changes, whilst staying loyal to the conditions laid down on ERM entry. The Government was criticised from within the Conservative Party for allowing interest rates to remain high for too long and for having surrendered sovereignty over monetary policy by agreeing that sterling should enter the EMS.

The resignation statements by Nigel Lawson, the former Chancellor, and Sir Geoffrey Howe confirmed that Mrs Thatcher had opposed ERM entry on the basis that this was likely to surrender the UK Government's sovereignty on economic policy. The criticism over loss of Parliamentary sovereignty in the conduct of economic policy tended to equate sovereignty with political sovereignty and the ability of the Government to utilise short-term economic measures to improve their electoral performance rather than the longer-term performance of the economy. The decision to enter the ERM in October 1990 had reduced the 'political' autonomy of the Government.

The Conservative Party in November 1990 could be perceived as the Party that was still trying to find an identity for its fourth term of office as the Government. The concepts of a 'cleaner', 'greener', 'safer' Britain, which had been articulated by Chris Patten, seemed to indicate increased intervention by the Government on environment issues, whilst the demands for additional spending by Kenneth Clarke at health and John McGregor at education also reinforced the view that spending ministers were reasserting their position as defenders of public services. In contrast, the No Turning Back Group of MPs were demanding continuity with the principles of the 'Thatcher Revolution' to continue to 'dismantle the remnants of the welfare state' by encouraging the private funding of health and education. This group of MPs argued that the Government should make its priority the cutting of the basic rate of tax to 15 per cent to allow people to purchase private insurance. Other options included the use of privatisation sales to finance welfare, and the privatisation of coal and railways. The One Nation Group, in contrast, emphasised that the boundaries of the public and private had been sufficiently redefined; it was now time to improve the services the Government provided.

The break with the past and the Autumn Statement of 1991

With hindsight, it now seems that the tensions that erupted within the Cabinet during the expenditure round of October 1990 overspilled into the leadership re-election in November 1990, when Mrs Thatcher was eventually forced to resign on the advice of her Cabinet colleagues.

The Autumn Statement of November 1991 was the last before the general election in 1992. It aimed to please a range of demands that were sometimes in conflict with each other. The confirmation by the Government to allow the PSBR to rise by £8 billion in 1992 was judged by the City as being better than expected, although for some commentators the increase in the PSBR did seem to represent the end of prudent government and the end of the Thatcher era. On previous forecasts it seemed that the Government was planning for a £20 billion deficit as a result of pressures for increased expenditures, so the outcome of £8 billion was actually much lower than expected. The Statement was also an attempt to persuade Conservative MPs that the Government was taking seriously increased public concern about public services, but was at the same time designed to reassure financial markets that this was not indicating a pre-election spending spree.

The Autumn Statement continued with the trend started by Norman Lamont in his first Budget, in March 1991, when he had announced that he would increase the PSBR for 1991–2 to £8 billion and for 1992–3 to £12 billion. Now in his Autumn Statement he had extended the PSBR further to £12 billion for 1991–2 and £20 billion for 1992–3.

Norman Lamont, however, set out to reject any arguments that suggested that the Autumn Statement represented a break with the commitment to reduce public expenditure as a ratio of GDP and to maintain a balanced budget. In the Autumn Statement of the previous year the Chancellor had made a commitment to continue to reduce public expenditure as a ratio of GDP, and had planned that as a ratio of 38 per cent. In the new Statement the ratio had been revised upwards to 42 per cent. Equally, in the previous Statement the Chancellor had planned for a deficit of £2 billion; now the deficit had also been revised upwards, to £12 billion. However, the Chancellor also emphasised that the new increases in expenditure for 1992–3 were an attempt to 'allow the automatic stabilisers to function', which seemed to indicate that both the increases in the PSBR and in the totals for public expenditure represented only a temporary response to the economic cycle:

> In the Autumn Statement we added £5.5bn to the planning total for 1992–93, but the great bulk of this increase, some £4–£5bn, can be attributed to the effects of the cycle. The ratio in 1992–93 will rise to 42 per cent. But it is still well below its level following the recession in the early 1980s when Mrs Thatcher was Prime Minister.

> (N. Lamont, cited in the *Financial Times*, 31 December 1991)

However, a more careful reading of the Autumn Statement confirmed the degree to which the Government had committed itself to expenditures that were not pro-cyclical. An additional £2.3 billion was allotted to the health programme as part of the Prime Minister's commitment to a high-quality health service, whilst education received an additional 8.6 per cent of new expenditure that was to be concentrated on school buildings and higher education. The Autumn Statement of November 1991 had added £11 billion of new spending for the period from 1992–3 to 1995–6, which put a limit on Conservative ambitions for further tax cuts – especially the pledge to reduce personal taxation to 20 per cent. Furthermore, despite the Chancellor's protestations that the bulk of the additional expenditures were inescapable, most of the increases had been pre-election 'discretionary' spending. The only inescapable expenditures were the cost of the unexpected increases in unemployment and the uprating of social security benefits in line with inflation, which made up some £2 billion of the £11 billion additional spending. The additional resources announced for health, education and transport all represented politically highly sensitive expenditures that set the framework for the debate in the election of April 1992.

The dilemma for the Government was that the likely slowdown in growth and the planned increases in the PSBR meant that there would be less options for reducing taxation, which does seem to indicate a shift from Mrs Thatcher's ideological commitment to lower public spending and lower personal taxation. The Autumn Statement was also anti-Thatcher in that the Government also announced additional subsidies to the railway network by forecasting an increase of 12.7 per cent of additional resources to the transport programme.

POLITICS AND THE CONSERVATIVE PARTY IN THE 1990s

Despite the election victory of April 1992, the Conservative Party still seems to be unable to resolve its crisis of identity. Since the departure of Mrs Thatcher in November 1990 there have been continuing tensions between those within the Party who associate the success of the Conservative Party with the ideas and policies articulated by Mrs Thatcher and those within the Party who want to emphasise the more pragmatic and caring aspects of John Major's leadership and government policy. One dimension of this tension that is likely to continue is between Conservatives who would like the Party to move closer to the views of the social market as articulated by the Christian Democratic parties in Europe and those who would like the Party to remain committed to policies introduced during the years of the Thatcher Governments.

It would be difficult to sustain a view that suggests that these tensions are a reflection of the arguments that emerged between market liberals and One Nation Conservatives during the 1970s. The debate on the Maastricht Treaty and the UK's approach to the future of Europe shows how this divide no longer holds in the 1990s. Those Conservatives who are committed to the politics of Thatcherism and associate themselves with market liberalism have continued to oppose the ERM because they argue that this would be an obstacle to UK parliamentary sovereignty in the conduct of economic policy. The decision therefore to leave the ERM in September 1992 was hailed as a victory by the pro-Thatcher Conservatives. They now believe that the Government can revert to what they describe as the 'successful' policies of the Thatcher years. Pro-Thatcher Conservatives favour a return to the control of the money supply, tight public expenditure controls and low interest rates – policies that they see as being good for Britain. The ERM, they argue, represents an 'interventionist' attempt to control exchange rates when exchange rates are best decided in the market-place. This group of Conservatives therefore supported Chancellor Lamont's view that leaving the ERM was good for Britain and that re-entry would only be considered when the times and conditions were right.

The argument of the Euro-sceptics is that the UK Government had surrendered its autonomy to manage interest rates and the exchange rate inside the ERM. However, one major criticism by market liberals during the 1970s on the conduct of economic policy was that the Government had used politics in the conduct of economic policy, which in turn had been harmful to the UK economy. The UK Government, they argued, had used public sector borrowing to increase public expenditure without increasing taxation, which had led to increases in the money supply and inflation. What was needed, according to market liberals, was less of a 'political' approach in the conduct of economic policy. They advocated that this approach needed to be replaced by a constitutional approach based on announced rules and procedures. The MTFS at one level therefore represented the attempt to conduct monetary policy according to predetermined rules. The rules for the conduct of monetary policy provided the means for gaining the confidence of the electorate about future inflation expectations. Market liberals argued for an independent central bank, free from political intervention, which in turn meant joining the ERM and Britain obeying the rules of the German Bundesbank, which is the independent central bank.

The decision by the UK Government to enter the ERM in November 1990 had only the reluctant support of Mrs Thatcher. Since Mrs Thatcher's departure others have argued that the EMS has obstructed the UK Government's ability to intervene in the economy. This group, which in the Cabinet now includes Peter Lilley, Michael Portillo and Michael Howard, is opposed to Britain's re-entry into the ERM and is also reluctant to accept the move towards an independent central bank and a constitutional approach in the conduct of economic policy.

In contrast, the pro-Europe Conservatives, who have been inclined to be more supportive of more interventionist economic policies and the social market, have been supportive of an EMU and independent central bank. Edward Heath is committed to a more caring One Nation Conservatism and yet is also committed to the EMU, even though this would mean less autonomy for the UK Government to produce interventionist policies.

The removal of Mrs Thatcher as Prime Minister in November 1990 by Conservative MPs, and her replacement by the then Chancellor of the Exchequer, John Major, could be perceived as confirming the shift of the politics of market liberalism towards a pragmatic approach to government. Mrs Thatcher had become associated with a 'Thatcher Revolution', the politics of Thatcherism, and a commitment to the rolling back of the State. She was still wholly committed to the process of introducing markets to public services, including health and education. In her conference speech to the Conservative Party in October 1990 Mrs Thatcher had indicated her commitment to the extension of vouchers in education and the continuation with the policies of introducing market ethics to more areas of the public sector. In contrast, John Major has emphasised his commitment to high-quality public services within the context of a market-orientated approach to economic policy. Mr Major, in his campaign to become Prime Minister after Mrs Thatcher's resignation, signalled his commitment to the National Health Service and public sector education as being central to his vision of creating a society of opportunity. During his period in office child benefit has been uprated twice and a commitment has been made to relate changes in child benefit to changes in inflation. John Major has also maintained his commitment to a National Health Service and to create what he calls 'a society which is at ease with itself'.

The Budgets of 1991 and 1992 together with the recent Autumn Statements have reinforced the view that the John Major Government is making a break with the Thatcher era. The Budgets confirmed the break with the Budgets of the Thatcher decade by attempting to be both more redistributive to lower income groups and more expansionary. The March 1991 Budget shifted the burden away from the poll tax towards VAT by increasing VAT from 15 per cent to 17.5 per cent, thus reducing the poll tax by over £100 for every individual, whilst the Budget of March 1992 introduced a lower tax rate of 20 per cent. The introduction of the council tax, which replaced the poll tax in April 1993, was related to property values rather than to being a tax on individuals. The Government has continued to extend national insurance contributions on company cars and petrol excise duties. Budgets in 1991 and 1992 also increased child benefits and benefits for unemployed families with children, and also announced the ending of the higher rate on mortgage tax relief.

The Autumn Statement of November 1992 emphasised the Government's willingness to increase the PSBR further, to £37 billion in 1993–4, in response to the impact of the recession. The attempt to redirect additions in public expenditure to capital expenditure projects, including housing construction, new railway projects and road building, indicates the acknowledgement by the Chancellor that it was feasible for the Government to utilise the levers of fiscal policy in times of recession.

The policy responses to the economic recession of the 1990s have been different to the polices pursued in the recession of the early 1980s. Instead of adding to public expenditure and the PSBR during the recession of 1981 and 1982, Sir Geoffrey Howe, the Chancellor of the Exchequer, announced further reductions in public expenditure together with a commitment to continue to reduce both public expenditure and the PSBR as a percentage of national income. The PSBR of 9 per cent of GDP, inherited from the previous Labour Government, had been blamed for being the major cause of UK inflation and high interest rates. Between 1980 and 1983 the Thatcher Government reduced the PSBR to 4 per cent of GDP despite an increase in unemployment to 3 million. In addition, the Government could claim that in 1987 it had managed to balance the budget and had also started to pay back some of the national debt. In both the 1987 and 1988 Budgets Nigel Lawson, the Chancellor of the Exchequer, had planned for a budget surplus of £14 billion in each year. It is therefore within the context of the Thatcher Government's response to the pressures of recession, together with the approach adopted on public expenditure, that the recent Autumn Statements are perceived to have been a break with Thatcherism:

> An Autumn Statement which added £11bn to departmental spending programmes and predicted growth of 2.5 per cent next year appeared to mark a decisive break by Mr John Major with the policies of the previous prime minister. Whilst Mr Lamont stressed that much of the spending was an unavoidable response to the recession, colleagues said that the outcome of the spending round demonstrated that Mrs Margaret Thatcher's ideological commitment to lower public spending had given way to political pragmatism.
>
> (*Financial Times*, 7 November 1991)

Can a new politics be discerned in the era of John Major as Prime Minister, and what are the implications for public expenditure? Whilst John Major seeks continuously to reinforce the view that he takes a pragmatic approach to policy: competing factions within the Conservative Party and their willingness to show dissent have tended to make life more difficult for the Major Government in this fourth Conservative term. The Government no longer has majorities of over 100; its majority now is 18 MPs. For the One Nation Conservatives, the election of John Major as leader of the Party and as Prime Minister is seen as reflecting a return to the Modern Conservatism associated with Ian Macleod, which sought to combine a commitment to a free market approach in economic policy together with a caring commitment to public services.

In contrast, market liberals argue that Mr Major is the successor to Mrs Thatcher and that he would not seek to undo the principles of the Thatcher Revolution, but would rather consolidate those achievements. His concern to introduce a Citizens' Charter in the public services confirms his commitment to ensuring that the present reforms in health and education are made to work. The revolution in the public sector, according to market liberals, has gone far, and now is the time to ensure that the reforms are implemented and secured. Market liberals argue that John Major would not return to the politics of Edward Heath, of seeking to appease professional and trade union interests in the public sector. Major's objective will continue to be that of breaking up monopolies and the bureaucracy and making services more responsive to the individual citizen, an objective that was, after all, central to the Thatcher era.

In one sense, therefore, the Autumn Statement of November 1992 reflects the attempt by the Prime Minister to seek to bring together these factions to support a common policy. The commitment to increase expenditure on construction projects is pleasing to those who would like to see a more interventionist approach by the Government. The recognition by the Government of the necessity of a policy on incomes in the public sector, together with exhortations for the private sector to follow the Government's example, is seen as a vindication of Edward Heath's approach in the early 1970s to dealing with inflation whilst seeking to reduce unemployment. In contrast, the commitment to reducing the PSBR over the cycle together with the emphasis on reducing interest rates and maintaining control over the money supply are perceived as a return to monetarist ideas.

THE UK ECONOMIC RECESSION SINCE 1990

Public expenditure decisions during the early 1980s were made in the context of a deepening recession. Unemployment between 1979 and 1982 increased sharply from 1.3 million in October 1979 to 3 million in October 1982. The reductions in public expenditure together with the increase in interest rates resulted in an overvalued sterling against the dollar and a fall in export markets. The Government in the meantime maintained its commitment to reduce public expenditure as a ratio of national income whilst giving more priority to reductions in personal taxation. The recession of the 1990s does raise the question of whether parallels can be drawn between the two recessions. Can the present recession also be attributed to policies of high interest rates, high sterling and tight fiscal policy? Between 1989 and 1992 unemployment increased from 1.7 million to 2.9 million. Inflation fell from 15 per cent to 3.7 per cent, whilst interest rates declined from 14 per cent to 8 per cent.

During the 1980s the experience of the British economy was similar to that of the 1970s. The policies of 'stop–go', which were supposed to have influenced economic policy in the 1970s, were also the policies of the 1980s despite the commitment of the Thatcher Government to the Medium Term Financial Strategy. The MTFS as outlined by the Chancellor in 1980 announced the paths for monetary growth, government borrowing and inflation. The adherence to the MTFS indicated that the Government would not become involved in mini

Budgets to fine-tune the economy, nor would it be tempted to utilise the electoral cycle as the means to conduct economic policy. Economic policy objectives had been established for the medium term. Despite its commitments to monetary targets, the Government found that changes in the money supply were constantly overshooting the announced target ranges without the Government increasing interest rates.

The UK experienced negative growth in the early 1980s to a growth of 4 per cent per annum in 1987 and 1988. The sterling exchange against the dollar also fluctuated widely from near parity in 1982 to between $2 and $1.80 in the late 1980s. Interest rates also fluctuated from a peak of 15 per cent in 1981 to 8 per cent in 1986 and back to 14 per cent in 1988.

Instead of fiscal policy to fine-tune the economy, the Government relied on interest rates, the exchange rate and taxation as a means of ensuring that there was a congruence between the economic cycle and the electoral cycle. The Thatcher Government allowed sterling to devalue by 25 per cent during its period in office as part of its strategy to improve UK competitiveness. Prior to the elections of 1983 and 1987 the Government allowed interest rates to fall and reduced personal taxation. After the 1987 election, despite the forecast that growth was likely to be unsustainable, the Chancellor, Nigel Lawson, again reduced personal taxation and interest rates. This gave an extra £6 billion boost to demand, which eventually led to the increase in interest rates in 1988 and the present recession.

The monetary context

Although the UK is now outside the new discipline of the ERM this does not mean that the UK Government has complete autonomy in making decisions on interest rates and the exchange rate; whether the policy is made explicit or remains implicit the Government will continue to have a policy for sterling. This means that UK interest rates will remain high whilst interest rates in Germany and other EC countries stay high.

The problem of rising unemployment and continued recession means that there are pressures on the Government to continue to reduce interest rates and allow sterling to devalue to help exports and growth. The question is whether the UK can go for growth alone when other countries are also in recession, and when the German Bundesbank is opposed to reducing interest rates. The pressure is therefore likely to increase on the UK Government to introduce a series of mini Budgets to fine-tune the economy, one example of which has been the Government's recent measures to increase expenditure on capital projects and the re-nationalising of 20,000 houses in an attempt to revive the housing market. The argument that the Government still has room to adjust its fiscal stance, either by increasing public expenditure or by reducing the rate of taxes such as VAT, indicates the extent to which Conservative MPs now seem to be less doctrinaire and more willing to resort to some form of Keynesian reflation.

The problem of consumer confidence

The second question is where the growth in the economy is likely to come from. Consumer demand has been falling sharply, which has also resulted in a fall in investment, especially in the housing construction, furniture and white goods industries. There has also been a sharp decline in car production. The UK growth rates of 2.3 per cent per annum over the last decade were achieved mainly through high levels of personal consumption, which grew at 2.4 per cent per annum. Despite the recent reductions in interest rates there seems to be a reluctance by consumers to be involved in the same levels of borrowing as in the credit explosion of the 1980s. The recent experience of high interest rates has meant that consumers are now involved in repaying their debts and increasing their savings ratio. The Autumn Statement of 1992 confirmed that the Government was still dependent on a consumer-led recovery. The emphasis on public expenditure control and reduced interest rates suggests that the Government hoped that with low inflation and low interest rates consumer confidence would return.

Despite continual reductions in interest rates in the USA, there seems to be at present no return to consumer confidence. The USA, like the UK, went through a period of dis-savings and an expansion of consumer credit. At present consumers in both countries seem to be saying 'once bitten, twice shy' – the increases in interest rates and the cost of borrowing after 1989 seemed to have taught consumers a lesson which they do not at present want to forget. The election of the Clinton administration seems to indicate the start of a turning point in American politics: a break with the politics of markets and a move towards more interventionist government.

Keynes did in an indirect way point to the ineffectiveness of using interest rates to influence demand when he argued that you could take a horse to water but you could not make it drink. The fall in interest rates will not necessarily increase consumer confidence nor is it likely to influence investment decisions, since the latter seem to depend on that same consumer confidence. Consumers are themselves dependent on the economic context – they are also employees dependent on stable employment and rising wages. With unemployment rising and becoming a threat to those in work it is less likely that people will take on new debt if they feel their jobs are vulnerable.

The UK system of industrial relations

A third problem concerns the issue of wage bargaining and how UK employees respond to the discipline of moderating their wage demands now that the UK has left the ERM. Whilst the country was inside the ERM, UK employees came under increased pressures to reduce their unit labour costs to match those of their European counterparts. To a limited extent this policy was successful as wage settlements continued to fall in manufacturing; however, the rate of growth was still higher than that of other European competitors. The question is, whether the UK outside the ERM has an anti-inflation strategy and a system of industrial relations that will allow for wages to be determined nationally, similar to the model developed in Germany. During the years of the Thatcher Government the objective was to move towards decentralised bargains and shift from the tripartitism that had developed during the years of the Heath Government and Labour's Social Contract.

The attempt by the Thatcher Government to break with what was seen as corporatist politics corresponded with its strategy on public expenditure. Whilst the major objective of the Government was to reduce public expenditure it could not continue with either the concept of the Social Contract of the Labour Government or with the tripartite structures of the Heath Government, since built into those structures were commitments to higher public expenditure. Mr Heath's U-turns had been the result of both employer and trade union pressure on his Government to increase subsidies and grants to industries, school meals, pensions and education. In contrast, Labour's Social Contract had been founded on price controls, food subsidies and subsidies to the nationalised industries, pensions and public sector pay. The Thatcher Governments were committed to a break with government being dependent on interest group politics.

Trade union legislation during the 1980s was aimed at reducing trade union influence in wage bargaining, and at creating a more flexible labour market that could respond to changes in the external climate without the Government having to resort to making bargains with interest groups. The role of government was to give leadership and to govern on behalf of the individual citizen, and not to be dependent on pressure group politics. The Thatcher Governments rejected the concept of social partnerships between government, trade unions and employers.

In the context of the 1990s, the question arises whether the UK system of decentralised bargaining will continue to be seen as a major achievement of the Thatcher years or whether the system will be seen as the major obstacle to economic prosperity. The attempt by John Major to provide strict guidelines for public sector pay does suggest that the Government is not willing to allow local pay bargains, at least in the public sector.

THE EMERGING POLITICAL CONSENSUS AND THE 1990s

Finally, there is the question of whether the changes emerging at both the economic and social levels are likely to produce a new political consensus for the 1990s. The extent to which both the Conservative Party and the Labour Party were implicitly in agreement on the future boundary between the public and the private sector during the April 1992 election confirms the extent to which the Labour Party has shifted from previous pledges in its approach to the public sector, and the degree to which John Major has come to accept the core principles of the welfare state. The Labour Party's approach to public expenditure was enshrined in its Policy Review Document *Looking to the Future*, which stated,

> Sustained and balanced economic growth makes the scope for public spending greater. But it must be clear at the outset that advance towards our objectives will necessarily depend on achieving that growth. We will not spend, nor will we promise to spend, more than Britain can afford.
>
> (Labour Party 1990: 8)

The argument that the reforms of the public sector initiated by the Government since 1979 represent the new framework of politics for the 1990s is obviously speculative. However, there are indicators that seem to suggest that the arguments for the 1990s will not relate to issues of boundaries but to the quality of public services. In seeking to provide an outline of the political consensus for the 1990s it can be pointed out that the Labour Party does not seek to challenge the essentials of the Thatcher reforms of the public sector. The Labour Party in the 1992 election confirmed its commitment to the principles of the Education Reform Act, 1988, although Labour would continue to argue the case that more resources are needed to make the reforms more effective. Local management of schools will remain, as will the devolved budgets to schools by local authorities. The new universities and colleges will retain their independence from local government, whilst competitive tendering for local services will also be retained. The re-election of a Conservative Government for a fourth term makes the re-national-isation of utilities more unlikely, although the Labour Party might argue in the future that more powers need to be devolved to the regulators, including OFGAS and OFTEL, to supervise the pricing policies in gas, electricity and telecommunications and to expand the rights of the consumer.

Although both the major political parties place competing emphases on which expenditure programmes to prioritise, there seems to be a blurring of ideas on the future role of public services. The Labour Party is now committed to issues of economy, efficiency and effectiveness in the public sector. Labour's approach points to a pragmatic approach on the services government should provide. Equally, its commitment to new resources for the public sector seems to be dependent on the future prospects of the economy.

The Conservative Party under the leadership of John Major seems to be shifting away from a Thatcherite approach to public services and towards a more caring public sector that offers high-quality services. The commitment to a Citizens' Charter for health and education reflects the Prime Minister's thinking on how to make education, health and transport more accountable to the consumer. Whilst the Government is committed to the privatisation of the coal industry and railways, the boundaries between the private and public sectors are likely to be consolidated, with a Conservative Government planning to redirect about 40 per cent of national income to the public sector for the foreseeable future. The Labour Party is equally committed to a Citizens' Charter, which seems to confirm the degree to which Labour has shifted from being the party that represents the interests of public sector employees towards providing public services that are more orientated to the consumer.

The attempt to provide a politics of public expenditure for the 1990s needs an understanding not only of the social and economic contexts but also the political dimension. Governments will always have a degree of political choice in the making of public policy and how they respond to external events. However, the question of how governments will in the future respond to these challenges depends on the extent to which a new political settlement is created. In the 1990s, European Community policies will have an increasing effect on the UK. The recent announcements in the Autumn Statement of November 1992 together with the attempt to provide an EC approach to fiscal policy indicate the degree to which governments are again becoming interested in the use of short-term fiscal policies to deal with economic issues. The implication is that the UK Government will move away from the concept of the Medium Term Financial Strategy towards the theme of mini Budgets and fiscal fine-tuning, similar to the strategies of the 1970s. It could also be argued that the discourse on social and environmental issues will have more of a European dimension, with UK employees comparing themselves more on issues of rights to their European counterparts, for example, in the areas of pensions, training, maternity leave and education. Equally, the UK Government will also have to adhere increasingly to European regulations on issues related to the environment; UK environmental groups are also looking to the European Courts to change UK policy. The question of how the UK Government is likely to respond to these issues depends on whether a new political settlement does emerge to deal with these challenges.

The climate for public expenditure decisions in the 1990s is qualitatively different from that of the 1970s and 1980s. During the previous two decades there was a general acceptance by both governments and electors that the levels of taxation had reached saturation point, whilst at the same time there was a disillusionment with government itself. The paradigm of the 1970s was that liberal democracy itself was in crisis. The welfare state had created a stalemate state, pluralist stagnation and political paralysis as functional groups competed with each other for increased resources. Governments and political parties had increased voter expectations of what governments could do, yet the claims made on governments had also resulted in the overload of the political system.

Despite frequent attempts to move the UK towards a process of social partnerships, both the Heath Government in 1974 and the Labour Government in 1979 were defeated by the trade unions, who saw their major objective as the protection of their members' interests. The post-war settlement, which had committed UK Governments to full employment and the welfare state, had resulted in the 1970s with governments being unable to produce a coherent policy to deal with inflation and economic stagnation.

CONCLUSIONS

The election of the Thatcher Government in 1979 confirmed a window of opportunity for an electorate willing a government to break with the past. The trade union reforms of the 1980s were accepted with the minimum of struggle from the trade unions themselves when compared to the mobilisation against the Trade Union Act, 1972. The Thatcher Government won the elections in 1983 and 1987 despite the fact that unemployment had peaked at 3 million. An unemployment rate of 1 million had been seen as being politically unacceptable during the years of the Heath Government.

The Thatcher Governments announced reductions in public expenditures. The moratorium on public sector housing imposed after 1983 meant that council house building per annum fell from a peak of 160,000 in 1975 to 20,000 a year in 1990, whilst the right to buy policies increased owner occupation from 60 per cent of the population in 1979 to 72 per cent in 1990. Housing expenditure was reduced from 1.4 per cent of GDP in 1979 to 0.4 per cent of GDP in 1990. Reductions in education expenditure also meant that the Government was spending less on education as a ratio of GDP; education expenditure fell from 5 per cent of GDP in 1979 to 4.4 per cent in 1990, whilst health care expenditure stayed relatively stable, falling from 4.8 per cent of GDP in 1979 to 4.6 per cent in 1990. The Government also de-nationalised all the major utilities except for coal and railways, and used most of the proceeds to reduce the PSBR and personal taxation. The UK PSBR fell from a ratio of 4 per cent of GDP in 1979 to a positive balance in 1989, whilst the basic rate of income tax was reduced from 33 per cent to 25 per cent. The higher rate of income tax was reduced from 83 per cent to 40 per cent. However, despite the Government commitment to supply side economics, the total tax burden actually increased from 34 per cent in 1979 to 36.7 per cent in 1990.

By 1990 the Thatcher Revolution had come to an end. The policies that were seen as being appropriate for the 1980s were no longer acceptable in the 1990s. Many Conservative MPs in 1990 had been sufficiently convinced that the Party was on the verge of losing the next election to remove Mrs Thatcher from the leadership of the Party. Mrs Thatcher still seemed committed to continuing with her revolution by introducing further privatisation to health and education. Whilst the electors had supported the privatisation of gas and British Telecom, they seemed unhappy about proposals to privatise health care and the possibility of introducing charges for health services. The prospect of introducing fees for treatment in the place of the National Health Service, which had been free at the point of delivery, became a major political issue. Voters seemed to have reached a new saturation level concerning further privatisation of the welfare state. The Conservative Party in 1990 was therefore on the defensive, arguing that the Government did not intend to privatise health care. The eventual resignation of Mrs Thatcher and her replacement by John Major seemed to signal the Conservative Party's acceptance that the 1990s would require a different approach.

During the years of the Thatcher Government there was a restructuring of the welfare state in terms of both the ethos and the resourcing of public services. The restructuring of services provided by local government has resulted in a qualitative break with the ethics of public sector administration as developed in the post-war period. The shift towards competitive tendering for local services means that local authorities are no longer monopoly producers of services; instead, local authority managers are now concerned with the setting up of contracts for private companies and adjusting to the role of a client–contractor relationship. The move towards devolved budgets and local management of schools means that local authorities have lost their education budget to local schools, where the head teacher and governors are now taking responsibility for the managing of the school budget. In health, the Griffiths proposals of 1987, to introduce internal markets, and the reforms of 1989 mean that health professionals will be increasingly asked to become the managers of budgets. In the meantime the Government has also managed to reduce social expenditure from 32 per cent of GDP in 1979 to 28 per cent of GDP in 1990. Social expenditure in 1990 was lower than in 1962.

The decisions by the Major Government to allow the PSBR to expand and to allow public expenditure to rise as a ratio of GDP do represent a break with the Thatcher Governments since 1983, where the central aim had been to reduce public expenditure in relation to national income. Total public expenditure fell continuously from 44 per cent of GDP in 1983 to 39 per cent in 1990. The Thatcher Government had planned for expenditure to continue falling in the 1990s. Under the recent plans expenditure is forecast to rise to 42 per cent in the 1990s, and is likely to remain at that level for the foreseeable future. The likelihood is that expenditure levels will actually increase beyond the levels indicated by the Government.

The issue of whether or not John Major reflects the beginnings of a new political consensus for the 1990s is still open to question. At present it is difficult to separate the new pragmatism about the public sector from the pressures of the electoral cycle. The increases in public expenditure on health and education reflect political expediency and the electoral pressures of the 1992 election. However, the decisions to protect capital expenditure programmes whilst allowing the PSBR to increase also confirm a break with the Thatcher era in the sense that John Major and the Cabinet seem to be committed at least to some form of 'reluctant' Keynesianism.

The question of whether or not a political consensus similar to that of the 1960s is likely to re-emerge is difficult to predict. The debates between Roy (now Lord) Jenkins when Chancellor and Ian Macleod, the Conservative Shadow Chancellor, always tended to be on issues related to the outcomes of public expenditure decisions and whether or not the Government was using public sector resources effectively. There was no attempt to redefine the boundaries between the private and the public sectors. The Conservative Party was equally committed to the NHS being funded from taxation and also to the financing of public sector utilities. During the 1970s and 1980s the boundaries were no longer fixed, and since 1979 there has been a redefinition of the public sector. In future years, governments will no longer be concerned with the funding of public utilities, which means that more resources will be available either to reduce personal taxation or to increase expenditure on social services. The major concern will be the successful management of the UK economy in the context of a more integrated Europe. Public expenditure decisions will therefore continue to be decisions that are political, that are made within an economic context and that will continue to have social implications.

Chapter 10

Conclusions: the challenges of the 1990s

INTRODUCTION: THE AFTERMATH OF THE 1992 ELECTION

The twin issues of taxation and public expenditure dominated most of the 1992 election campaign. The re-election of a Conservative Government for a fourth term has reinforced the view that the UK voters seemed to prefer the party that made pledges to reduce taxation rather than the party that was more likely to increase taxation. Despite what voters had said to the opinion pollsters – that they would give a higher level of priority to increased spending in contrast to lower taxation – in the privacy of the ballot box they voted against an increase in taxation. During the 1992 election electors were offered very distinct choices between individual and public consumption, with the Conservative Government pledged to make the reduction of taxation central to its election strategy, in contrast to the Labour Party and the Liberal Democrats, who argued for increases in taxation and national insurance to provide the additional revenues to fund increases in public expenditure. However, whilst the election campaign seemed to generate different visions there was also emerging a wider degree of consensus when contrasted to the previous decade. Indeed, whilst the 1980s could be associated with the breakdown of the politics of collectivism, the election of 1992 confirmed the degree to which a new politics was emerging for the 1990s.

During the 1992 election campaign the Conservative Party wanted to show that it was committed to reducing taxation whilst improving the quality of public services:

> But lower taxes and a prudent approach to borrowing do not mean public spending must fall; quite the reverse. A light-taxed economy generates more economic growth, and more revenue. High taxes

kill the goose that lays the golden eggs. In the course of its last five years in office, Labour was forced to cut public spending in real terms. By contrast the Conservatives have been able to raise public spending by nearly a quarter in real terms.

(Conservative Central Office 1992: 7)

The declaration that the Conservatives had been able to increase public spending in real terms was turned from a policy failure into a policy of virtue and a commitment to caring. Whilst in 1979 Mrs Thatcher had argued that public expenditure was at the heart of Britain's economic problems and that her Government was committed to reducing expenditure, by contrast Mr Major wanted to emphasise that increases in public expenditure had come to represent achievement in 1992.

The 1992 Conservative manifesto reflected the degree to which the Conservative Party was willing to present itself as the Party that gave precedence not only to the rights of the individual and the success of a market economy but also high-quality public services. The Conservative Party had replaced Margaret Thatcher with John Major in 1990 and had entered the election campaign with commitments to major increases in public expenditure on health, education and railways. The Autumn Statement of 1991 together with the March 1992 Budget confirmed the extent to which the Conservative Party had shifted from the politics of anti-collectivism, associated with the Thatcher Government, to a politics that sought to combine market efficiency with public provision. The additional increases in public expenditure together with the increases to the PSBR confirmed the break with the Thatcher approach to public finance. During the election campaign, without wanting to appear disloyal, Mrs Thatcher seemed to hint at – although indirectly – her disapproval of the increases in government borrowing when she argued that governments must be prepared to say no if they were not to appear weak before their electors by giving way to demands:

My Government did not have to borrow for four years in order to meet our outgoings . . . although when you have a recession expenditure rises and income doesn't, to coin a phrase, you have to say no, no, no and to coin a double phrase you have to go on and on saying no, no, no.

(M. Thatcher, speech at Chelmsford, 30 March 1992, cited in *Financial Times*, 31 March 1992)

The study of the policy review statements of the Labour Party also confirm the extent to which its politics had changed during the years of the Thatcher Government. Without directly challenging Clause IV in the manner of Hugh Gaitskell, Neil Kinnock, as leader of the Labour Party, had managed to shift the Party from any commitments to re-nationalisation except for the water industry. In the 1992 election campaign it was that much more difficult for critics to argue that Labour was likely to be profligate with public expenditure or had failed to cost its electoral pledges. Labour went into the 1992 election with an alternative budget showing the costing of its programme over a period of 22 months. The Party pointed to specific spending pledges on pensions and child benefits and also on education, health and training. Labour leaders could dismiss as misleading the shadow costings of £40 billion estimated by the Conservative Party and the £27 billion outlined by Cooper and Lybrand, since Labour had not made pledges to major increases in public expenditure. The Labour Party could point to differences in emphasis between specific commitments and long-term policy objectives. The aim of restoring the ratio of public expenditure in health and education to that of 1979 could be described as a long-term objective, which depended in turn on the future of the UK economy. If the UK economy prospered so would the public sector. Growth in public expenditure would be realised because the economy was able to produce that growth:

> Sustained and balanced economic growth makes the scope for public spending greater. But it must be clear at the outset that advance towards our objectives will necessarily depend on achieving that growth. We will not spend, nor will we promise to spend, more than Britain can afford . . . Where there is extra growth, we believe that investment must have a greater priority than tax cuts. The first priority is the restoration of public investment and service.
>
> (Labour Party 1990: 8)

Labour argued that its policies differed from those of the Conservative Party because Labour was not making pledges to reduce taxation, which meant that the Party would always have the extra revenues to finance the public sector, in contrast to the Conservatives who had pledged to use the additional resources to reduce personal taxation.

THE BREAK WITH KEYNESIAN ECONOMICS

The study of public expenditure over the last two decades confirms that governments have been influenced by competing discursive societies, with each discursive group seeking to gain the ear of government and to transmit its ideas into public policy. It was further suggested that the language that was in ascendance was associated with the agenda of market liberal principles and monetarist macro economics. These ideas challenged the discourses of collectivism, of Keynesian economics and tripartite politics. Within the context of the 1970s and 1980s there is evidence of an attempt to establish certain identities in relation to public expenditure. The degree of change can be gauged from two *Times* editorials. In 1971, *The Times'* comment was: 'Keynesian economics have been adopted as the basis of demand management through the budget since 1944 . . . it is morally, economically, socially and politically intolerable that unemployment should remain this high' (*The Times*, 19 November 1971). By 1976 perceptions of government had shifted. The assumption that government could influence the level of employment ceased to be regarded as legitimate: 'We need to end all illusions. The illusion that government can create prosperity because they can print money. The illusion that government can create livelihoods and maintain full employment because they can finance particular jobs' (*The Times*, 20 September 1976).

There are many and often competing explanations why governments over the last two decades were seeking to make the containment of public expenditure central to their policies. Hood and Wright (1981) have described the period as encompassing 'hard times', that it was a period when growth in the economy could no longer be assumed and when governments had to alter their expenditure plans to correspond with the new environment: 'In the last decade the winds have become more persistently chilling: hard times are no longer "just around the corner". The "treble affluence" of the 1950's and 1960's – rising GDP, public expenditure and take-home pay – began to crumble' (Hood and Wright 1981: 3).

The No Growth State was not, however, to be perceived as some temporary setback, a period through which expenditure programmes could be protected until better times. It had, according to some commentators, heralded a permanent shift, and a break in perceptions and expectations of government. The combination of persistent high levels of unemployment, economic recessions and inflation has confirmed the degree to which Keynesian conventional wisdom has been abandoned both intellectually and practically. Intellectually Keynesians worked on the assumption that unemployment and inflation represented alternatives; the presence of high levels of unemployment and inflationary pressures would suggest that Keynesian solutions are no longer relevant. Practically, the retreat from Keynes also implied that governments could no longer look to Keynesian techniques to provide the levers to resolve these problems. These challenges, the argument continues, have led to a market liberal and monetarist counter-revolution, bringing in their wake a questioning of the assumed world of continuous growth in public expenditure. Judge (1982a) has argued that

> The changing nature of economic ideology is probably the most important single reason for the reduced political priority associated with public expenditure . . . The result of this [monetarist] counter revolution is that the role of public expenditure has changed dramatically.
>
> (Judge 1982a: 47)

The election of the first Thatcher Government in 1979 seemed to confirm the voters' willingness to make the break with the consensus politics of the post-war years. The winds of change experienced during the years of the Labour Government after 1975 had swept Mrs Thatcher's Government into power with the pledge that it would seek to reduce the frontiers of the State. A further three election victories seem to indicate the degree to which the UK had moved away from the consensus politics of the post-war settlement. The Conservative Governments have maintained their popularity and their levels of electoral support despite the increase in the rate of unemployment and the growing inequalities of income. Whilst the one million unemployed had been politically unacceptable during the years of the Heath Government and 1.3 million a disgrace for the Labour Government, the level of 3 million unemployed in the 1980s was seen as unavoidable and not necessarily the fault of the Government. Whether unemployment continues to be a non-issue in the 1990s seems to depend on whether the Government can improve the living standards of those in work. If those in work are contented, the unemployed will continue to be at the margin of the political process. On the other hand, if unemployment is perceived to be the obstacle to prosperity it could become a more central issue.

Furthermore, whilst part of the wartime coalition Government's agreement had been to reduce poverty, a pledge to which both Labour and Conservative Governments had adhered in the 1960s and 1970s, that commitment seemed to be broken during the years of the Thatcher Government. The government policy on taxation meant that those in higher income groups received the highest benefits, whilst increases in indirect taxation resulted in a higher tax burden for those on low incomes. The failure to uprate pensions and child benefits also seemed to erode the income of vulnerable groups.

THE BREAK WITH POLITICAL PARALYSIS AND PLURALIST STAGNATION

In addition to the break with the economics of Keynes was an argument that was concerned with the political dimension of public expenditure. According to this view the public sector was heading towards political ungovernability and fiscal overload. Rose and Peters (1979) warned that increased taxation to finance higher levels of public expenditure was no longer an option since this was leading to government becoming bankrupt, whilst Beer (1982) pointed to 'pluralistic stagnation' and political paralysis:

> In another form, pluralistic stagnation arises (as) defence of a quiescent status quo. The participants, many in number, defend a variety of interests. Individual groups may be so placed strategically in the managed economy to be able to veto government action. Or perhaps several, which view some proposal or set of proposals as injurious, constitute an electoral threat strong enough to prevent change.
>
> (Beer 1982: 25)

Thus, the new emergent political consensus of the 1980s was of governments in the UK seeking to change a culture, of altering people's expectations about the claims that could legitimately be made of government. The politics of social democracy founded on the twin principles of commitment to full employment and an expanding welfare state had to be replaced by the belief that governments must follow where the market-place beckons. Employment in the 1990s depends on people's willingness to price themselves into jobs and produce goods and services that are competitive. The emphasis in welfare provision has also shifted from public provision to a mixed economy of welfare. Privatisation is perceived to be the means of breaking with public sector monopolies in the provision of services, and the dominance of the bureaucracy and public sector professionals, and creating a shift towards individual choice and consumer-orientated services.

THE POLITICAL DILEMMAS OF CHANGE AND CONTINUITY

The concern of this study has been to construct an argument that describes the changes in public expenditure as a dual process, in that whilst certain expenditure did seem to represent a break with the past, other areas of expenditure have reinforced a process of continuity. British governments have continued to provide funding for health and education and have also continued to protect the more visible and vociferous vested interests through subsidies to mortgagers, agriculture, industry, roads and education grants.

The study of public expenditure by programme confirms, first, that the rate of growth in public expenditure has been contained quite successfully since the 1960s and therefore that any argument suggesting that the break with the post-war consensus could be associated with a specific year in the mid-1970s would be misleading. However, it is important to emphasise that since the mid-1980s there has been a shift from the process of containment towards reductions, in the sense that whilst the economy as a whole has been growing, the rate of growth in public expenditure has not been allowed to grow in relation to national income. This means that in 1992 public expenditure by programme as a ratio of GDP was below that of 1962.

Second, the breakdown of expenditure programmes by economic component confirms that there was both a quantitative and qualitative shift in the dynamics between capital and current expenditures. Whilst between 1951 and 1967 capital and current expenditures were being simultaneously expanded, in contrast the experience from 1968 was one of continuous reductions in capital expenditure whilst current expenditures continued to be expanded. It would also seem that these changes were systematically related, in that there was a causal relationship between the increases in current expenditure and the reductions in capital expenditure. Capital expenditures continued to be reduced under both Labour and Conservative Governments from the mid-1970s.

Third, these trends seem to substantiate the Heclo and Wildavsky (1982) argument that it was the macro discursive societies that were in ascendance. The new dictum that 'it is finance which decides expenditure and not expenditure finance' reinforced the dominance of a specific perception of public expenditure. Capital expenditure was aggregated with consumption expenditure despite the differential impacts of these components on economic activity, an observation picked up by *The Times*:

> The [Thatcher] Government's difficulty is that it includes public
> investment in its anathema for public expenditure. This is seriously
> misleading. There is a fundamental difference between government
> spending on current consumption and investment in capital
> programmes. Public investment must lead the way for it will
> provide the underpinning to re-assure private industry's thinking of
> expanding its output.
>
> (*The Times*, 11 March 1981)

In this context, the 1970s and 1980s were different because it would
seem that macro considerations, such as the aggregate economy,
taxation and government borrowing, had become the criteria for
deciding the levels of public expenditure. According to the present
Government, it was the programme approach that had caused
expenditure to continue to grow, whilst it has pointedly insisted that
expenditure was now, as it should be, in the hands of the macro
analysts:

> There will be some who will argue that it makes little sense to
> consider, still less to decide upon, public spending totals without a
> clear view of the implications for individual programmes. This
> government believes that such thinking has been largely responsible
> for the upward drift of public expenditure over many years. It is
> necessary to turn the argument around the other way, to decide first
> what can and should be afforded, then to set expenditure plans for
> individual programmes consistently with that decision.
>
> (HMSO 1984b: 13)

THE PROCESSES OF CONSTRAINTS AND POLITICAL AUTONOMY

This text also seeks to question the thesis that correlates expenditure
changes with changes in party government. The findings confirm that
changes in expenditure were not related to party government but that
after 1970, growth and restraint were associated with both the
Conservative and Labour years. Indeed, what seems to have happened
in the 1970s and 1980s is a continuation of a bipartisan approach.
Whilst the 1950s and 1960s could be described as the era of Butskellism
and collectivist politics, the 1970s and 1980s could be perceived as
representing the politics of retrenchment and contraction. This does
not imply that parties do not matter, but rather that the party in
government has tended to work within a series of political constraints.

The concept of a politics of public expenditure cannot be adequately explained through a process of modelling the political dimension, since the concept of politics itself emphasises a process of indeterminacy and expediency, of political judgement and political choice. The concept of a politics of public expenditure therefore requires a framework that captures the dual process of constraints and autonomy, or, as Von Beyme (1984) suggests:

> The final answer to our question 'do parties matter' is they do matter. But as to the extent to which they matter we will not find out by the computerisation of global figures but rather by a con-figurative, comparative analysis of policies and policy mixes under similar social conditions and comparable political challenges.
>
> (Von Beyme 1984: 28)

The concern is to provide a series of biographies and accounts of the records of governments on issues relating to public expenditure with the aim of outlining the series of 'events' and the process of 'autonomy' that allowed governments to negotiate between constraints that were not always within their immediate influence, and the attempts by governments to reflect their political priorities.

Within this context of constraint and autonomy it was argued that it would be misleading to suggest that the Heath Government did attempt to break with the post-war settlement or that the Government betrayed the 'Quiet Revolution'. Instead it was pointed out that the Heath Government did not forswear the role of public expenditure as an instrument of economic management. Indeed, when in November 1971 the Government announced increases in expenditure, it explicitly argued that it wanted to utilise resources that would have otherwise been left idle. Public expenditure between 1970 and 1974 remained a tool aimed at economic stabilisation, whilst inflation was seen as a political problem generated by strategic groups. Monetarist solutions were dismissed as being irrelevant. Governments could, it was believed, influence the level of economic activity to reduce the level of unemployment. The Heath Government still accepted that it was possible for governments to achieve low levels of inflation and low unemployment within the constraints of a politics of consent.

Equally, on taking office in February 1974 the Labour Government announced increases in expenditures on subsidies, thus reversing the policies of the previous government. In contrast to the Heath Government, Labour ministers argued that government had to seek a social contract as a way of finding solutions to Britain's economic problems. Increases in expenditure on food subsidies, rent controls and higher pensions were presented as the Government's commitments to fulfil its part of the bargain. The Social Contract implied that the Government was committed to providing more resources for the public sector to improve and protect the social wage.

However, from April 1975 the Government became involved in a series of packages of cuts. These represented more than reversals of the previous plans; they signalled a shift in governmental perceptions of the role of public expenditure. The study of the Labour Government also confirms that the Labour Party, the trade unions and leaders of the Labour Government were in agreement. There was no betrayal by ministers as some people would like us to believe. The Labour movement had accepted that there was no alternative:

> It [the Labour Government] presided over the largest cuts in real public expenditure that have occurred in the last fifty years. These cuts were on a scale similar to the famous Geddes axe of 1922 . . . Changes also took place during 1974–79 to public expenditure's macro economic role. Public expenditure was to be controlled in order to meet the government's public sector borrowing requirement targets and hence its monetary targets. Monetary policy was to be dominant and fiscal policy was henceforth to be accommodative.

> (Artis and Cobham 1991: 72)

The Thatcher Governments failed in their initial attempts to reduce public expenditure as a proportion of the national income, but since 1985 brought public expenditure under control and also managed to reduce the ratio of public expenditure as a ratio of national income to below the levels of the 1960s. Analysing the impact of Thatcherism on public expenditure, it was suggested that Thatcherism could be associated within a fundamentalist approach to government, seeking to break with the politics of social democracy. It is an interpretation that suggests that these governments had been evangelical in their pursuit of a specific economic dogma and that they succeeded in altering the political terrain by repudiating the claims of full employment and a redistributive welfare state, replacing them with the ethos of the market-place, choice and individualism. In the meantime the continuous high levels of unemployment reflect the abandonment of public expenditure as an instrument of economic policy.

In contrast, there has been the sceptical interpretation of the Thatcher years, mainly influenced by the writings of market liberals

(Rose 1984c; Brittan 1983). The Government, according to this view, continued to protect subsidies directed at specific interest groups and, furthermore, was not radical in seeking to remove monopolies in welfare provision through the privatisation of health care and education provision. The primary aim of the Government was always to win the next election, which meant working within the politics of statecraft and the constraints of the political market. This implies that the Thatcher Government could not be radical in the sense that it could push forward policies without thinking out the consequences. It is an approach that rejects the views that the Government was either dogmatic or that it had a coherent strategy that it failed to achieve; instead, it was a government that, like all previous governments, sought to remain the incumbent government.

The Thatcher Government failed to reduce public expenditure during its early stages because capital expenditure had already been drastically reduced, and because ministers were not fully committed to Mrs Thatcher's vision. If that Government was going to fulfil its pledges, therefore, it had to embrace more radical departures on expenditures, which were also more politically sensitive. Ministers had, for example, rejected the CPRS report in 1983 because they argued that its recommendations were too radical. Furthermore, the eventual removal of Mrs Thatcher as leader of the Conservative Party in 1990 confirmed the extent to which the Conservatives were concerned about the forthcoming election and the need of the Party to embrace a more pragmatic approach to public services.

THE NEW POLITICS OF INDIVIDUAL CITIZENSHIP

The political process has also reinforced a shift in the political practice of government, away from the politics of consent towards a politics of parliamentarism, which Jessop (1979) has defined thus:

> Parliamentarism involves the fusion of political representations mediated through the participation of 'citizens' in the policy making of an elected government . . . Corporatism involves the fusion of political representation mediated through a system of public 'corporations' which are constituted on the basis of their members' functions.
>
> (Jessop 1979: 194–5)

The concept of a politics of corporatism involves a process that seeks to integrate functional groups into the process of government. However, the term corporatist would be inappropriate to describe the UK political system since there was neither an acceptance by governments to surrender their parliamentary role nor by trade unions to surrender the concept of free collective bargaining. The political process was that of tripartitism, where the economic objectives of achieving full employment and holding down inflation were resolved within the framework of negotiated consent. Trade unions were asked to moderate their wage demands in order to assist in the control of inflation whilst the government would seek to hold down prices, maintain growth in the economy and redistribute income through the mechanism of public expenditure.

THE BREAK WITH THE POLITICS OF CONSENT AND FUNCTIONAL DEMOCRACY

During the years of the Heath Government, there were concessions on pensions, growth in the economy and the control of prices in exchange for an agreement on the process of wage bargaining. Equally, the 1974–9 Labour Government constructed, with the trade unions, the Social Contract, which again involved the commitment by the Government to increase pensions, to control prices and to secure growth in the economy in exchange for income restraint. The experience of securing incomes policy by consensus has, therefore, inevitably implied the expansion of public expenditure. Incomes policy represented the willingness of trade unions to surrender, or at least suspend, their *raison d'être*, namely to bargain with employers on behalf of their members. It suggested that the trade unions would be willing to negotiate, at least in the short term, their right to engage in unrestricted collective bargaining for an agreement that would give them more influence in policy-making.

Public expenditure is of interest to trade unions for three reasons. First, because of its demand management potential. Expanded public expenditure is perceived as increasing demand in the economy and lowering unemployment. A high level of unemployment threatens trade union organisations with loss of membership and thereby weakens their bargaining position with employers on behalf of their members (Bain and Elsheikh 1976, 1982). Second, there is the more visible and direct interest that the public sector is an important area of employment in its own right:

To make this point is to underline the importance of the organisation and role of labour – trade unions and professional organisations – in explaining the growth of public consumption. The most immediate beneficiaries of the welfare state – i.e. education and health services – are those working in the programmes provided.

(Klein 1982: 27)

Third, besides these more immediate self-interested objectives, there are other areas of public expenditure that are seen as having an impact on the living standards of trade union members. Indirectly, but also in the longer term, this includes the social wage aspect of public expenditure, such as pensions, housing costs, food subsidies, health care and education provision:

> Equally important, however, is the fact that strong labour movements tend to act as proxy groups for the less organised sectors. An altruistic ideology, is buttressed by self interest . . . pensions in particular can be seen as a deferred payment.
>
> (Klein 1982: 31)

The Heath Government failed to secure a voluntary incomes policy because of its unwillingness to compromise on housing and food subsidies, which the Government saw as too politically costly. However, this says something more about the strength of the trade unions during this period. High trade union membership, the success of the miners' and power workers' strikes in 1971 and 1972, the successful campaign against the Trade Union Act, 1972, together with a post-war historic perspective of full employment allowed the trade unions to bargain with the Government from a position of strength. British trade unions felt that the best way to serve their members was to protect the voluntary tradition in industrial relations, whilst the issues of employment and welfare remained the problems of government.

In contrast to the Heath years, the trade union response to public expenditure reductions during the years of the last Labour Government could be described as reluctant acquiescence to the demands of the Government, because of fear of an alternative government. However, this strategy did eventually lead to the Winter of Discontent in 1979, which contributed to the eventual electoral defeat of that Government.

THE POLITICS OF THE STRONG STATE AND INDIVIDUAL CITIZENSHIP

Since 1979 the political strategy has changed from the politics of consent to one favouring the strong State and individual citizenship.

The Thatcher Governments did not seek to reduce inflation by consent since this would have led to the likely compromise of their political priorities. Hence the Government declared its intention of reducing inflation through the control of the money supply and of government borrowing whilst at the same time using the legislative process to reduce trade union immunities. According to Gamble (1988) the strong State and increased forms of State intervention are congruous within the politics of Thatcherism:

> The key to the paradox of how the Thatcher government can be at one and the same time opposed to state intervention and the most interventionist government of recent times lies in the doctrine of the free economy and the strong state . . . For the economy to be 'free', for markets to be unhindered in their operation and for individual property rights to govern the economic processes of production . . . then the state must be strong – strong enough to ensure open and fair competition in all markets.
>
> (Gamble 1988: 21)

In the context of the strong State the objective was therefore not to integrate functional groups within the process of government but rather to provide strong government that was able to reflect the wishes of the individual citizens as voters. Functional groups within this context were perceived as a distortion of the democratic relationship between the citizen and the government. Functional groups only represent the vested interests of strategic groups, of business organisations, trade unions, bureaucracies and professionals. Utilising the principles of market liberalism, the Thatcher Government sought to break up the monopoly positions of these groups within the public sector, to introduce a policy of competition and consumer choice. The process of breaking up the powers of vested interest groups including local government required a strong State. The reforms in the Health Service, education system and public sector housing have required a government with the political will to embark on a process that recognises the rights of the citizens as consumers rather than the interests of producer groups.

THE CHALLENGES OF THE 1990s

Commitments to the classless society

On becoming Prime Minister in April 1992, John Major reiterated his vision of wanting to see a Britain that was at ease with itself. The major battles against big government and functional groups that seemed to have undermined the democratic system had now been won. The challenge for the 1990s was therefore how to create a democracy founded on the rights of the individual citizen. The setting up of a ministry responsible for the Citizens' Charter under William Waldegrave represents an attempt by Mr Major to make citizenship within the context of public policy a reality. The question is whether the removal of intermediary agencies, including local government, education and local health authorities would actually enhance the rights of the individual, or would these rights be undermined in the context of a more centralising State? If schools chose to opt out from local authority control would parents have more, or less, choice? Whilst education was controlled by local authorities parents did have the political choice of removing their local councillors. Grant maintained schools have a number of appointed governors who are not elected and, furthermore, parents have to seek redress through the Secretary of State for Education.

One major question for the 1990s must be whether the reforms in the public sector would meet the criterion of providing services that are directed to the needs of the individual as a consumer or whether individuals would experience less choice – and would choice only be meaningful for those who opt for private provision? The argument of the new administration is that it would like to see high-quality public sector services that will attract individuals who at present choose private provision. It is within this framework of voluntarism that John Major hopes to create a classless society of opportunity.

Paradoxically, this argument for a classless society reflects the views articulated in Tony Crosland's approach to socialism. He also had argued, in the 1950s, that high-quality public services represented the mechanism for achieving a classless society. The difference between Crosland's vision and that of John Major is that Crosland argued for additional increases in public expenditure, in contrast to John Major's approach, which seeks to make the public services more efficient and open to competition.

Private affluence and public squalor

Public expenditure reflects a dilemma for all governments in modern democracies as they attempt to provide popular services at the minimum cost and without increasing the tax burden on individuals. The tensions between private and collective consumption have resulted in major problems of reconciling private affluence with public squalor. At a global level there are now major problems of pollution and depletion of resources, yet governments attending the Earth Summit in Rio in 1992 found themselves in difficulty because of their inability to commit public finances to deal with problems of the environment. Most governments are aware that their short-term political success depends on their ability to secure high levels of private consumption for their electors, even when private consumption seems to conflict with the arguments for sustainable growth. Equally, there are also problems at a global level of income redistribution between the rich and poor countries and the role of governments as a mechanism to redistribute income.

Yet whilst at the international level the role of governments is becoming increasingly central to dealing with the challenges of the environment, at a national and local level the role of government has been in retreat over the past two decades. The politics of consent founded on the economics of Keynes and the public provision of services that had gained ascendance in most countries in the aftermath of the Second World War has been replaced by market liberal economics and individualism in the 1990s. The retreat from social democratic politics is now an international phenomenon.

At both a national and local level the shift towards increased private affluence and public squalor means that, eventually, public services do deteriorate. Long-term neglect in infrastructure expenditure means that the costs of repairing public buildings, sewerage facilities and communications becomes prohibitive for governments, which in turn means further neglect and deterioration.

Allowing earnings differentials to increase between private and public sector employees means that, whilst teachers and doctors might tolerate low pay in the short term, they will eventually see themselves as being used as cheap labour and will start to behave as cheap labour, by withdrawing from their commitment to professionalism. The problem for government is that if concessions are made on wages there is then less money available to be spent on maintaining or improving the service. The Autumn Statement of November 1992 confirmed this dilemma, with the Government on the one hand seeking to protect public sector projects, whilst on the other relying on low pay settlements in the public sector.

The study of public expenditure confirms that we want to have our cake and eat it. We look forward to reductions in personal income tax because that means more money for individual consumption, but we do not connect this to services we consume in the public sector. The public sector is now too large for us to hope that services can be improved if we can get others to pay the costs. Redistribution from high income earners through the tax system cannot improve welfare services drastically. At the end of the day, we all get the sort of welfare we deserve.

References

Alford, R. and Friedland, R. (1985) *Powers of Theory: The State, Capitalism and Democracy*, Cambridge University Press, Cambridge.

Alt, J. (1979) *The Politics of Economic Decline*, Cambridge University Press, Cambridge.

Alt, J. and Chrystal, K.A. (1977) *Endogenous Government Behaviour*, University of Essex, Discussion Paper No. 108.

—— (1979) *Public Sector Behaviour: The Status of the Political Business Cycle*, University of Essex, Discussion Paper No. 128.

—— (1981) 'Electoral cycles, budget controls and public expenditure', *Journal of Public Policy* 1: 37–59.

—— (1983) *Political Economics*, Wheatsheaf, Brighton.

Artis, M. and Cobham, D. (eds) (1991) *Labour's Economic Policies 1974–79*, Manchester University Press, Manchester.

Bacon, R. and Eltis, W.A. (1978) *Britain's Economic Problem: Too Few Producers*, Macmillan, London.

Bain, G.S. (1984) *Industrial Relations in Britain*, Basil Blackwell, Oxford.

Bain, G.S. and Elsheikh, F. (1976) *Union Growth and the Business Cycle*, Basil Blackwell, Oxford.

—— (1982) 'Union growth and the business cycle', *British Journal of Industrial Relations*, April: 34–43.

Ball, R.J. (1981) *Money and Employment*, Macmillan, London.

Barnet, C. (1986) *The Audit of War*, Macmillan, London.

Barnett, J. (1982) *Inside the Treasury*, Andre Deutsch, London.

Baumol, W.J. (1967) 'Macro economics of unbalanced growth: the anatomy of urban crisis', *Amercian Economic Review* 57: 415–26.

Beck, M. (1976) 'Public sector growth: a real perspective', *Journal of Public Finance*, November: 313–56.

Beer, S. (1965) *Modern British Politics*, Faber & Faber, London.

—— (1982) *Britain Against Itself: The Political Contradictions of Collectivism*, Faber & Faber, London.

Benn, T. (1979) *Arguments for Socialism*, Penguin, Harmondsworth.

Bevan, A. (1978) *In Place of Fear*, Quartet, London.

Birch, A.(1984) 'Overload, ungovernability and delegitimation: the theories and the British case', *British Journal of Political Science* 3: 135–60.

Black Report (1980) *Inequalities and Health*, DHSS, London.

Blackaby, F.T. (1979) *British Economic Policy 1960–1974*, Cambridge University Press, Cambridge.

—— (1980) 'In Praise of Mr. Heath', *The Listener*, 21 February.

Blackstone, T. (1980) 'Education', in N. Bosanquet and P. Townsend (eds) *Labour and Inequality: A Fabian Study of Labour in Power 1974 to 1979*, Heinemann, London.

Blake, R. (1985) *The Conservative Party from Peel to Thatcher*, Fontana, London.

Bleaney, M. (1985) *The Rise and Fall of Keynesian Economics*, Macmillan, London.

Borcherding, T.E. (1977) *Budgets and Bureaucrats: the Sources of Government Growth*, Duke University Press, Durham, NC.

Bosanquet, N. and Townsend, P. (eds) (1980) *Labour and Inequality: A Fabian Study of Labour in Power 1974 to 1979*, Heinemann, London.

Bow Group (1971) *Freedom to Spend*, Conservative Politics Centre, London.

Boyson, R. (1978) *Centre Forward; A Radical Conservative Programme*, Temple Smith, London.

Breton, A. (1974) *The Economic Theory of Representative Government*, Macmillan, London.

Brittan, S. (1977) *The Economic Consequences of Democracy*, Maurice Temple Smith, London.

—— (1983) *The Role and Limits to Government*, Maurice Temple Smith, London.

Bruce-Gardyne, J. (1974) *Whatever Happened to the Quiet Revolution?*, Knight, London.

—— (1984) *Mrs Thatcher's First Administration: The Prophets Confounded*, Macmillan, London.

Buchanan, J. (1978) *The Economics of Politics*, IEA Readings No. 18, Goron Pro-Print, West Sussex.

Bulpitt, J. (1982) 'Conservatism, Unionism and the problem of territorial management', in P. Madgwick and R. Rose (eds) *The Territorial Dimension in UK Politics*, Macmillan, London.

—— (1985) *The Discipline of the New Democracy: Mrs Thatcher's Domestic Statecraft*, paper presented to the Political Studies Association Conference, April 1985.

Burch, M. (1983) *Mrs Thatcher's Approach to Leadership in Government: June 1979 to June 1983, Parliamentary Affairs* 36: 399–416.

Burton, J. (1985) *Why No Cuts?*, Institute of Economic Affairs, London.

Butler, R. (1971) *The Art of the Possible*, Hamilton, London.

Butt, R. (1986) *The Unfinished Task: The Conservative Record in Perspective*, Centre for Policy Studies, London.

Callaghan, J. (1987) *Time and Chance*, Collins, London.

Cameron, D. (1978) 'The expansion of the public economy: a comparative analysis', *American Political Science Review* 72: 1,243–69.

Castle, B. (1980) *The Castle Diaries 1974 to 1976*, Weidenfeld & Nicolson, London.

Castles, F. (1982) *The Impact of Parties*, Sage, London.

Clark, G.L. and Dear, M. (1984) *State Apparatus: Structures and Language of Legitimacy*, Allen & Unwin, London.

Clarke, P. (1992) *A Question of Leadership: From Gladstone to Thatcher*, Penguin, Harmondsworth.

Clarke, R. (1968) *Public Expenditure Management and Control*, Macmillan, London.

—— (1973) 'Parliament and public expenditure', *Political Quarterly* 1, April: 17–24.

Coates, D. (1980) *Labour in Power? A Study of the Labour Government 1974–79*, Longman, London.

Congdon, T.Q. (1982) *Monetary Control in Britain*, Macmillan, London.

Connolly, W.E. (1984a) *The Terms of Political Discourse*, Martin Robertson, Oxford.

—— (1984b) *Legitimacy and the State*, Basil Blackwell, Oxford.

Conservative Central Office (1970) *A Better Tomorrow: The Conservative Manifesto 1970*, Conservative Party, London.

—— (1977) *The Right Approach to the Economy*, Conservative Party, London.

—— (1979) *The Conservative Manifesto 1979*, Conservative Party, London.

—— (1983) *The Conservative Manifesto 1983*, Conservative Party, London.

—— (1987) *The Conservative Manifesto 1987*, Conservative Party, London.

—— (1992) *The Best Future for Britain: The Conservative Manifesto 1992*, Conservative Party, London.

Conservative Party (1947) *The Industrial Charter*, Conservative Party, London.

—— (1949) *Conservative Conference Verbatim Report*, Conservative Party, London.

—— (1951) *The Conservative Party Manifesto – The 1951 Election*, Conservative Party, London.

—— (1970) *Verbatim Conference Report*, Conservative Party, London.

—— (1971) *Verbatim Conference Report*, Conservative Party, London.

—— (1981) *Conservative Conference Verbatim Report*, Conservative Party, London.

Conservative Political Centre (1950) *One Nation: A Tory Approach to Social Problems*, Conservative Party, London.

Conservative Research Department (1972) *Fighting Inflation*, Conservative Party, London.

—— (1976) *The Problem of Public Expenditure*, Conservative Party, London.

Cosgrave, P. (1978) *Margaret Thatcher*, Hutchinson, London.

CPAG (1979) *Abandoning Social Priorities*, CPAG, London.

—— (1983) *Thatcherism and the Poor*, CPAG, London.

Crosland, C.A.R. (1967) *The Future of Socialism*, Cape, London.

Crosland, S. (1982) *Tony Crosland*, Cape, London.

Crossman, R. (1952) *New Fabian Essays*, Turnstile, London.

Culyer, A. and Wright, K. (1978) *Economic Aspects of Health*, Martin Robertson, Oxford.

Dean, A. (1981) 'Public and private sector pay and the economy', in J.L. Fallick and R.F. Elliott (eds) *Incomes Policies, Inflation and Relative Pay*, Allen & Unwin, London.

Desai, M. (1981) *Testing Monetarism*, Frances Pinter, London.

Downs, A. (1957) *An Economic Theory of Democracy*, Harper & Row, New York.

—— (1965) 'Why the government budget is too small in a democracy', in E. Phelps, *Private Wants and Public Needs*, Harvester, New York.

Duke, V. and Edgell, S. (1983) *Public Expenditure Cuts in Britain and Consumption Sectoral Cleavages*, paper presented to the Political Studies Association Conference, April 1983.

Duncan, G. (1985) 'A crisis of social democracy?', *Parliamentary Affairs* 3, Summer: 267–81.

Dunleavy, P. (1979) 'The political implications of sectoral cleavages and state employment', *Journal of Political Studies* 27: 18–23.

—— (1980) *Urban Political Analysis*, Macmillan, London.

—— (1991) *Democracy, Bureaucracy and Public Choice*, Harvester Wheatsheaf, London.

Durbin, E. (1940) *The Politics of Democratic Socialism*, Faber & Faber, London.

Fallick, J.L. and Elliott, R.F. (eds)(1981) *Incomes Policies, Inflation and Relative Pay*, Allen & Unwin, London.

Fine, B. and Harris, L. (1979) *Re-Reading Capital*, Macmillan, London.

Fishbein, W.H. (1984) *Wage Restraint by Consensus*, Routledge, London.

Fisher, N. (1973) *Iain Macleod*, Andre Deutsch, London.

Foote, G. (1986) *The Labour Party's Political Thought: A History*, Croom Helm, London.

Frey, B. (1978) *Modern Political Economy*, Martin Robertson, London.

—— (1985) *Democratic Economic Policy: A Theoretical Introduction*, Blackwell, Oxford.

Frey, B. and Schneider, F. (1978) 'A political economic model of the UK', *Economic Journal* 88: 243–53.

Friedman, M. and R. (1985) *The Tyranny of the Status Quo*, Penguin, Harmondsworth.

Galbraith, J.K. (1981) 'Up from monetarism and other wishful thinking', *New York Review of Books*, August: 104–6.

Gamble, A. (1974) *The Conservative Nation*, Macmillan, London.

—— (1979a) 'Thatcher make or break', *Marxism Today*, November: 14–20.

—— (1979b) 'The Conservative Party', in H. Drucker, *Multi Party Britain*, Macmillan, London.

—— (1980) 'Economic policy', in Z. Layton-Henry, *Conservative Party Politics*, Macmillan, Basingstoke.

—— (1988) *The Free Economy and the Strong State*, Macmillan, London.

Gilmour, I. (1977) *Inside Right*, Hutchinson, London.

Goldman, S. (1976) *Growth and Control of Public Expenditure*, Institute of Fiscal Studies, London.

Gough, I. (1979) *The Political Economy of the Welfare State*, Macmillan, London.

—— (1983) 'Thatcherism and the welfare state', in S. Hall and M. Jacques (eds) *The Politics of Thatcherism*, Lawrence & Wishart, London.

Gouldner, A. (1980) *The Two Marxisms*, Macmillan, London.

Gray, J. (1989) *Limited Government: A Positive Agenda*, Institute of Economic Affairs, London.

Greenleaf, W.H. (1983) *The Ideological Heritage*, Methuen, London.

Hahn, F. (1982) *Money and Inflation*, Basil Blackwell, Oxford.

Hall, S. and Jacques, M. (eds)(1983) *The Politics of Thatcherism*, Lawrence and Wishart, London.

Harrison, A. (1989) *The Control of Public Expenditure 1979–1989*, Transaction, Oxford.

Hatfield, J.M. (1978) *The House the Left Built*, Gollancz, London.

Havel, V. (1992) *Summer Meditations*, Faber & Faber, London.

Hayek, F. (1946) *The Road to Serfdom*, Routledge, London.

Heald, D. (1983) *Public Expenditure*, Martin Robertson, Oxford.

Healey, D.T. (1989) *The Time of My Life*, Michael Joseph, London.

Heclo, H. and Wildavsky, A. (1982) *The Private Government of Public Money*, Macmillan, London.

Heller, A. (1990) *Can Modernity Survive?*, Polity, Cambridge.

Heller, A. and Feher, F. (1988) *The Postmodern Political Condition*, Polity, Cambridge.

Hill, J. (ed)(1991) *The State of Welfare: The Welfare State in Britain since 1974*, Clarendon, Oxford.

Hirschman, A. (1970) *Exit, Voice and Loyalty*, Harvard University Press, Cambridge, Mass.

HMSO (1970) *New Policies for Public Spending*, Cmnd 4515, HMSO, London.

—— (1971a) *Public Expenditure 1969/70 to 1974/75*, Cmnd 4578, HMSO, London.

—— (1971b) *Public Expenditure to 1975/76*, Cmnd 4829, HMSO, London.

—— (1971c) *A Fair Deal for Housing*, Cmnd 4628, HMSO, London.

—— (1972a) *Public Expenditure to 1976/77*, Cmnd 5178, HMSO, London.

—— (1972b) *Education: A Framework for Expansion*, Cmnd 5176, HMSO, London.

—— (1973) *Public Expenditure to 1977/78*, Cmnd 5519, HMSO, London.

—— (1975) *Public Expenditure to 1978/79*, Cmnd 5879, HMSO, London.

—— (1976a) *Cash Limits in Public Expenditure*, Cmnd 6440, HMSO, London.

—— (1976b) *Public Expenditure to 1979/80*, Cmnd 6393, HMSO, London.

—— (1977) *The Government's Expenditure Plans 1976/77 to 1980/81*, Cmnd 6721, HMSO, London.

—— (1978a) *The Government's Expenditure Plans 1978/79 to 1981/82*, Cmnd 7049, HMSO, London.

—— (1978b) *National Income and Expenditure to 1977*, HMSO, London.

—— (1979a) *The Government's Expenditure Plans 1979/80 to 1982/83*, Cmnd 7439, HMSO, London.

—— (1979b) *The Government's Expenditure Plans 1980/81*, Cmnd 7746, HMSO, London.

—— (1979c) *National Income and Expenditure to 1978*, HMSO, London.

—— (1980a) *The Government's Expenditure Plans 1980/81 to 1983/84*, Cmnd 7841, HMSO, London.

—— (1980b) *National Income and Expenditure to 1979*, HMSO, London.

—— (1981a) *The Government's Expenditure Plans 1981/82 to 1983/84*, Cmnd 8175, HMSO, London.

—— (1981b) *National Income and Expenditure to 1980*, HMSO, London.

—— (1982a) *The Government's Expenditure Plans 1982/83 to 1984/85*, Cmnd 8494, HMSO, London.

—— (1982b) *National Income and Expenditure to 1981*, HMSO, London.

—— (1983a) *The Government's Expenditure Plans 1983/84 to 1985/86*, Cmnd 8789, HMSO, London.

—— (1983b) *National Income and Expenditure to 1982*, HMSO, London.

—— (1984a) *The Government's Expenditure Plans 1984/85 to 1986/87*, Cmnd 9143, HMSO, London.

—— (1984b) *The Next Ten Years: Public Expenditure and Taxation into the 1990s*, Cmnd 9189, HMSO, London.

—— (1985) *The Government's Expenditure Plans 1985/86 to 1987/88*, Cmnd 9428, HMSO, London.

—— (1986) *The Government's Expenditure Plans 1986/87 to 1988/89*, Cmnd 9702, HMSO, London.

—— (1987) *The Government's Expenditure Plans 1987/88 to 1989/90*, Cm 56, HMSO, London.

—— (1988) *The Government's Expenditure Plans 1988/89 to 1990/91*, Cm 288, HMSO, London.

—— (1989) *The Government's Expenditure Plans 1989/90 to 1991/92*, Cmn 621, HMSO, London.

—— (1990a) *The Government's Expenditure Plans 1990/91 to 1992/93*, Cm 1004, HMSO, London.

—— (1990b) *National Income and Expenditure to 1989*, HMSO, London.

—— (1991) *Public Expenditure Analyses to 1993/94*, Cm 1520, HMSO, London.

Hodgson, G.(1981) *Labour at the Crossroads*, Martin Robertson, Oxford.

Hoffman, J.D. (1964) *The Conservative Party in Opposition 1945–51*, Gibbon & Kee, London.

Hogg, Q. (1947) *The Case for Conservatism*, Penguin, Harmondsworth.

Hogwood, B.W. (1992) *Trends in British Public Policy*, Open University Press, Buckingham.

Holmes, M. (1982) *Political Pressure and Economic Policy*, Butterworth, London.

—— (1985a) *The First Thatcher Government 1979 to 1983*, Wheatsheaf, Brighton.

—— (1985b) *The Labour Government 1974 to 1979: Political Aims and Economic Reality*, Macmillan, London.

—— (1989) *Thatcherism: Scope and Limits 1983–87*, Macmillan, London.

Hood, C., Huby, M. and Dunsire, A. (1984) 'Bureaucrats and budgeting benefits: how do British central government departments measure up?', *Journal of Public Policy* 4: 163–79.

Hood, C. and Wright, M. (1981) *Big Government in Hard Times*, Martin Robertson, Oxford.

Horne, A. (1988) *Macmillan*, 2 vols, Macmillan, London.

House of Commons (1971) *3rd Report of the Expenditure Committee on Public Expenditure Plans 1970/71*, HC 349, HMSO, London.

—— (1972) *7th Report Taken Before the Expenditure Committee: Public Expenditure and Economic Management*, HC 515, HMSO, London.

—— (1973) *5th Report Taken Before the Expenditure Committee: The White Paper on Public Expenditure to 1976/77*, HC 149, HMSO, London.

—— (1974) *9th Report of the Expenditure Committee: Public Expenditure, Inflation and the Balance of Payments*, HC 328, HMSO, London.

—— (1975a) *First Report of the Expenditure Committee: The Financing of Public Expenditure*, HC 69, HMSO, London.

—— (1975b) *3rd Report of the Expenditure Committee: The White Paper on Public Expenditure to 1978/79*, HC 278 i & ii, HMSO, London.

—— (1976a) *4th Report of the Expenditure Committee: The White Paper on Public Expenditure to 1979/80*, HC 299, HMSO, London.

—— (1976b) *8th Report of the Expenditure Committee: The Chancellor's Statement of 22 July 1976*, HC 622, HMSO, London.

—— (1978) *2nd Report of the Expenditure Committee: The Government's Expenditure Plans 1978/79 to 1981/82*, HC 257, HMSO, London.

—— (1979) *4th Report of the Expenditure Committee: The Government's Expenditure Plans 1979/80 to 1982/83*, HC 237, HMSO, London.

—— (1980a) *Select Committee on the Treasury and Civil Service: Monetary Policy*, HC 720, HMSO, London.

—— (1980b) *Select Committee on the Treasury and the Civil Service: Monetary Policy*, HC 163 i, ii and iii, HMSO, London.

—— (1981a) *2nd Report from the Treasury and Civil Service Committee: The Government's Economic Policy*, HC 79, HMSO, London.

—— (1981b) *5th Report from the Treasury and Civil Service Committee: The Government's Expenditure Plans 1981/82*, HC 232, HMSO, London.

—— (1982a) *1st Report from the Treasury and Civil Service Committee: The Government's Economic Policy*, HC 28, HMSO, London.

—— (1982b) *5th Report from the Treasury and Civil Service Committee: The Government's Expenditure Plans to 1984/85*, HC 316, HMSO, London.

Howard, A. (1987) *RAB: A Life of R.A. Butler*, Cape, London.

Howell, D. (1976) *British Social Democracy*, Routledge, London.

Institute of Fiscal Studies (1976) *Public Expenditure, Growth and Control*, Mendip, Bath.

Jay, D. (1937) *The Socialist Case*, Eden & Eden, London.

Jenkins, P. (1987) *Mrs Thatcher's Revolution*, Cape, London.

Jenkins, S. (1985) 'The Star Chamber, PESC and the Cabinet', *Political Quarterly* 1, April–June: 7–12.

Jessop, B. (1977) 'Recent theories of the capitalist state', *Cambridge Journal of Economics* 1, (iv): 313–70.

—— (1979) 'Corporatism, parliamentarism and social democracy', in P.C. Schmitter and G. Lehmbruch (eds) *Trends Towards Corporatist Intermediation*, Sage, London.

—— (1983) *The Capitalist State*, Martin Robertson, Oxford.

—— (1985) *Nicos Poulantzas: Marxist Theory and Political Strategy*, Macmillan, London.

Jessop, B., Bonnett, K., Bromley, S. and Ling, T. (1988) *Thatcherism*, Cambridge University Press, Cambridge.

Johnson, C. (1991) *The Economy Under Mrs Thatcher 1979–1990*, Penguin, Middlesex.

Joseph, K. (1975) *Stranded in the Middle Ground*, Conservative Political Studies, London.

Judge, K. (1981) 'State pensions and the growth of social welfare expenditure', in *Journal of Social Policy* 2: 503–30.

—— (1982a) 'The growth and decline of social expenditure', in A. Walker (ed.) *Public Expenditure and Social Policy*, Heinemann Educational, London.

—— (1982b) 'Is there a crisis in the welfare state?', *International Journal of Sociology and Social Policy* 2 (1): 13–24.

Judge, K. and Hampson, R. (1980) 'Political advertising and the growth of public expenditure', *International Journal of Social Economics*, MCB, Bradford.

Kahn, Lord (1976) 'Thoughts on the behaviour of wages and monetarism', *Lloyds Bank Review* 119, May: 8–14.

Kaldor, Lord N. (1982a) *The Economic Consequences of Mrs Thatcher*, Duckworth, London.

—— (1982b) *The Scourge of Monetarism*, Oxford University Press, Oxford.

Kalecki, M. (1943) 'Political aspects of full employment', *Political Quarterly* 14: 322–31.

Kavanagh, D. (1987) *Thatcherism and British Politics, The End of Consensus?*, Oxford University Press, Oxford.

Kavanagh, D. and Seldon, A. (eds) (1989) *The Thatcher Effect: A Decade of Change*, Oxford University Press, Oxford.

Keegan, W. (1984) *Mrs Thatcher's Economic Experiment*, Allen Lane, London.

—— (1989) *Mr. Lawson's Gamble*, Allen Lane, London.

Keegan, W. and Pennant Rea, R. (1979) *Who Runs The Economy?*, Temple Smith, London.

King, A. (1985) *The British Prime Minister*, Macmillan, London.

Klein, R.(1974) *Social Policy and Public Expenditure 1974: An Interpretative Essay*, Centre for Studies in Social Policy (CSSP), London.

—— (1975) *Inflation and Priorities*, CSSP, London.

—— (1976a) 'The politics of public expenditure: American theory and British practice', *British Journal of Political Science* 2: 319–46.

—— (1976b) *Constraints and Choice*, CSSP, London.

—— (1982) *Public Expenditure in an Inflationary World*, Brookings Institute project on inflation (unpublished).

Klein, R. and O'Higgins, M. (1985) *The Future of Welfare*, Basil Blackwell, Oxford.

Kymlicka, W. (1990) *Contemporary Political Philosophy*, Clarendon Press, Oxford.

Labour Party (1973) *Labour's Programme 1973*, The Labour Party, London.

—— (1974) *Election Manifesto: Britain Will Win with Labour*, The Labour Party, London.

—— (1975) *Jobs and Prices*, The Labour Party, London.

—— (1976) *Annual Conference Report*, The Labour Party, London.

—— (1990) *Looking to the Future*, The Labour Party, London.

—— (1991) *Opportunity Britain*, The Labour Party, London.

—— (1992) *It's Time to Get Britain Working Again*, The Labour Party, London.

Labour Party/TUC (1979) *The Attack on Inflation*, The Labour Party, London.

Laclau, E. and Mouffee, C. (1985) *Hegemony and Socialist Strategy*, Verso, London.

Laidler, D. (1981) 'Monetarism: an interpretation and assessment', *Economic Journal* 91: 1–28.

Larkey, P., Stolp, C. and Winder, M. (1981) 'Theorizing about the growth of government', *Journal of Public Policy*, October: 157–220.

Lawson, N. (1992) *The View From No. 11. Memoirs of a Tory Radical*, Bantham, London.

Layton-Henry, Z. (1980) *Conservative Party Politics*, Macmillan, Basingstoke.

Le Grand, J. (1985) 'Comment on "Inequality, Redistribution and Recession" ', *Journal of Social Policy*, July: 309–12.

Levitt, M.S. (1984) 'The growth of government expenditure', *NIER*, May: 34–42.

—— (1987) *New Priorities in Public Spending*, Gower, London.

Likierman, A. (1988) *Public Expenditure: The Public Spending Process*, Penguin, Harmondsworth.

Lindsay, T. and Harrington, M. (1978) *The Conservative Party 1918 to 1979*, Macmillan, London.

Lipsey, D. and Leonard, D. (1981) *The Socialist Agenda*, Cape, London.

Longstreth, F.H. (1983) *Financial Markets and the Political Business Cycle in Britain*, paper presented to the Political Studies Association Annual Conference, Newcastle, April 1983.

McCracken, P. (1977) *Toward Full Employment and Price Stability*, OECD, Paris.

MacKintosh, J. (1982) 'Has social democracy failed in Britain?', in D. Marquand *John P. MacKintosh on Parliament and Social Democracy*, Longman, London.

McLennan, G. (1984) *The Idea of the Modern State*, Open University Press, Milton Keynes.

Macleod, I. and Powell, E. (1952) *Social Services: Needs and Means*, Conservative Party, London.

Macmillan, H. (1969) *Tides of Fortune*, Macmillan, London.

MacPherson, C.R. (1984) *Democractic Theory: Essays in Retrieval*, Clarendon, Oxford.

Mace, J. (1984) 'Education and science', in J. Cockle (ed.) *Public Expenditure Policy 1984–85*, Macmillan, London.

Maddison, A. (1984) 'The welfare state 1883 to 1983', in *Banco Nazionale Di Lavoro*, March 1984.

Madgwick, P. and Rose, R. (1982) *The Territorial Dimension in UK Politics*, Macmillan, London.

Mandel, E. (1978) *Late Capitalism*, Verso, London.

—— (1980) *The Second Slump*, Verso, London.

Marquand, D. (1982) *John P. MacKintosh on Parliament and Social Democracy*, Longman, London.

Maudling, R. (1978) *Memoirs*, Sedgewick and Jackson, London.

Maynard, G. (1980) *The Economy under Mrs Thatcher*, Basil Blackwell, Oxford.

Middlemas, K. (1986) *Industry, Unions and Government*, Macmillan, London.

Miliband, R. (1983) *Class Power and State Power*, Verso, London.

Minford, P. (1980) *Memorandum to the Treasury and Civil Service Committee: Monetary Policy*, HC 720, HMSO, London.

—— (1984) 'State expenditure – a study in waste', *Economic Affairs Supplement*, April–June.

Mishra, R. (1984) *The Welfare State in Crisis*, Harvester, London.

Morgan, K.O. (1984) *Labour in Power 1945–51*, Clarendon, Oxford.

Mosley, P. (1984) *The Making of Economic Policy*, Wheatsheaf, Brighton.

Mullard, M. (1987) *The Politics of Public Expenditure*, Routledge, London.

—— (1992) *Understanding Economic Policy*, Routledge, London.

Mullard, M., Butcher, H., Law, I. and Leach, R. (1990) *Local Government and Thatcherism*, Routledge, London.

Musgrave, R.A. and Musgrave, P.B. (1975) *Public Finance in Theory and Practice*, McGraw Hill, London.

NEC/Cabinet Working Paper (1976) RE 1793/July 1976/CONFIDENTIAL.

Newton, P. and Karran, T.J. (1985) *The Politics of Local Expenditure*, Macmillan, London.

Nickell, S. and Layard, R. (1985) 'The cause of British unemployment', *NIER 1985*: 62–85, NIESR, London.

NIESR (1980) *Memorandum to the Treasury and Civil Service Committee: Monetary Policy*, HC 720, HMSO, London.

—— (1983) 'Public sector borrowing', NIER 1983: 50–5, NIESR, London.

—— (1987) *The Growth and Efficiency of Government Spending*, Cambridge University Press, Cambridge.

Niskanen, W. (1971) *Bureaucracy and Representative Government*, Aldine Press, Chicago.

Nordaus, W. (1975) 'The political business cycle', *Review of Economic Studies* 42: 169–90.

Norton, P. (1978) *Conservative Dissidents*, Macmillan, London.

—— (1985) *Parliament in the 1980's*, Basil Blackwell, Oxford.

O'Connor, J. (1973) *The Fiscal Crisis of the State*, St. Martin's Press, New York.

O'Gorman, F. (1986) *British Conservatism*, Longman, London.

O'Higgins, M. (1984) 'Welfare, re-distribution and inequality', mimeo, University of Bath.

—— (1985) 'Inequality, redistribution and recession: the British experience 1976 to 1982', *Journal of Social Policy*, July: 279–307.

OECD (1978) *Public Expenditure Trends*, OECD, Paris.

—— (1983) *The Growth and Control of Social Expenditure 1960 to 1980*, OECD, Paris.

Offe, C. (1984) *Contradictions and the Welfare State*, Hutchinson, London.

Olson, M. (1965) *The Logic of Collective Action*, Harvard University Press, Cambridge, Mass.

Outram, Q. (1975) *The Significance of Public Expenditure Plans*, CSSP, London.

Panitch, L. (1979) 'The development of corporatism in liberal democracies', in P.C. Schmitter and G. Lehmbruch (eds) *Trends Towards Corporatist Intermediation*, Sage, London.

—— (1980) 'Recent theorization of corporatism', *British Journal of Sociology* 2: 159–87.

Parry, G. (1985) 'Welfare state and welfare society', *Government and Opposition* 20: 287–96.

Patten, C. (1980) 'Policy making in opposition', in Z. Layton-Henry (ed.) *Conservative Party Politics*, Macmillan, Basingstoke.

Peacock, A. and Wiseman, J. (1961) *The Growth of Public Expenditure in the UK*, Princeton University Press, Princeton, USA.

Pelling, H. (1984) *The Labour Governments 1945–51*, Macmillan, London.

Piachaud, D. (1980) 'Social security', in N. Bosanquet and P. Townsend (eds) *Labour and Inequality: A Fabian Study of Labour in Power 1974 to 1979*, Heinemann, London.

Pimlott, B. (ed.) (1984) *Fabian Essays in Socialist Thought*, Heinemann, London.

Pliatzky, L. (1976) *The Control of Public Expenditure*, Institute of Fiscal Studies, Mendip, Bath.

—— (1982) *Getting and Spending*, Basil Blackwell, Oxford.

—— (1989) *The Treasury Under Mrs Thatcher*, Basil Blackwell, Oxford.

Pollard, S. (1982) *The Wastage of the British Economy*, Croom Helm, London.

Poulantzas, N. (1980) *State, Power and Socialism*, Verso, London.

Price, R.W.R. (1979) 'Public expenditure policy and control', NIER November 1979: 68–76, NIESR, London.

Pym F. (1985) *The Politics of Consent*, Sphere, London.

Ramanadhan, V.V. (ed.) (1989) *Privatisation in Developing Countries*, Routledge, London.

Riddell, P. (1983) *The Thatcher Government*, Martin Robertson, London.

—— (1989) *The Thatcher Decade*, Martin Robertson, London.

Rose, R. (1984a) *Understanding Big Government*, Sage, London.

—— (1984b) 'The programme approach to the growth of government', *British Journal of Political Science* 15: 1–28.

—— (1984c) *Do Parties Make a Difference?*, Macmillan, London.

—— (1989) 'Inheritance before choice in public policy', *Studies in Public Policy*, No. 180, University of Strathclyde, discussion paper.

Rose, R. and Peters, G. (1979) *Can Governments Go Bankrupt?*, Macmillan, London.

Saunders, P. (1988) 'Explaining international differences in public expenditure', *Public Finance*, June: 271–94.

Savage, P. and Robins, L. (eds) (1990) *Public Policy under Thatcher*, Macmillan, London.

Schmitter, P.C. and Lehmbruch, G. (eds) (1979) *Trends Towards Corporatist Intermediation*, Sage, London.

Seldon, A. (1981) *Churchill's Indian Summer: Conservative Government 1951–55*, Hodder & Stoughton, London.

Shapiro, M. (1984) *Language and Politics*, Basil Blackwell, Oxford.

Shonfield, A. (1984) *In Defence of the Mixed Economy*, Oxford University Press, Oxford.

Skidelsky, R. (ed.) (1988) *Thatcherism*, Chatto & Windus, London.

Stewart, M. (1977) *The Jekyll and Hyde Years*, Dent, London.

Strachey, J. (1956) *Contemporary Capitalism*, Labour Publications, London.

Strinati, D. (1982) *Capitalism, the State and Industrial Relations*, Croom Helm, London.

Tarschys, D. (1975) 'The growth of public expenditure, nine modes of explanation', *Yearbook of Scandinavian Political Studies* 61(4): 1010–19.

—— (1985) 'Curbing public expenditure: current trends', *Journal of Public Policy*, February: 23–68.

Tawney, R.H. (1931) *Equality*, Bell & Hyman, London.

—— (1954) *The Radical Tradition*, Faber & Faber, London.

Taylor, C.L. (1983) *Why Government Grows?*, Sage, London.

Taylor-Gooby, P. (1985) *Public Opinion, Ideology and State Welfare*, Routledge and Kegan, London.

Tobin, J. (1981) 'The monetarist counter revolution – an appraisal', *Economic Journal*, March: 21–37.

Trinder, C. (1990) *Trends and Cycles in Public Sector Pay*, Public Finance Foundation, London.

Tufte, E. (1978) *The Political Control of the Economy*, Princeton University Press, Princeton, USA.

Tullock, G. (1976) *The Vote Motive*, Institute of Economic Affairs, London.

Tumlir, J. (1984) *Economic Policy as a Constitutional Problem*, Institute of Economic Affairs, London.

Veljanovski, C. (1987) *Selling the State: Privatisation in Britain*, Weidenfeld & Nicolson, London.

Von Beyme, K. (1984) 'Do parties matter?', *Government and Opposition* 19: 5–29.

Walker, A. (ed.) (1982) *Public Expenditure and Social Policy*, Heinemann Educational, London.

Walshe, G. (1987) *Planning Public Expenditure in the UK*, Macmillan, London.

Walters, A. (1986) *Britain's Economic Renaissance*, Oxford University Press, Oxford.

Webb, S. and Webb, B. (1962) *Fabian Essays*, Allen & Unwin, London.

White, G. and Chapman, H. (1987) 'Long term trends in public expenditure', *Economic Trends* 408, October: 124–8.

Whiteley, P. (1983) *The Labour Party in Crisis*, Methuen, London.

Wilding, P. (1982) *Professional Power and Social Welfare*, Routledge, London.

Wilensky, H. (1975) *The Welfare State and Equality*, University of California Press, California, USA.

Willetts, D. (1992) *Modern Conservatism*, Penguin, Harmondsworth.

Wright, A. (1983) *British Socialism*, Longman, London.

Yaffe, D. (1978) *The Marxist Theory of Crisis, Capital and the State. Economy and Society*, Verso, London.

Young, H. (1990) *One of Us: A Biography of Margaret Thatcher*, Pan, London.

Index